双语名著无障碍阅读丛书

经典集锦

毛姆短篇小说选

Selected Short Works of Maugham

[英国] 威廉·萨默赛特·毛姆 著
潘华凌 译

中国出版集团
中译出版社

图书在版编目(CIP)数据

毛姆短篇小说选 / (英) 毛姆著；潘华凌译. —北京：中译出版社，2016.3
(2019.4重印)
（双语名著无障碍阅读丛书）
ISBN 978-7-5001-4603-2

Ⅰ. ①毛… Ⅱ. ①毛… ②潘… Ⅲ. ①英语－汉语－对照读物 ②短篇小说－小说集－英国－现代 Ⅳ. ①H319.4: I

中国版本图书馆CIP数据核字(2016)第048068号

出版发行 / 中译出版社
地　　址 / 北京市西城区车公庄大街甲4号物华大厦6层
电　　话 / (010) 68359827； 68359303（发行部）； 53601537（编辑部）
邮　　编 / 100044
传　　真 / (010) 68357870
电子邮箱 / book@ctph.com.cn
网　　址 / http: // www.ctph.com.cn

总 策 划 / 张高里　贾兵伟
策划编辑 / 胡晓凯
责任编辑 / 胡晓凯　张美珍

封面设计 / 潘　峰
排　　版 / 北京竹页文化传媒有限公司
印　　刷 / 山东华立印务有限公司
经　　销 / 新华书店北京发行所

规　　格 / 710毫米×1000毫米　1/16
印　　张 / 19.25
字　　数 / 411千字
版　　次 / 2016年4月第一版
印　　次 / 2019年4月第三次

ISBN 978-7-5001-4603-2　定价：29.00元

版权所有　侵权必究
中　译　出　版　社

出版前言

多年以来，中译出版社有限公司（原中国对外翻译出版有限公司）凭借国内一流的翻译和出版实力及资源，精心策划、出版了大批双语读物，在海内外读者中和业界内产生了良好、深远的影响，形成了自己鲜明的出版特色。

二十世纪八九十年代出版的英汉（汉英）对照“一百丛书”，声名远扬，成为一套最权威、最有特色且又实用的双语读物，影响了一代又一代英语学习者和中华传统文化研究者、爱好者；还有“英若诚名剧译丛”“中华传统文化精粹丛书”“美丽英文书系”，这些优秀的双语读物，有的畅销，有的常销不衰反复再版，有的被选为大学英语阅读教材，受到广大读者的喜爱，获得了良好的社会效益和经济效益。

“双语名著无障碍阅读丛书”是中译专门为中学生和英语学习者精心打造的又一品牌，是一个新的双语读物系列，具有以下特点：

选题创新——该系列图书是国内第一套为中小学生量身打造的双语名著读物，所选篇目均为教育部颁布的语文新课标必读书目，或为中学生以及同等文化水平的社会读者喜闻乐见的世界名著，重新编译为英汉（汉英）对照的双语读本。这些书既给青少年读者提供了成长过程中不可或缺的精神食粮，又让他们领略到原著的精髓和魅力，对他们更好地学习英文大有裨益；同时，丛书中入选的《论语》《茶馆》《家》等汉英对照读物，亦是热爱中国传统文化的中外读者所共知的经典名篇，能使读者充分享受阅读经典的无限乐趣。

无障碍阅读——中学生阅读世界文学名著的原著会遇到很多生词和文化难点。针对这一情况，我们给每一本读物原文中的较难词汇和不易理解之处都加上了注释，在内文的版式设计上也采取英汉（或汉英）对照方式，扫清了学生阅读时的障碍。

优良品质——中译双语读物多年来在读者中享有良好口碑，这得益于作者和出版者对于图书质量的不懈追求。“双语名著无障碍阅读丛书”继承了中译双语读物的优良传统——精选的篇目、优秀的译文、方便实用的注解，秉承着对每一个读者负责的精神，竭力打造精品图书。

愿这套丛书成为广大读者的良师益友，愿读者在英语学习和传统文化学习两方面都取得新的突破。

目录
CONTENTS

William Somerset Maugham

Rain

It was nearly bed-time and when they awoke next morning land would be in sight. Dr. Macphail lit his pipe and, leaning over the **rail**①, searched the heavens for the Southern Cross. After two years at the front and a wound that had taken longer to heal than it should, he was glad to settle down quietly at Apia for twelve months at least, and he felt already better for the journey. Since some of the passengers were leaving the ship next day at Pago-Pago they had had a little dance that evening and in his ears **hammered**② still the **harsh**③ notes of the mechanical piano. But the **deck**④ was quiet at last. A little way off he saw his wife in a long chair talking with the Davidsons, and he strolled over to her. When he sat down under the light and took off his hat you saw that he had very red hair, with a bald **patch**⑤ on the crown, and the red, **freckled**⑥ skin which accompanies red hair; he was a man of forty, thin, with a **pinched**⑦ face, precise and rather **pedantic**⑧; and he spoke with a Scots accent in a very low, quiet voice.

Between the Macphails and the Davidsons, who were **missionaries**⑨, there had arisen the **intimacy**⑩ of shipboard, which is due to **propinquity**⑪

雨

快到睡觉的时间了。翌日早晨，船上的乘客醒过来时，便可见到陆地了。麦克费尔医生点燃了烟斗，身子倚靠在船的护栏上，眼睛遥望着九霄云外，寻找那南十字星座。他在前线待了两年，负伤后，伤口久拖不愈。能够在阿皮亚[1]平静安宁地待上至少十二个月，他对此感到高兴。他已经觉得身体更加硬朗了，能够进行这次旅行。由于有些乘客翌日要在帕果帕果[2]下船，他们当晚跳了一会儿舞。所以，他的耳畔仍然响着机械钢琴刺耳的键音。不过，甲板上终于还是平静下来了。他看见自己的夫人正在不远处和戴维森夫妇坐在一张长椅上交谈着，他便信步走到了她身边。他坐在灯光下，摘下头上的帽子时，您便可以清楚看到，他长着一头深红色的头发，头顶秃了一块。皮肤红润，布满了雀斑，与红头发相映成趣。他已经年过四十了，身体瘦削，窄窄的脸庞，显得刻板迂腐。他说话时带苏格兰口音，声音很低沉，语气很温和。

麦克费尔夫妇和身为传教士的戴维森夫妇之间有了那种同在一条船上的亲密感。他们的这种亲密关系与其

① rail [reil] n. 栏杆，扶手

② hammer ['hæmə] v. 敲出节拍

③ harsh [hɑ:ʃ] a. 刺耳的

④ deck [dek] n. 甲板

⑤ patch [pætʃ] n. 一小块

⑥ freckled ['frekld] a. 有雀斑的

⑦ pinched ['pintʃt] a. 皱缩的

⑧ pedantic [pi'dæntik] a. 学究式的

⑨ missionary ['miʃənəri] n. 传教士

⑩ intimacy ['intiməsi] n. 亲密

⑪ propinquity [prəu'piŋkwiti] n.（观点、兴趣方面的）类似

1 阿皮亚（Apia）位于太平洋中南部的西萨摩亚首都和主要港口，是座美丽的热带城市，依山傍水，风光绮丽。本书注释除特别注明者之外，均由译者提供。

2 帕果帕果（Pago-Pago）位于太平洋中南部的美属萨摩亚首府和主要港口，地处图图伊拉岛南岸中部帕果帕果湾内。

rather than to any community of taste. Their chief tie was the disapproval they shared of the men who spent their days and nights in the smoking-room playing poker or **bridge**[①] and drinking. Mrs. Macphail was not a little **flattered**[②] to think that she and her husband were the only people on board with whom the Davidsons were willing to associate, and even the doctor, shy but no fool, half unconsciously acknowledged the **compliment**[③]. It was only because he was of an **argumentative**[④] mind that in their cabin at night he permitted himself to **carp**[⑤].

"Mrs. Davidson was saying she didn't know how they'd have got through the journey if it hadn't been for us," said Mrs. Macphail, as she neatly brushed out her **transformation**[⑥]. "She said we were really the only people on the ship they cared to know."

"I shouldn't have thought a missionary was such a big **bug**[⑦] that he could afford to **put on frills**[⑧]."

"It's not frills. I quite understand what she means. It wouldn't have been very nice for the Davidsons to have to mix with all that rough **lot**[⑨] in the smoking-room."

"The founder of their religion wasn't so **exclusive**[⑩]," said Dr. Macphail with a chuckle.

"I've asked you over and over again not to joke about religion," answered his wife. "I shouldn't like to have a nature like yours, Alec. You never look for the best in people."

He gave her a sidelong glance with his pale, blue eyes, but did not reply. After many years of married life he had learned that it was more **conducive**[⑪] to peace to leave his wife with the last word. He was undressed before she was, and climbing into the upper **bunk**[⑫] he settled down to read himself to sleep.

When he came on deck next morning they were close to land. He looked at it with greedy eyes. There was a thin strip of silver beach rising quickly to hills covered to the top with luxuriant vegetation. The coconut trees, thick and green, came nearly to the water's edge, and among them you saw the grass houses of the Samoaris; and here and there, gleaming white, a little church. Mrs. Davidson

说是由于志趣相投，不如说是由于观念相近。他们走得很近的主要纽带是，他们都看不惯那些男士们没日没夜地待在吸烟室里，打扑克，玩桥牌，或者喝酒。麦克费尔夫人想到，自己和丈夫成了这船上戴维森夫妇唯一愿意结交的人，着实感到很有面子。连这位生性腼腆但并不愚笨的医生都有意无意地认可这种恭维。正是因为他内心好辩，所以晚上在他们的船舱里，他会放任自己挑剔找茬。

“戴维森夫人可是说过了，若是没有我们在，她真不知道他们该如何度过这段旅行过程，”麦克费尔夫人说着，一边干净利索地梳理着自己的假发，“她说过，我们确实是这艘船上他们唯一愿意交往的人。”

“我真不应该觉得传教士是什么了不起的大人物，居然装腔作势摆架子。”

“不是什么摆架子。她的言下之意我很理解。戴维森夫妇若是混迹在吸烟室里那批举止粗鲁的人中间，那才真是很不成体统呢。”

“他们所信奉的宗教的创始人才不会如此这般地与人格格不入呢。”麦克费尔医生说着，咯咯笑了起来。

“我对你说了多少回了，不要拿宗教的问题开玩笑，”夫人回答说，“我真不应该喜欢你这种性格的人，亚力克。你从不注意看别人的优点。”

他淡蓝色的眼睛斜睨了夫人一眼，但没有回话。他们已经结婚很多年，他懂得了，夫妻间要想和睦相处，最有效的办法就是让夫人说最后一句话。他比她先脱下衣服，爬到了上铺，躺下来看会儿书，看着看着睡着了。

翌日早晨，麦克费尔医生登上甲板时，他们已经离岸边很近了。他尽情地观赏着陆地。眼前是一片狭长的银色海滩，紧接着就是起伏的群山，山野草木茂盛，一片苍翠，直至山顶。椰子林浓密翠绿，几乎延伸到了海边。您可以看到萨摩亚人的草屋点缀其间，时不时还可以看见一座闪着亮光的白色小教堂。戴维森夫人也上了

① bridge [bridʒ] *n.* 桥牌
② flatter ['flætə] *v.* 恭维
③ compliment ['kɔmplimənt] *n.* 恭维话
④ argumentative [ˌɑːgju'mentətiv] *a.* 爱争论的
⑤ carp [kɑːp] *v.* 挑剔，找碴儿
⑥ transformation [ˌtrænsfə'meiʃən] *n.*（女用）假发
⑦ bug [bʌg] *n.* 要人，名士
⑧ put on frills 摆架子
⑨ lot [lɔt] *n.* 某一类人
⑩ exclusive [ik'skluːsiv] *a.* 排外的
⑪ conducive [kən'djuːsiv] *a.* 有益的
⑫ bunk [bʌŋk] *n.* 铺位

came and stood beside him. She was dressed in black, and wore round her neck a gold chain, from which **dangled**[1] a small cross. She was a little woman, with brown, dull hair very elaborately arranged, and she had **prominent**[2] blue eyes behind invisible **pince-nez**[3]. Her face was long, like a sheep's, but she gave no impression of foolishness, rather of extreme alertness; she had the quick movements of a bird. The most remarkable thing about her was her voice, high, **metallic**[4], and without inflection; it fell on the ear with a hard monotony, irritating to the nerves like the pitiless **clamour**[5] of the **pneumatic**[6] drill.

"This must seem like home to you," said Dr. Macphail, with his thin, difficult smile.

"Ours are low islands, you know, not like these. Coral. These are volcanic. We've got another ten days' journey to reach them."

"In these parts that's almost like being in the next street at home," said Dr. Macphail **facetiously**[7].

"Well, that's rather an exaggerated way of putting it, but one does look at distances differently in the South Seas. So far you're right."

Dr. Macphail sighed faintly.

"I'm glad we're not stationed here," she went on. "They say this is a terribly difficult place to work in. The steamers' touching makes the people unsettled; and then there's the **naval**[8] station; that's bad for the natives. In our district we don't have difficulties like that to **contend with**[9]. There are one or two traders, of course, but we take care to make them behave, and if they don't we make the place so hot for them they're glad to go."

Fixing the glasses on her nose she looked at the green island with a ruthless stare.

"It's almost a hopeless task for the missionaries here. I can never be sufficiently thankful to God that we are at least **spared**[10] that."

Davidson's district consisted of a group of islands to the North of Samoa; they were widely separated and he had frequently to go long distances by **canoe**[11]. At these times his wife remained at their headquarters and managed the mission.

① dangle ['dæŋgl] *v.* 悬挂
② prominent ['prɔminənt] *a.* 突出的
③ pince-nez ['pænsnei] *n.* [法语] 夹鼻眼镜
④ metallic [mi'tælik] *a.* (声音) 刺耳的
⑤ clamour ['klæmə] *n.* 噪音
⑥ pneumatic [njuː'mætik] *a.* 风动的
⑦ facetiously [fə'siːʃəsli] *ad.* 滑稽地
⑧ naval ['neivəl] *a.* 海军的
⑨ contend with 对付
⑩ spare [spɛə] *v.* 宽恕
⑪ canoe [kə'nuː] *n.* 独木舟

甲板，站立在他身边。夫人一身黑色，脖子上戴着一条金项链，下端挂着一个十字架。她个头娇小，头发呈棕褐色，缺乏光泽，但经过了精心梳理。她戴着一副夹鼻眼镜，眼镜后面是一双突出的蓝眼睛。她长着一张瘦长的绵羊脸，但是，给人的印象不仅不显愚笨，反而十分机警干练。她像一只鸟儿，动作敏捷。她最为引人注目的是她说话时的声音，高声大气，声音刻板。听起来显得生硬单调，犹如风钻无情的喧闹声刺激着神经。

“眼前的情景一定让您感觉回到了家乡啊。”麦克费尔医生说，脸上勉强地挤出了一丝微笑。

“我们家乡是一片低矮的海岛，您知道的，和这儿的情形不一样，是珊瑚岛。这儿的是火山岛。我们还有十天的行程才能抵达那儿呢。”

“处在这样的区域，十天行程几乎就像是在家乡逛隔壁的街道啊。”麦克费尔医生语气诙谐地说。

“啊，这样说夸张了一点吧，不过，南太平洋一带，人们对距离的看法是有差异的。因此您说的也对啊。”

麦克费尔医生轻轻地叹息了一声。

“我很高兴，我们不在这驻守，”戴维森夫人接着说，“人们说这地方很可怕，难以开展工作。游船进出，弄得人们心绪不宁。其次，这儿还是海军驻地，当地的居民可遭殃了。我们待的那个地方，无需面对诸如此类的困难。当然，有那么一两个贸易商人，但我们会盯着他们，让他们中规中矩。他们若是不守规矩，我们就会让他们觉得那地方水深火热，还是离开的好。”

戴维森夫人用手固定了一下鼻梁上的眼镜，然后目不转睛，盯着眼前郁郁葱葱的海岛看。

“传教士若是要在此地传教，那几乎就是一项没有希望完成的任务。我对上帝始终怀有无限的感激之情，因为我们至少免除了在此地传教的使命。”

戴维森负责的教区包括萨摩亚以北的一组群岛。岛屿分布的区域很辽阔。他往往需要驾着独木舟经历漫长的航程。那时候，他夫人一般留在总部，处理传教的事务。麦

Dr. Macphail felt his heart sink when he considered the efficiency with which she certainly managed it. She spoke of the **depravity**① of the natives in a voice which nothing could hush, but with a **vehemently**② **unctuous**③ horror. Her sense of delicacy was singular. Early in their acquaintance she had said to him:

"You know, their marriage customs when we first settled in the islands were so shocking that I couldn't possibly describe them to you. But I'll tell Mrs. Macphail and she'll tell you."

Then he had seen his wife and Mrs. Davidson, their deckchairs close together, in earnest conversation for about two hours. As he walked past them backwards and forwards for the sake of exercise, he had heard Mrs. Davidson's **agitated**④ whisper, like the distant flow of a mountain **torrent**⑤, and he saw by his wife's open mouth and pale face that she was enjoying an alarming experience. At night in their cabin she repeated to him with **bated**⑥ breath all she had heard.

"Well, what did I say to you?" cried Mrs. Davidson, **exultant**⑦, next morning. "Did you ever hear anything more dreadful? You don't wonder that I couldn't tell you myself, do you? Even though you are a doctor."

Mrs. Davidson scanned his face. She had a dramatic eagerness to see that she had achieved the desired effect.

"Can you wonder that when we first went there our hearts sank? You'll hardly believe me when I tell you it was impossible to find a single good girl in any of the villages."

She used the word *good* in a severely technical manner.

"Mr. Davidson and I talked it over, and we made up our minds the first thing to do was to **put down**⑧ the dancing. The natives were crazy about dancing."

"I was not **averse**⑨ to it myself when I was a young man," said Dr. Macphail.

"I guessed as much when I heard you ask Mrs. Macphail to have a turn with you last night. I don't think there's any real harm if a man dances with his wife, but I was relieved that she wouldn't. Under the circumstances I thought it better

克费尔医生想到夫人处理传教事务一定会有的那种效率时，内心感到很沮丧。夫人说到土著居民的罪恶行径时，那说话的声音，根本无法使之安静下来，只能用一种强烈而又虚情假意的恐惧应对。她感知微妙情况的能力很独特。早在他们刚认识的那阵子，她便对他说过：

“您知道吧，我们刚到那些岛屿时，土著居民的婚姻习俗令人惊愕不已，我都简直无法在您面前描述。不过，我可以告诉麦克费尔夫人，她再来告诉您。”

随后，麦克费尔医生看见自己夫人和戴维森夫人两个人的甲板躺椅挨在一块儿，两人真挚热情地交谈了大概有两个小时。他为了活动活动身子骨，来回从她们身边经过时，他听见了戴维森夫人情绪激动的低语，犹如远处山涧的激流。只见自己夫人正张开着嘴，脸色苍白。他由此看出，她正在享受着体验惊恐的过程。夜间，夫妇俩到了自己的船舱时，夫人压低着嗓门，把自己听到的所有情况复述给他听。

“对吧，我对您说什么来着？”翌日早晨，戴维森夫人大声嚷嚷着，兴致勃勃，“您听说过比这更加骇人听闻的事情吗？我不能把事情亲口告诉您，您不会感到奇怪，对吧？即便您是位医生也罢。”

戴维森夫人审视了一番医生的脸。她满怀激情，迫不及待地希望看到自己的话已经取得了期待中的效果。

“我们初到那儿时，心都是凉的。您对此不会感到奇怪吧？我若是告诉您，那儿的任何村落里都不可能寻觅到一位好姑娘，您简直不会相信我说的话。”

她严格按照字面意义使用了“好”这个词。

“这件事情我和戴维森先生讨论过了，我们已经做出了决定，首先要干的一件事就是禁止跳舞。那些土著人对舞蹈如痴如醉。”

“我本人年轻时可并不讨厌跳舞啊。”麦克费尔医生说。

“昨晚，我听见您邀请麦克费尔夫人陪您跳一回合时，我就猜到了。我觉得，一位男士若是同自己的夫人跳舞，实际上并不会有什么坏处。但是，她不陪，我心

① depravity [di'prævəti] *n.* 堕落
② vehemently ['vi:imәntli] *ad.* 强烈地
③ unctuous ['ʌŋktjuəs] *a.* 虚情假意的
④ agitated ['ædʒiteitid] *a.* 激动的
⑤ torrent ['tɔrənt] *n.* 湍流
⑥ Bated 屏息的；屏住呼吸
⑦ exultant [ig'zʌltənt] *a.* 兴高采烈的
⑧ put down 制止
⑨ averse [ə'və:s] *a.* 反对的

that we should keep ourselves to ourselves."

"Under what circumstances?"

Mrs. Davidson gave him a quick look through her pincenez, but did not answer his question.

"But among white people it's not quite the same," she went on, "though I must say I agree with Mr. Davidson, who says he can't understand how a husband can stand by and see his wife in another man's arms, and as far as I'm concerned I've never danced a step since I married. But the native dancing is quite another matter. It's not only immoral in itself, but it distinctly leads to immorality. However, I'm thankful to God that we **stamped it out**①, and I don't think I'm wrong in saying that no one has danced in our district for eight years."

But now they came to the mouth of the harbour and Mrs. Macphail joined them. The ship turned sharply and steamed slowly in. It was a great **landlocked**② harbour big enough to hold **a fleet of**③ battleships; and all around it rose, high and steep, the green hills. Near the entrance, getting such breeze as blew from the sea, stood the governor's house in a garden. The Stars and Stripes dangled **languidly**④ from a flagstaff. They passed two or three trim bungalows, and a tennis court, and then they came to the **quay**⑤ with its warehouses. Mrs. Davidson pointed out the **schooner**⑥, **moored**⑦ two or three hundred yards from the side, which was to take them to Apia. There was a crowd of eager, noisy, and good-humoured natives come from all parts of the island, some from curiosity, others to barter with the travellers on their way to Sydney; and they brought pineapples and huge bunches of bananas, *tapa* cloths, necklaces of shells or sharks' teeth, *kava*-bowls, and models of war canoes. American sailors, neat and trim, clean-shaven and frank of face, **sauntered**⑧ among them, and there was a

里感觉轻松了。面对如此情形，我们还是事不关己不予干预为妙。”

“面对什么情形？”

戴维森夫人透过夹鼻眼镜扫了医生一眼，但没有回答他的问题。

“但是，白人中间，情况就很不一样了，”她接着说，“尽管我必须得说，我认同戴维森先生的看法。他说，他不明白，做丈夫的为何要袖手旁观，看着自己的夫人让另一位男士搂着。就我而言，打从我结婚嫁人之后，就没有跳过一步舞。但是，土著人的舞蹈则是另外一回事。那种舞蹈不仅本身不道德，而且一定会导致伤风败俗行为的发生。然而，感谢上帝，我们压制了那种舞蹈。若是说八年来，我们那个地区没有任何人跳过舞，我觉得，这话没有说错。”

这时候，他们的船已经抵达港口了。麦克费尔夫人来到了他们身边。轮船急速转了弯，然后缓慢向前。这是一座由陆地环绕的大海港，规模大得足以容纳一支舰队。海港的四周耸立着巍峨陡峭的苍翠群山。临近入口，沐浴着徐徐吹来的海风，总督府坐落在一座花园当中。旗杆上懒洋洋地飘扬着星条旗[1]。他们的船掠过了两三幢整齐的孟加拉式平房，还有一处网球场，然后抵达了配有一个个仓库的码头。戴维森夫人指着一艘停泊在距离岸边两三百码远的纵帆船，他们将要乘着该船前往阿皮亚。岸边有一大群来自海岛四面八方的土著居民，他们态度热切，叽叽喳喳，兴致勃勃。其中有些人出于好奇看热闹来了，另外一些则打算同前往悉尼的旅客做些交易。他们带来了凤梨、大串的香蕉、塔巴土布、用贝壳或者鲨鱼齿制作成的项圈、卡瓦胡椒木碗，还有打仗用的独木舟模型。驻岛的美国水兵们穿行在人群中间，一

① stamp out 消灭

② landlocked ['lændlɔkt] *a.* 内陆的

③ a fleet of 一队……

④ languidly ['læŋgwidli] *ad.* 懒洋洋地

⑤ quay [kiː] *n.* 码头

⑥ schooner ['skuːnə] *n.* 纵帆船

⑦ moor [muə] *v.*（用缆、索）固定

⑧ saunter ['sɔːntə] *v.* 闲逛，漫步

1 星条旗（The Stars and Stripes）是美国的国旗。由十三道红白相间的宽条构成，左上角还有一个包含了五十颗白色小五角星的蓝色长方形。五十颗小星代表了美国的五十个州，而十三条间纹则象征着美国最早建国时的十三个殖民地。红色象征勇气，白色象征真理，蓝色则象征正义。旗帜的正式名称为“合众国旗”（The Flag of the United States）。

little group of officials. While their luggage was being landed the Macphails and Mrs. Davidson watched the crowd. Dr. Macphail looked at the yaws from which most of the children and the young boys seemed to suffer, **disfiguring**① sores like **torpid**② **ulcers**③, and his professional eyes **glistened**④ when he saw for the first time in his experience cases of elephantiasis, men going about with a huge, heavy arm or dragging along a **grossly**⑤ disfigured leg. Men and women wore the lava-lava.

"It's a very indecent costume," said Mrs. Davidson. "Mr. Davidson thinks it should be prohibited by law. How can you expect people to be moral when they wear nothing but a strip of red cotton round their **loins**⑥?"

"It's suitable enough to the climate," said the doctor, wiping the sweat off his head.

Now that they were on land the heat, though it was so early in the morning, was already **oppressive**⑦. Closed in by its hills, not a breath of air came in to Pago-Pago.

"In our islands," Mrs. Davidson went on in her high-pitched tones, "we've practically **eradicated**⑧ the lava-lava. A few old men still continue to wear it, but that's all. The women have all taken to the Mother Hubbard, and the men wear trousers and **singlets**⑨. At the very beginning of our stay Mr. Davidson said in one of his reports: the inhabitants of these islands will never be thoroughly Christianised till every boy of more than ten years is made to wear a pair of trousers."

But Mrs. Davidson had given two or three of her birdlike glances at heavy grey clouds that came floating over the mouth of the harbour. A few drops began to fall.

"We'd better take shelter," she said.

They made their way with all the crowd to a great shed of **corrugated**⑩

个个衣着整齐，干净利落，脸上修饰得很干净，态度坦诚。另外还有少数一些官员。行李运上岸时，麦克费尔夫妇和戴维森夫人注视着岸上的人群。麦克费尔医生看到，大部分孩子和青年小伙子似乎都患有雅司病[1]，有损形象的疮疤犹如慢性溃疡留下的伤疤。他那双充满了职业敏感性的眼睛闪闪发亮了，因为这是他职业生涯中第一次目睹了象皮病[2]的病例。那些男人或甩着粗大笨重的手臂四处行走，或拖着臃肿变形的大腿艰难前行。男男女女都围着萨摩亚印花布短围裙。

“这种着装很不成体统，”戴维森夫人说，“戴维森先生认为，应该通过立法来禁止这种穿戴。人们若是衣不附体，只是在胯间围着一块红布条，你如何能够指望他们树立道德情操啊？”

“这种穿戴挺适合当地气候的。”医生说着，一边擦了擦额头上的汗。

他们这时已经上岸了。虽说是清晨，但炎热已经让人感觉透不过气来。帕果帕果地处群山怀抱，外面吹不进一丝风来。

“我们的那些岛屿上，”戴维森夫人说，说话声音很高亢，“实际上已经杜绝了人们围那种短围裙。极少数老年男子仍然围着它，但仅此而已。妇女都开始喜爱穿宽大的长罩衣了，男子则穿上了长裤和汗衫。我们在那儿居住的开始阶段，戴维森先生在一份报告中表述称，这些岛屿上的居民们不可能完全皈依基督教，除非规定十岁以上的少年小伙都穿上长裤。”

但是，海口的上空飘来一团团黑压压的乌云，戴维森夫人用鸟儿一样敏锐的目光瞥了两三眼云团。稀稀拉拉的雨点开始落了下来。

“我们最好还是避一避吧。”她说。

他们随着一大群人走向一处顶上盖着瓦楞铁皮的大

① disfiguring [dis'figəriŋ] *a.* 有损外观的
② torpid ['tɔːpid] *a.* 缓慢的
③ ulcer ['ʌlsə] *n.* 溃疡
④ glisten ['glisən] *v.* 闪闪发光
⑤ grossly [grəusli] *ad.* 很，非常
⑥ loin [lɔin] *n.* 腰部
⑦ oppressive [ə'presiv] *a.* 压抑的
⑧ eradicate [i'rædikeit] *v.* 杜绝
⑨ singlet ['siŋglit] *n.* 汗衫
⑩ corrugated ['kɔrugeitid] *a.* 有瓦楞的

1　雅司病（yaws）是一种经皮肤接触感染雅思螺旋体而发生的皮肤病，对皮肤造成的损害很像是梅毒导致的，此病主要流行于热带地区。

2　象皮病（elephantiasis）是一种由丝虫引起的人体寄生虫病。

iron, and the rain began to fall in torrents. They stood there for some time and then were joined by Mr. Davidson. He had been polite enough to the Macphails during the journey, but he had not his wife's sociability, and had spent much of his time reading. He was a silent, rather **sullen**① man, and you felt that his **affability**② was a duty that he imposed upon himself Christianly; he was by nature reserved and even **morose**③. His appearance was singular. He was very tall and thin, with long limbs loosely jointed; hollow cheeks and curiously high cheek-bones; he had so **cadaverous**④ an air that it surprised you to notice how full and sensual were his lips. He wore his hair very long. His dark eyes, set deep in their **sockets**⑤, were large and tragic; and his hands with their big, long fingers, were finely shaped; they gave him a look of great strength. But the most striking thing about him was the feeling he gave you of suppressed fire. It was impressive and vaguely troubling. He was not a man with whom any intimacy was possible.

He brought now unwelcome news. There was an epidemic of **measles**⑥, a serious and often fatal disease among the Kanakas, on the island, and a case had developed among the crew of the schooner which was to take them on their journey. The sick man had been brought ashore and put in hospital on the **quarantine**⑦ station, but telegraphic instructions had been sent from Apia to say that the schooner would not be allowed to enter the harbour till it was certain no other member of the crew was affected.

"It means we shall have to stay here for ten days at least."

"But I'm urgently needed at Apia," said Dr. Macphail.

"That can't be helped. If no more cases develop on board, the schooner will be allowed to sail with white passengers, but all native traffic is prohibited for three months."

"Is there a hotel here?" asked Mrs. Macphail.

Davidson gave a low chuckle.

"There's not."

"What shall we do then?"

棚。天开始下起了瓢泼大雨。他们在棚下站了好一阵，戴维森先生随后过来了。旅途当中，戴维森先生对麦克费尔夫妇恭谦礼让，但没有夫人那样的交际能力，大部分时间都消磨在阅读上。他是个沉默寡言的人，甚至有点闷声不响。您会感觉到，他和蔼可亲的态度是一种责任，是他本着作为一名基督徒赋予自己的责任。他性格内向，甚至怪癖。他的音容相貌很独特，身材又高又瘦，修长的四肢松松垮垮地连接在躯体上，脸颊凹陷，颧骨高得出奇。他形容枯槁，死气沉沉，但您会惊讶地注意到，他的两片嘴唇倒是丰满而又性感。他留着长长的头发。一双黑色的眼睛深陷在眼窝里，显得巨大而又悲悯。他的那双手长着又大又长的指头，显得结构完美，让他看上去拥有巨大的力量。但是，他身上最让人觉得不同凡响的是，他就像是一团被压制住了的火。那团火让人印象深刻，却又隐隐地燃烧着。他属于那种不可能亲密接触的人。

现在他带来了令人沮丧的消息。岛上正流行麻疹，这是南太平洋诸岛上的居民中间的一种严重而且常常致命的疾病。那艘纵帆船上船员中已经发现了一例病例，即他们准备搭乘继续自己行程的那艘。那位病患已经送上岸了，安置进了检疫站的医院。但是，阿皮亚那边发来电报说，除非确认纵帆船上的其他船员没有受到疾病的感染，否则，船只不允许入港。

“这等于说，我们得滞留此地，至少得待上十天。”

“但是，阿皮亚那边迫切需要我过去啊。”麦克费尔医生说。

“那没有办法啊。如若不出现新病例，纵帆船可以载着白人乘客航行。但是，对于所有土著居民，三个月内禁止通行。”

“这儿有旅馆吗？”麦克费尔夫人问了一声。

戴维森咯咯地低声笑了起来。

“没有。”

“我们该怎么办呢？”

① sullen ['sʌlən] *a.* 闷闷不乐的

② affability [ˌæfə'biləti] *n.* 亲切

③ morose [mə'rəus] *a.* 孤僻的

④ cadaverous [kə'dævərəs] *a.* 形容枯槁的

⑤ socket ['sɔkit] *n.* 凹穴

⑥ measles ['mi:zlz] *n.* 麻疹

⑦ quarantine ['kwɔrənti:n] *n.* 检疫

"I've been talking to the governor. There's a trader along the front who has rooms that he rents, and my proposition is that as soon as the rain **lets up**① we should go along there and see what we can do. Don't expect comfort. You've just got to be thankful if we get a bed to sleep on and a roof over our heads."

But the rain showed no sign of stopping, and **at length**② with umbrellas and waterproofs they set out. There was no town, but merely a group of official buildings, a store or two, and at the back, among the coconut trees and **plantains**③, a few native dwellings. The house they sought was about five minutes' walk from the **wharf**④. It was a frame house of two storeys, with broad **verandas**⑤ on both floors and a roof of corrugated iron. The owner was a **half-caste**⑥ named Horn, with a native wife surrounded by little brown children, and on the ground-floor he had a store where he sold canned goods and cottons. The rooms he showed them were almost bare of furniture. In the Macphails' there was nothing but a poor, worn bed with a ragged mosquito net, a **rickety**⑦ chair, and a washstand. They looked round with dismay. The rain poured down without ceasing.

"I'm not going to unpack more than we actually need," said Mrs. Macphail.

Mrs. Davidson came into the room as she was unlocking a **portmanteau**⑧. She was very brisk and alert. The cheerless surroundings had no effect on her.

"If you'll take my advice you'll get a needle and cotton and start right in to mend the mosquito net," she said, "or you'll not be able to get a **wink**⑨ of sleep tonight."

"Will they be very bad?" asked Dr. Macphail.

"This is the season for them. When you're asked to a party at Government House at Apia you'll notice that all the ladies are given a pillowslip to put their—their lower extremities in."

"I wish the rain would stop for a moment," said Mrs. Macphail. "I could try to make the place comfortable with more heart if the sun were shining."

① let up 停止

② at length 最后

③ plantain ['plæntin] n. 车前草

④ wharf [hwɔ:f] n. 码头

⑤ veranda [və'rændə] n. 走廊

⑥ half-caste ['hɑ:fkɑ:st] a. 混血儿的

⑦ rickety ['rikəti] a. 摇晃的

⑧ portmanteau [pɔ:t'mæntəu] n. 旅行皮箱

⑨ wink [wiŋk] n. 小睡

"我已经同总督谈过了。海滨人行道那儿有位店老板，他有几间房子出租。我建议，等到雨一停，我们就去那儿，看看有没有办法解决。别指望舒适惬意。我们若是能有一张床睡觉，头顶上方有屋顶挡着，就该感恩戴德啦。"

但是，大雨好像没有要停下来的迹象，最后，他们撑着雨伞、穿着雨衣出发了。这儿没有集镇，只有几幢办公用的建筑，一两家店铺，后面的椰树林和大蕉丛中，有几处土著居民的住宅。他们要寻找的房子距离码头大概五分钟路程。这是一幢两层的木板房，两层都有宽敞的露台，房顶是瓦楞铁皮的。房主是位欧亚混血种，名叫霍恩，娶了一位土著女人做妻子，养了一小拨棕色皮肤的孩子。他在一楼开了个店铺，经营罐头食品和布匹。他领着他们去看的房间几乎没有什么家具。麦克费尔夫妇准备住的房间里，只有一张破旧的床，上面挂着一顶破烂不堪的蚊帐，一把摇摇晃晃的椅子，以及一个脸盆架。他们神情沮丧，环顾了一番四周。倾盆大雨还没有停下。

"除了取出要用的东西，我不准备打开行李。"麦克费尔夫人说。

戴维森夫人一边打开手提包一边走了进来。她态度轻快爽朗，并没有受到眼前令人沮丧的环境的影响。

"你们听我的建议好了，立刻拿出针线和布片来，补一补蚊帐，"她说，"否则，你们今晚别想合眼。"

"这儿的蚊子很厉害吗？"麦克费尔医生说。

"现在是蚊子活跃的季节。你们若是受到邀请，去参加一个在阿皮亚政府官邸举行的聚会，你们就会注意到，所有小姐夫人们都会领到一个枕套，用以包住她们的——她们的下半身[1]。"

"但愿雨能够停一停就好了，"麦克费尔夫人说，"若是有阳光照耀，我可以更加精心地设法收拾一番，让这儿显得舒适一些。"

1 戴维森夫人意思是说她们的腿部，但她不能直截了当这样说，因为她觉得那样说不文明。

"Oh, if you wait for that, you'll wait a long time. Pago-Pago is about the rainiest place in the Pacific. You see, the hills, and that bay, they attract the water, and one expects rain at this time of year anyway."

She looked from Macphail to his wife, standing helplessly in different parts of the room, like lost souls, and she **pursed**[1] her lips. She saw that she must take them in hand. **Feckless**[2] people like that made her impatient, but her hands **itched**[3] to put everything in the order which came so naturally to her.

"Here, you give me a needle and cotton and I'll mend that net of yours, while you go on with your unpacking. Dinner's at one. Dr. Macphail, you'd better go down to the wharf and see that your heavy luggage has been put in a dry place. You know what these natives are, they're quite capable of storing it where the rain will beat in on it all the time."

The doctor put on his waterproof again and went downstairs. At the door Mr. Horn was standing in conversation with the quartermaster of the ship they had just arrived in and a second-class passenger whom Dr. Macphail had seen several times on board. The quartermaster, a little, **shrivelled**[4] man, extremely dirty, nodded to him as he passed.

"This is a bad job about the measles, doc," he said. "I see you've fixed yourself up already."

Dr. Macphail thought he was rather familiar, but he was a timid man and he did not **take offence**[5] easily.

"Yes, we've got a room upstairs."

"Miss Thompson was sailing with you to Apia, so I've brought her along here."

The quartermaster pointed with his thumb to the woman standing by his side. She was twenty-seven perhaps, plump, and in a coarse fashion pretty. She wore a white dress and a large white hat. Her fat calves in white cotton stockings **bulged**[6] over the tops of long white boots in glace **kid**[7]. She gave Macphail an **ingratiating**[8] smile.

"The feller's tryin' to soak me a dollar and a half a day for the meanest-

“噢，您若是等待阳光，那可得等很长时间啊。帕果帕果是太平洋区域雨量最多的地方。您看看，那些群山和那个海湾，它们会招来雨水啊。不管怎么说，一年当中的这个时候，人们总是会遇到雨的。”

麦克费尔夫妇站立在房间里不同的位置，一副失魂落魄的样子。戴维森夫人把目光从麦克费尔医生身上移到他夫人身上，并且噘起了嘴唇。她看出，自己必须要承担起照顾他们的责任了。她看到眼前这样的无能之辈便没有了耐性，但双手直痒痒，一定把一切安排得井井有条。况且这对她来说也是顺理成章的事情。

“得了，你们把针线和布片给我吧，我来替你们缝补蚊帐，你们接着打开行李。一点钟吃午餐。麦克费尔医生，您最好去一趟码头，看看你们的大件行李是否放在干燥处。您可知道，那些土著人都是些什么货色。他们很可能会把行李堆放在成天淋着雨的地方呢。”

医生再次穿上雨衣下楼了。霍恩先生在门口边同他们刚刚乘的那艘船上的舵手和一位二等舱里的乘客交谈。麦克费尔医生有几次在甲板上见到过那位乘客。舵手身材瘦小干瘪，浑身脏兮兮的。麦克费尔医生经过他们身边时，舵手朝他点了点头。

“发生了麻疹这样的疾病真是很糟糕啊，医生，”舵手说，“我看你们已经安顿下来了。”

麦克费尔医生觉得，此人态度过于冒昧，不过，他是个羞怯内敛的人，不那么容易动气。

“不错，我们在楼上安排了一个房间。”

“汤普森小姐同你们一块儿乘船前往阿皮亚，所以，我便把她领到这儿来了。”

舵手用大拇指指着站在他身边的一位小姐。她大概二十七岁的样子，体态丰满，打扮显得粗俗，有几分姿色。她身穿白色衣裙，头戴一顶白色大帽子。套着白色棉质长筒袜的两条粗腿肚子露在白色羊皮长靴子上面，显得鼓鼓囊囊。她对着麦克费尔医生莞尔一笑。

“这家伙想要敲我竹杠子，一天收一块五，就那么

① purse [pəːs] *v.* 使缩拢
② feckless ['feklis] *a.* 无能的
③ itch [itʃ] *v.* 渴望
④ shriveled ['ʃrivəld] *a.* 干瘦的
⑤ take offence 生气
⑥ bulge [bʌldʒ] *v.* 鼓起
⑦ kid [kid] *n.* 小山羊皮
⑧ ingratiating [in'greiʃieitiŋ] *a.* 迎合的

sized room," she said in a hoarse voice.

"I tell you she's a friend of mine, Jo," said the quartermaster. "She can't pay more than a dollar, and you've sure got to take her for that."

The trader was fat and smooth and quietly smiling. "Well, if you put it like that, Mr. Swan, I'll see what I can do about it. I'll talk to Mrs. Horn and if we think we can make a reduction we will."

"Don't try to pull that stuff with me," said Miss Thompson. "We'll settle this right now. You get a dollar a day for the room and not one bean more."

Dr. Macphail smiled. He admired the **effrontery**① with which she bargained. He was the sort of man who always paid what he was asked. He preferred to be over-charged than to **haggle**②. The trader sighed.

"Well, to oblige Mr. Swan I'll take it."

"That's the goods," said Miss Thompson. "Come right in and have a shot of **hooch**③. I've got some real good **rye**④ in that grip if you'll bring it along, Mr. Swan. You come along too, doctor."

"Oh, I don't think I will, thank you," he answered. "I'm just going down to see that our luggage is all right."

He stepped out into the rain. It swept in from the opening of the harbour in sheets and the opposite shore was all blurred. He passed two or three natives **clad**⑤ in nothing but the lava-lava, with huge umbrellas over them. They walked finely, with leisurely movements, very upright; and they smiled and greeted him in a strange tongue as they went by.

It was nearly dinner-time when he got back, and their meal was laid in the trader's **parlour**⑥. It was a room designed not to live in but for purposes of prestige, and it had a **musty**⑦, melancholy air. A suite of stamped **plush**⑧ was arranged neatly round the walls, and from the middle of the ceiling, protected

个巴掌大的房间。”她说着，声音粗声粗气。

“我告诉你，她是我的朋友啊，乔[1]，”舵手说，“她支付的房费不能超过一块钱一天，你就照顾她一下吧。”

店老板人长得胖胖的，脸盘子圆圆的，微笑着，“那好吧，既然您都这么说了，斯旺，我来想办法解决这个问题吧。我同我太太商量一下，我们若是能够降低收费，那就会降的。”

“别想着跟我推三阻四，”汤普森小姐说，“我们这就把事情给确定下来。给你一天一块钱房费，多一分都不行。”

麦克费尔医生微笑着。他很佩服她的这种不讲情面的杀价手段。他自己则属于那种人家开价多少就给多少的人。他宁可多出点钱，也不去讨价还价。店老板叹息了一声。

“那好吧，看斯旺先生的面子，那就这样吧。”

“这还差不多，”汤普森小姐说，“进屋喝一杯自酿的酒吧。斯旺先生，您若是帮我把那个旅行箱搬进来，我那里面可是有真正上等的黑麦酒呢。您也一块儿来吧，医生。”

“噢，我恐怕不能来，谢谢您，”医生回答说，“我正要到码头去看看我们的行李是否妥帖呢。”

他走进了外面的雨中。倾盆大雨从海港入口处斜着飘过来，对岸一片模糊。他在途中遇到了两三个土著人，他们什么都没有穿，只是胯间围着印花布的短围裙，撑着大雨伞。他们大大方方地行走着，举止悠闲，身子挺直。他们从他身边经过时，微笑着用奇怪的语言同他打招呼。

麦克费尔医生返回住处时，差不多到午饭时间了。他们的午餐已经摆在店老板的客厅里。说它是客厅，其实平时并没有人进去，只是装点门面而已，里面弥漫着一股发霉和阴沉的气息。墙壁边整整齐齐地摆着一套丝

① effrontery [i'frʌntəri] *n.* 冒犯胆大

② haggle ['hægl] *v.* 讨价还价

③ hooch [huːtʃ] *n.* 烈性酒

④ rye [rai] *n.* 黑麦

⑤ clad [klæd] *v.* clothe 的一种过去式与过去分词

⑥ parlour['pɑːlə] *n.* 客厅

⑦ musty ['mʌsti] *a.* 发霉的

⑧ plush [plʌʃ] *n.* 长毛绒

1 此处是对霍恩的昵称。

from the flies by yellow tissue-paper, hung a **gilt**① **chandelier**②. Davidson did not come.

"I know he went to call on the governor," said Mrs. Davidson, "and I guess he's kept him to dinner."

A little native girl brought them a dish of Hamburger steak, and after a while the trader came up to see that they had everything they wanted.

"I see we have a fellow **lodger**③, Mr. Horn." said Dr. Macphail.

"She's taken a room, that's all," answered the trader. "She's getting her own board."

He looked at the two ladies with an **obsequious**④ air.

"I put her downstairs so she shouldn't be in the way. She won't be any trouble to you."

"Is it someone who was on the boat?" asked Mrs. Macphail.

"Yes, ma'am, she was in the second cabin. She was going to Apia. She has a position as cashier waiting for her."

"Oh!"

When the trader was gone Macphail said:

"I shouldn't think she'd find it exactly cheerful having her meals in her room."

"If she was in the second cabin I guess she'd rather," answered Mrs. Davidson. "I don't exactly know who it can be."

"I happened to be there when the quartermaster brought her along. Her name's Thompson."

"It's not the woman who was dancing with the quartermaster last night?" asked Mrs. Davidson.

"That's who it must be," said Mrs. Macphail. "I wondered at the time what she was. She looked rather **fast**⑤ to me."

"Not good style at all," said Mrs. Davidson.

They began to talk of other things, and after dinner, tired with their early rise, they separated and slept. When they awoke, though the sky was still grey

① gilt [gilt] *a.* 镀金的
② chandelier [ˌʃændə'liə] *n.* 枝形吊灯
③ lodger ['lɔdʒə] *n.* 房客
④ obsequious [əb'siːkwiəs] *a.* 奉承的
⑤ fast [fɑːst] *a.* 放荡的

绒面的长沙发。天花板的正中央悬着一盏镀金的枝形吊灯，周围围着黄色的薄纸，防止苍蝇聚集。戴维森没有到场。

“我知道，他拜访总督去了，”戴维森夫人说，“估计总督要留下他吃午饭了。”

一位土著小姑娘给他们端上了一盘汉堡牛排。过了一会儿，店老板来了，看看他们点的东西是否都上齐了。

“我知道，我们多了一位同住的房客，霍恩先生。”麦克费尔医生说。

“她就是租了个房间，仅此而已，”店老板回答说，“伙食她自理。”

他看着两位夫人，一副谄媚讨好的姿态。

“我把她安顿在楼下了，因此，她不至于妨碍什么。她不会给你们添麻烦的。”

“是搭乘那艘纵帆船的吗？”麦克费尔夫人问了一声。

“不错啊，夫人，她在二等舱。她去阿皮亚，在那儿谋到了一份出纳员的差事。”

“噢！”

店老板离开后，麦克费尔说：

“我寻思着，让她独自一人留在房间里用餐，一定会很枯燥乏味的。”

“她既然是乘坐二等舱的，我看她这样也挺不错的，”戴维森夫人说，“我真不知道那是哪路人。”

“那位舵手把她领过来时，我正好在场。她叫汤普森。”

“不就是昨晚同舵手跳舞的那个女人吗？”戴维森夫人问了一声。

“一定就是，”麦克费尔夫人说，“我当时就纳闷着，她是什么货色啊。我觉得她有点放荡。”

“反正很不正派。”戴维森夫人说。

他们开始把话题转到别的事情上。午餐过后，由于他们当天起床很早，感觉很疲倦，于是，各自分开睡觉去了。他们醒来之后，天空虽然依旧灰蒙蒙的，乌云低

and the clouds hung low, it was not raining and they went for a walk on the high road which the Americans had built along the bay.

On their return they found that Davidson had just come in.

"We may be here for a fortnight," he said **irritably**①. "I've argued it out with the governor, but he says there is nothing to be done."

"Mr. Davidson's just longing to get back to his work," said his wife, with an anxious glance at him.

"We've been away for a year," he said, walking up and down the verandah. "The mission has been in charge of native missionaries and I'm terribly nervous that they've let things slide. They're good men, I'm not saying a word against them, God-fearing, devout, and truly Christian men—their Christianity would put many so-called Christians at home to the blush—but they're pitifully lacking in energy. They can **make a stand**② once, they can make a stand twice, but they can't make a stand all the time. If you leave a mission in charge of a native missionary, no matter how trustworthy he seems, in course of time you'll find he's let abuses creep in."

Mr. Davidson stood still. With his tall, spare form, and his great eyes flashing out of his pale face, he was an impressive figure. His sincerity was obvious in the fire of his gestures and in his deep, ringing voice.

"I expect to have my work cut out for me. I shall act and I shall act promptly. If the tree is rotten it shall be cut down and cast into the flames."

And in the evening after the high tea which was their last meal, while they sat in the **stiff**③ parlour, the ladies working and Dr. Macphail smoking his pipe, the missionary told them of his work in the islands.

"When we went there they had no sense of sin at all," he said. "They broke the commandments one after the other and never knew they were doing wrong.

垂，但雨停了。于是他们去大路上散步，大路是由美国人沿着海滨修起来的。

他们返回到住处时，发现戴维森刚刚回来。

“我们说不定得在这儿待上两个星期呢，”戴维森说，显得很焦躁，“我和总督争论了一番，但他说，这是没有办法的事情。”

① irritably['irətəbli] *ad.* 生气地

“戴维森先生一门心思想着要回到自己的岗位上去，”他夫人说，心急火燎地瞥了他一眼。

“我们已经离开有一年时间了，”他说，一边在露台上来回走着，“教会的事务全部由当地的教士们负责处理，我十分揪心，担心他们放任不管。他们都是好人，我不会说半句责备他们的话，敬畏上帝，笃信虔诚，是真正的基督徒——他们的基督精神会令国内许多所谓基督徒汗颜——但是，很可惜的是，他们缺乏能力。他们能够坚持原则一次，他们能够坚持原则两次，但他们不可能一直都坚持原则。您若是把教会的事务交给某位当地的教士去处理，不管他看起来有多么值得信赖，时间久了，您便会发现，他让那些弊病陋习死灰复燃了。”

② make a stand 采取坚定立场

戴维森先生平静地站立着。他身材高大，体型瘦削，那双硕大的眼睛在苍白的脸庞上朝外闪烁着，给人留下深刻印象。他热情似火的手势，深沉而又响亮的声音，从中可以明显看出他的真诚性格。

“我希望我的工作能够有人替我安排好。我要行动，我要立刻采取行动。大树若是腐烂了，那就应该砍倒，扔进火里去。”

③ stiff [stif] *a.* 过于死板的

傍晚茶[1]是他们这一天最后的一道餐食。傍晚，他们用过茶点之后，便在缺乏生气的客厅里坐了下来。两位夫人在干着手上的活儿。麦克费尔医生抽着烟斗。传教士给大家讲述自己在群岛上的工作。

“我们刚去那儿时，土著居民毫无罪恶观念，”戴维森先生说，“他们一条接着一条地触犯戒律，但根本

1　傍晚茶（high tea）是指傍晚五六点钟时吃的茶点，常有肉食，糕饼和茶等等。

And I think that was the most difficult part of my work, to **instil**① into the natives the sense of sin."

The Macphails knew already that Davidson had worked in the Solomons for five years before he met his wife. She had been a missionary in China, and they had become acquainted in Boston, where they were both spending part of their leave to attend a missionary congress. On their marriage they had been appointed to the islands in which they had laboured ever since.

In the course of all the conversations they had had with Mr. Davidson one thing had shone out clearly and that was the man's **unflinching**② courage. He was a medical missionary, and he was liable to be called at any time to one or other of the islands in the group. Even the whaleboat is not so very safe a **conveyance**③ in the stormy pacific of the wet season, but often he would be sent for in a canoe, and then the danger was great. In cases of illness or accident he never hesitated. A dozen times he had spent the whole night **baling**④ for his life, and more than once Mrs. Davidson had given him up for lost.

"I'd beg him not to go sometimes," she said, "or at least to wait till the weather was more settled, but he'd never listen. He's **obstinate**⑤, and when he's once made up his mind, nothing can move him."

"How can I ask the natives to put their trust in the Lord if I am afraid to do so myself?" cried Davidson. "And I'm not, I'm not. They know that if they send for me in their trouble I'll come if it's humanly possible. And do you think the Lord is going to abandon me when I am on his business? The wind blows at his bidding and the waves toss and rage at his word."

Dr. Macphail was a timid man. He had never been able to get used to the **hurtling**⑥ of the shells over the **trenches**⑦, and when he was operating in an advanced dressing-station the sweat poured from his brow and dimmed his spectacles in the effort he made to control his unsteady hand. He shuddered a little as he looked at the missionary.

"I wish I could say that I've never been afraid," he said.

① instil [in'stil] v. 逐渐灌输

② unflinching [ˌʌn'flintʃiŋ] a. 不畏缩的

③ conveyance [kən'veiəns] n. 运输工具

④ bail [beil] v. 舀出船舱里的水

⑤ obstinate ['ɔbstinit] a. 固执的

⑥ hurtling ['həːtliŋ] n. 飞驰

⑦ trench [trentʃ] n. 战壕

就不知道，自己犯下了罪过。我觉得，自己工作中最艰难的一部分就是向土著居民们灌输关于罪恶的观念。”

麦克费尔夫妇已经知道，戴维森认识自己的夫人之前，已经在所罗门群岛[1]担任传教工作五年。而他夫人则一直在中国传教。他们是在波士顿相识的，当时两个人都是利用休假时间参加海外传教士大会。他们婚后便被派往那些岛屿，一直工作到现在。

麦克费尔夫妇同戴维森先生经过多次交谈之后，有一个情况非常鲜明，那就是，此人具有毫不退却的勇气。他是位从事医疗工作的传教士，随时都有可能被人请到群岛上的某一处去看病。雨季期间，太平洋上暴风雨频发，波涛汹涌，连捕鲸船都不是很安全，但他却常常驾着一叶扁舟出海，冒着巨大的危险。遇到有病患或者事故，他从来都毫不犹豫。有十多次，他整夜都在把船上的水往外舀，这才死里逃生，而且不止一次，戴维森夫人认为他已经回不来了。

“我有时候会恳求他不要出去，”她说，“或者至少等到风浪小一点再说，但他毫不理会。他固执己见，一旦对某事打定了注意，那就任何情况都动摇不了他。”

“我若是自己都担心受怕，那又如何能够要求土著居民们相信上帝呢？”戴维森大声说，“我不能担心受怕，不能。他们知道，他们若是遇到了什么麻烦有求于我，只要人力可以实现的，我一定会到。当我在替上帝履行职责时，你们认为，上帝会抛弃我吗？暴风是因上帝嘱咐而刮起来的，波涛也是因上帝的吩咐而汹涌的。”

麦克费尔医生是个生性胆怯的人。他无法忍受战壕上空子弹来回穿梭的情景。每当他在前沿阵地的某处绷扎所做手术时，他要竭尽全力控制自己颤抖的手，因此额头上大汗淋漓，眼镜的镜片给弄得模糊了。他注视着眼前这位传教士时，不禁微微地颤抖了起来。

“我若是能够说自己什么都不害怕那该有多好啊。”

1　所罗门群岛（the Solomons）是南太平洋上的一个岛国，地处澳大利亚东北部，由近一千个岛屿组成。

"I wish you could say that you believed in God," retorted the other.

But for some reason, that evening the missionary's thoughts travelled back to the early days he and his wife had spent on the islands.

"Sometimes Mrs. Davidson and I would look at one another and the tears would stream down our cheeks. We worked without ceasing, day and night, and we seemed to make no progress. I don't know what I should have done without her then. When I felt my heart sink, when I was very near despair, she gave me courage and hope."

Mrs. Davidson looked down at her work, and a slight colour rose to her thin cheeks. Her hands trembled a little. She did not trust herself to speak.

"We had no one to help us. We were alone, thousands of miles from any of our own people, surrounded by darkness. When I was broken and **weary**① she would put her work aside and take the Bible and read to me till peace came and settled upon me like sleep upon the **eyelids**② of a child, and when at last she closed the book she'd say: 'We'll save them in spite of themselves.' And I felt strong again in the Lord, and I answered: 'Yes, with God's help I'll save them. I must save them.'"

He came over to the table and stood in front of it as though it were a **lectern**③.

"You see, they were so naturally **depraved**④ that they couldn't be brought to see their **wickedness**⑤. We had to make sins out of what they thought were natural actions. We had to make it a sin, not only to commit **adultery**⑥ and to lie and thieve, but to expose their bodies, and to dance and not to come to church. I made it a sin for a girl to show her bosom and a sin for a man not to wear trousers."

"How?" asked Dr. Macphail, not without surprise.

"I instituted fines. Obviously the only way to make people realize that an action is sinful is to punish them if they commit it. I fined them if they didn't

麦克费尔医生说。

“您若是能够说自己笃信上帝那才好呢。”对方反驳了一句。

但是，由于某种原因，当天傍晚，传教士的思绪回到了他和夫人初到群岛的那些日子。

“有时，我会和戴维森夫人相互对视，泪流满面。日日夜夜，我们没完没了地工作着，但似乎毫无进展。当时若是没有她在身边，我真不知道自己该怎么办。当我感到心灰意冷时，当我近乎于绝望时，她会赋予我勇气和希望。”

戴维森夫人目光朝下看着自己手上的活儿，她瘦削的面颊上泛起了红晕，双手微微颤抖着，说不出话来。

“我们得不到任何人的帮助。我们孤军奋战，我们的所有亲人都远在数千英里之外。黑暗笼罩着我们。每当我意志消沉、疲惫不堪时，她就会放下自己手上的活儿，拿起《圣经》念给我听，直到我情绪平和下来，犹如一个孩子睡意袭来。最后，她会合上《圣经》，并且说：‘尽管他们目前的状况很不堪，但我们一定要拯救他们。’于是，我再次对上帝有了坚强的信念，并且回答说‘对，有了上帝的帮助，我将拯救他们。我一定要拯救他们。’”

他迈步向前走向桌子，站立在桌子前面，仿佛把它当成了教堂的诵经台。

“您知道的，那些土著居民们天生就是那么堕落，都无法教化他们认清自己的邪恶。我们只好从他们习以为常的行为中指出，哪些是罪恶行为。我们定性的罪恶行为不仅仅限于奸淫、说谎和偷盗，而且还包括袒露他们的身体、跳舞以及不去教堂参加礼拜。我把姑娘裸露胸部定性为罪行，把男子不穿长裤也定性为罪行。”

“如何实现呢？”麦克费尔医生问了一声，很是惊讶。

“实施惩罚手段。很显然，我们若是要促使人们认识到某一种行为是有罪的，唯一的方法就是，一旦他们犯了事情，那就对他们实行惩罚。他们若是不上教堂做

① weary ['wiəri] *a.* 疲倦的

② eyelid ['aiˌlid] *n.* 眼皮

③ lectern ['lektəːn] *n.*（教堂中的）读经台

④ depraved [di'preivd] *a.* 堕落的

⑤ wickedness ['wikidnis] *n.* 罪恶

⑥ adultery [ə'dʌltəri] *n.* 通奸行为

come to church, and I fined them if they danced. I fined them if they were improperly dressed. I had a **tariff**①, and every sin had to be paid for either in money or work. And at last I made them understand."

"But did they never refuse to pay?"

"How could they?" asked the missionary.

"It would be a brave man who tried to stand up against Mr. Davidson," said his wife, tightening her lips.

Dr. Macphail looked at Davidson with troubled eyes. What he heard shocked him, but he hesitated to express his disapproval.

"You must remember that in the last resort I could expel them from their church membership."

"Did they mind that?"

Davidson smiled a little and gently rubbed his hands.

"They couldn't sell their **copra**②. When the men fished they got no share of the catch. It meant something very like starvation. Yes, they minded quite a lot."

"Tell him about Fred Ohlson," said Mrs. Davidson.

The missionary fixed his **fiery**③ eyes on Dr. Macphail.

"Fred Ohlson was a Danish trader who had been in the islands a good many years. He was a pretty rich man as traders go and he wasn't very pleased when we came. You see, he'd had things very much his own way. He paid the natives what he liked for their copra, and he paid in goods and whiskey. He had a native wife, but he was **flagrantly**④ unfaithful to her. He was a **drunkard**⑤. I gave him a chance to mend his ways, but he wouldn't take it. He laughed at me."

Davidson's voice fell to a deep **bass**⑥ as he said the last words, and he was silent for a minute or two. The silence was heavy with **menace**⑦.

"In two years he was a ruined man. He'd lost everything he'd saved in a quarter of a century. I broke him, and at last he was forced to come to me like a beggar and **beseech**⑧ me to give him a passage back to Sydney."

① tariff ['tærif] n. 收费表

② copra ['kɔprə] n. 干椰肉

③ fiery ['faiəri] a. 激昂的

④ flagrantly ['fleigrəntli] ad. 明目张胆

⑤ drunkard ['drʌŋkəd] n. 酒鬼

⑥ bass [beis] n. 低音

⑦ menace ['menəs] n. 威胁

⑧ beseech [bi'si:tʃ] v. 哀求

礼拜，我就罚他们的款。他们若是跳舞了，我罚他们的款。他们若是穿着不得体，我也罚他们的款。我制定了一个处罚的清单，犯下的每一桩罪行都得支付钱款或者通过做工来抵。最后，我终于让他们明白了。”

“但是，他们就从来都没有拒绝支付吗？”

“他们怎么可能呢？”传教士反问了一声。

“哪个人若是敢于对抗戴维森先生，那他算是够勇敢的人，”戴维森夫人说，紧抿着双唇。

麦克费尔医生看着戴维森，目光显得很惶恐。他听了刚才的话后，深感震惊，但不愿意表达自己对此不认同的想法。

“您可别忘了，我最后的杀手锏就是把他们开除出教会。”

“他们在乎这个吗？”

戴维森微微地笑了一下，双手轻柔地揉搓着。

“他们无法卖掉自己的那些椰子干。男人们捕来的鱼，他们也分不到一条半条的。那就意味着要忍饥挨饿。是啊，他们可在乎着呢。”

“告诉他关于弗雷德·奥尔森的情况吧。”戴维森夫人说。

传教士目光炯炯有神，看着麦克费尔医生。

“弗雷德·奥尔森是位丹麦商人，在群岛待了很多年。作为商人，他挺富有的。我们到达那儿时，他可不怎么高兴。您要知道，他一向我行我素惯了，向土著居民购买椰子干时，想给人家多少钱就给多少钱，有时候还会用食物和威士忌冲抵。他娶了个土著女人做妻子，但他明目张胆，做出对妻子不忠的事情。他是个酒鬼。我给了他机会，让他改过自新，但是，他不好好把握，竟然还嘲笑我。”

戴维森说最后这句话时，声音降得很低。他沉默了一两分钟。沉默中充满着威胁。

“才两年时间，他成了个落魄的人。他苦苦积攒了二十五年的财富消失殆尽。我让他破了产，他最后不得不

"I wish you could have seen him when he came to see Mr. Davidson," said the missionary's wife. "He had been a fine, powerful man, with a lot of fat on him, and he had a great big voice, but now he was half the size, and he was shaking all over. He'd suddenly become an old man."

With **abstracted**① gaze Davidson looked out into the night. The rain was falling again.

Suddenly from below came a sound, and Davidson turned and looked questioningly at his wife. It was the sound of a **gramophone**②, harsh and loud, **wheezing out**③ a **syncopated**④ tune.

"What's that?" he asked.

Mrs. Davidson fixed her pincenez more firmly on her nose.

"One of the second-class passengers has a room in the house. I guess it comes from there."

They listened in silence, and presently they heard the sound of dancing. Then the music stopped, and they heard the **popping**⑤ of **corks**⑥ and voices raised in **animated**⑦ conversation.

"I daresay she's giving a farewell party to her friends on board," said Dr. Macphail. "The ship sails at twelve, doesn't it?"

Davidson made no remark, but he looked at his watch.

"Are you ready?" he asked his wife.

She got up and folded her work.

"Yes, I guess I am," she answered.

"It's early to go to bed yet, isn't it?" said the doctor.

"We have a good deal of reading to do," explained Mrs. Davidson. "Wherever we are, we read a chapter of the Bible before retiring for the night and we study it with the **commentaries**⑧, you know, and discuss it thoroughly. It's a wonderful training for the mind."

The two couples bade one another good night. Dr. and Mrs. Macphail were left alone. For two or three minutes they did not speak.

"I think I'll go and fetch the cards," the doctor said at last.

像个乞丐似的来找我，恳求我给资助买张船票返回悉尼。”

“我真是希望您能够看到他来找戴维森先生时的那副模样，”传教士的夫人说，“他原本是个相貌堂堂、身体强壮的人，身上肉也不少，说话声音洪亮，但这时候已经不成人样了，走路都颤颤巍巍的，突然就变成了一个年迈的老人了。”

戴维森出神地注视着室外的夜色。天又下雨了。

突然，楼下传来一阵声响。戴维森转过身，看着自己的夫人，满腹疑问。那是留声机的声音，声音又响又刺耳，沙沙地奏出多切分音的曲调。

“怎么回事啊？”戴维森问了一声。

戴维森夫人固定一下鼻梁上的眼镜。

“楼下有个房间里住了一位二等舱的乘客。我估计声音是从那儿传来的。”

他们静静地倾听着，立刻听出了有跳舞的脚步声。音乐随即停止了，他们又听见了开酒瓶的声音，还有高声大气的交谈声。

“我肯定，她一定是在给船上的朋友们举行告别聚会，”麦克费尔医生说，“那艘船十点钟启航对吧？”

戴维森没有接话，但看了看自己的表。

“你弄好了吗？”他问了一声自己夫人。

夫人站起身，收拾起手上的活儿。

“对，弄好了。”她回答说。

“现在上床睡觉还早了点对吧？”医生说。

“我们还要朗读很多书上的内容呢，”戴维森夫人解释说，“我们不管到什么地方，就寝之前，都要朗读《圣经》中的一章，结合注释，还要做一番研究，您知道，还要进行详尽的讨论。这对心智是一种绝佳的训练啊。”

两对夫妇相互道了晚安。麦克费尔医生和夫人原地待着。他们有两三分钟时间没有开口说话。

“我觉得我该去把扑克牌拿来。”医生最后开口说。

① abstracted [æbˌstræktid] *a.* 出神的

② gramophone ['græməfəun] *n.* 留声机

③ wheeze out 沙沙声地奏出

④ syncopated [ˌsiŋkəpeitid] *a.* 切分（音）的

⑤ popping ['pɔpiŋ] *n.* 砰的一声

⑥ cork [kɔːk] *n.* 瓶塞

⑦ animated ['ænimeitid] *a.* 活跃的

⑧ commentary ['kɔməntəri] *n.* 注解

Mrs. Macphail looked at him doubtfully. Her conversation with the Davidsons had left her a little uneasy, but she did not like to say that she thought they had better not play cards when the Davidsons might come in at any moment. Dr. Macphail brought them and she watched him, though with a vague sense of guilt, while he laid out his **patience**① . Below the sound of **revelry**② continued.

It was fine enough next day, and the Macphails, **condemned**③ to spend a fortnight of idleness at Pago-Pago, set about making the best of things. They went down to the quay and got out of their boxes a number of books. The doctor called on the chief **surgeon**④ of the naval hospital and went round the beds with him. They left cards on the governor. They passed Miss Thompson on the road. The doctor took off his hat, and she gave him a "Good morning, doc." in a loud, cheerful voice. She was dressed as on the day before, in a white **frock**⑤, and her shiny white boots with their high heels, her fat legs bulging over the tops of them, were strange things on that **exotic**⑥ scene.

"I don't think she's very suitably dressed, I must say," said Mrs. Macphail. "She looks extremely common to me."

When they got back to their house, she was on the veranda playing with one of the trader's dark children.

"Say a word to her," Dr. Macphail whispered to his wife. "She's all alone here, and it seems rather unkind to ignore her."

Mrs. Macphail was shy, but she was in the habit of doing what her husband bade her.

"I think we're fellow lodgers here," she said, rather foolishly.

"Terrible, ain't it, bein' **cooped**⑦ up in a **one-horse**⑧ **burg**⑨ like this?" answered Miss Thompson. "And they tell me I'm lucky to have gotten a room. I don't see myself livin' in a native house, and that's what some have to do. I don't know why they don't have a hotel."

They exchanged a few more words. Miss Thompson, loud-voiced and **garrulous**⑩, was evidently quite willing to gossip, but Mrs. Macphail had a

麦克费尔夫人满腹狐疑地看着丈夫。她和戴维森夫人交谈过后，心里感到有点忐忑不安。但是，她又不想说，自己觉得，戴维森夫人随时都有可能进来，还是不要玩扑克牌的好。麦克费尔医生拿来了扑克牌。丈夫在玩单人纸牌时，她看着他玩，不过心里隐隐地怀着负罪感。楼下狂欢的喧闹声还在继续。

① patience ['peiʃəns] *n.* 单人牌戏之一
② revelry ['revəlri] *n.* 狂欢
③ condemn [kən'dem] *v.* 使处于

翌日天气晴朗。麦克费尔夫妇既然不得不在帕果帕果待上两个星期，无所事事地打发时光，便着手做出安排，尽量让日子过得充实些。他们到了下面的码头，从他们的行李箱取出了许多书。医生前往海军医院，去拜访了那儿的外科主任，还陪同主任一块儿去查了病房。他们还在总督官邸留下了名片。他们途中还遇见了汤普森小姐。医生脱帽致意，她则对他说了声“上午好，医生”，声音很大，喜气洋洋。她的衣着打扮还和头天的一样，一身白色，脚上是一双白得铮亮的高跟靴子，上方露着两条粗腿，鼓鼓囊囊的，这在这样一处异国他乡的环境里，显得怪异离奇。

④ surgeon ['səːdʒən] *n.* 外科医生
⑤ frock [frɔk] *n.* 女服
⑥ exotic [ˌig'zɔtik] *a.* 异国情调的

“我觉得，她的穿着打扮很不得体，我必须得这样说，”麦克费尔夫人说，“在我眼中，她显得极度俗气。”

他们回到住处时，汤普森小姐正在露台上同店老板那些皮肤黝黑的孩子中的一个玩耍。

“和她打声招呼吧，”麦克费尔医生轻声对夫人说，“她独自一人在这里，忽略她显得不够厚道啊。”

麦克费尔夫人很羞怯，但是，她已经习惯了，丈夫怎么吩咐她，她就怎么做。

“我看我们是同住这儿一个屋檐下的房客呢。”她说，话说得有点不着要领。

“困在这么个鬼地方，真可怕啊，对吧？”汤普森小姐接话说，“而他们却告诉我说，我弄到了一个房间，算是有运气。不能想象我正住在当地房子里，但有些人就是不得不这么做。我真是弄不明白，他们怎么就不开一家旅馆呢。”

⑦ coop [kuːp] *v.* 将…限制在狭小空间
⑧ one-horse ['wʌn'hɔːs] *a.* 偏僻的
⑨ burg [bəːg] *n.* 小村

她们接着再交谈了几句。汤普森小姐说话大声大气，喋喋不休。很显然，她愿意再聊下去，但麦克费尔夫人

⑩ garrulous ['gærjuləs] *a.* 喋喋不休的

poor stock of small talk and presently she said:

"Well, I think we must go upstairs."

In the evening when they sat down to their high tea, Davidson on coming in said:

"I see that woman downstairs has a couple of sailors sitting there. I wonder how she's gotten acquainted with them."

"She can't be very particular," said Mrs. Davidson.

They were all rather tired after the idle, aimless day.

"If there's going to be a fortnight of this I don't know what we shall feel like at the end of it," said Dr. Macphail.

"The only thing to do is to portion out the day to different activities," answered the missionary. "I shall set aside a certain number of hours to study and a certain number to exercise, rain or fine—in the wet season you can't afford to pay any attention to the rain—and a certain number to **recreation**[①]."

Dr. Macphail looked at his companion with **misgiving**[②]. Davidson's programme oppressed him. They were eating Hamburger steak again. It seemed the only dish the cook knew how to make. Then below the gramophone began. Davidson started nervously when he heard it, but said nothing. Men's voices floated up. Miss Thompson's guests were joining in a well-known song and presently they heard her voice too, hoarse and loud. There was a good deal of shouting and laughing. The four people upstairs, trying to make conversation, listened despite themselves to the **clink**[③] of glasses and the scrape of chairs. More people had evidently come. Miss Thompson was giving a party.

"I wonder how she gets them all in," said Mrs. Macphail, suddenly breaking into a medical conversation between the missionary and her husband.

It showed whither her thoughts were wandering. The **twitch**[④] of Davidson's face proved that, though he spoke of scientific things, his mind was busy in the same direction. Suddenly, while the doctor was giving some experience of practice on the Flanders front, rather **prosily**[⑤], he sprang to his feet with a cry.

不善于闲聊，于是很快便说：

“恐怕我们该要上楼了。”

黄昏时分，他们坐下来喝傍晚茶时，戴维森进门便说：

“我看见楼下住着的那个女的同几位水手在一块儿。我不知道她是怎么认识他们的。”

“她不可能是个很讲究的人。”戴维森夫人说。

他们度过了无所事事、漫无目标的一天之后，全都感到很疲倦。

“若是两个星期里都像这样过日子，我真不知道到最后我们会对此有怎么样的一种感觉。”麦克费尔医生说。

“唯一的办法就是把日子分成段，开展不同的活动，”传教士回答说，“我会留出一定的时间用于学习，一定的时间用于锻炼，无论下雨还是天晴——雨季期间，您不可能顾及到天是否下雨——还要留出一定时间用于娱乐。”

麦克费尔医生打量着自己的同伴，目光中充满了疑虑。他听到了戴维森的计划后觉得喘不过气来。他们又吃汉堡牛排。厨子好像就只会做这道菜似的。然后，楼下的留声机又开始响起来了。戴维森听到声音后，怔了一下，神情不安，但没有吭声。有男人的声音飘了上来。汤普森小姐的客人们正在合唱一支广为人知的歌曲。他们很快也听到了她的声音，沙哑高亢。喊声笑声，闹哄哄的一片。楼上的四个人想要交谈一番，但却不由自主地听到碰杯的叮当声，椅子移动的刮擦声。显然又来了一些人，汤普森小姐举行聚会呢。

“我不知道，她怎么就把那些人全都邀请来了。”麦克费尔夫人说，突然打断了传教士和她丈夫之间关于医疗方面的谈话。

这句话表明了她的思绪所关注的地方。戴维森脸上抽搐的表情说明，尽管他在说着有关科学方面的事情，但他的心绪也沉浸在同一个方面。医生正在平铺直叙地谈着在弗兰德斯前线救治伤员的经历的当儿，猛然间，戴维森先生一跃身子站起来，大叫了一声。

① recreation [ˌrekri'eiʃən] *n.* 娱乐（活动）

② misgiving [ˌmis'giviŋ] *n.* 疑虑

③ clink [kliŋk] *n.* 丁当声

④ twitch [twitʃ] *n.* 抽搐

⑤ prosily ['prəuzili] *ad.* 单调地

"What's the matter, Alfred?" asked Mrs. Davidson.

"Of course! It never occurred to me. She's out of Iwelei."

"She can't be."

"She came on board at Honolulu. It's obvious. And she's carrying on her trade here. Here."

He uttered the last word with a passion of indignation.

"What's Iwelei?" asked Mrs. Macphail.

He turned his gloomy eyes on her and his voice trembled with horror.

"The **plague**① spot of Honolulu. The Red Light district. It was a **blot**② on our civilization."

Iwelei was on the edge of the city. You went down side streets by the harbour, in the darkness, across a rickety bridge, till you came to a deserted road, all **ruts**③ and holes, and then suddenly you came out into the light. There was parking room for motors on each side of the road, and there were **saloons**④, **tawdry**⑤ and bright, each one noisy with its mechanical piano, and there were barbers' shops and tobacconists. There was a stir in the air and a sense of expectant **gaiety**⑥. You turned down a narrow alley, either to the right or to the left, for the road divided Iwelei into two parts, and you found yourself in the district. There were rows of little bungalows, trim and neatly painted in green, and the pathway between them was broad and straight. It was laid out like a garden-city. In its respectable regularity, its order and **spruceness**⑦, it gave an impression of **sardonic**⑧ horror; for never can the search for love have been so systematized and ordered. The pathways were lit by a rare lamp, but they would have been dark except for the lights that came from the open windows of the bungalows. Men wandered about, looking at the women who sat at their windows, reading or sewing, for the most part taking no notice of the passers-by; and like the women they were of all nationalities. There were Americans, sailors

① plague [pleig] *n.* 瘟疫
② blot [blɔt] *n.* 耻辱
③ rut [rʌt] *n.* 凹槽
④ saloon [sə'lu:n] *n.* 酒吧
⑤ tawdry ['tɔ:dri] *n.* 花哨而不值钱的服饰
⑥ gaiety ['geiəti] *n.* 狂饮
⑦ spruceness['spru:snis] *n.* 整洁
⑧ sardonic [sɑ:'dɔnik] *a.* 嘲弄的

"怎么回事啊，阿尔弗雷德？"戴维森夫人问了一声。

"当然啦！我真是没有想到啊，她是从伊韦雷出来的。"

"不可能。"

"她是在火奴鲁鲁[1]上的船。这很明显啊。她在这儿做起生意来了。在这儿。"

他说最后这句话时情绪激动，义愤填膺。

"伊韦雷是什么地方啊？"麦克费尔夫人问了一句。

戴维森先生用阴郁的目光看着她，说话的声音颤抖着，充满了恐惧感。

"那是火奴鲁鲁的一个瘟疫盛行的地方，红灯区，是我们文明世界的一个污点。"

伊韦雷地处火奴鲁鲁城的边缘。黑暗中，您若是顺着港口附近的旁街小巷一路前行，跨过一座摇摇晃晃的桥梁，最后踏上一条人迹罕至的路，坑坑洼洼的，走着走着，突然便到达一片灯火通明处。道路的两边还有停车位。有形形色色的酒吧，色彩斑斓，灯光通亮。每一家酒吧都传出闹哄哄的声音，还夹杂着机械钢琴声。还有理发店和烟草铺。那儿弥漫着一种令人心旌摇曳的氛围，有一种随时可以寻欢作乐的感觉。您拐进一条狭窄的巷子，向左或向右都可以，因为小巷子把伊韦雷一分为二。这时候，您便置身于那个红灯区了。那儿有一排排小平房，整整齐齐的，外表漆成了绿色，平房之间的通道宽敞笔直，区域内的布局像是一座花园城市。区域的外观体面规整，井然有序，洁净漂亮，给人一种嘲讽而又恐怖的印象，因为从来没有哪儿的猎艳活动如此形成系统且井然有序的。过道上偶尔有盏灯亮着，但若不是有平房敞开着的窗口射出的灯光，那会是漆黑一片的。男人们四处徘徊，眼睛注视着坐在窗户边看书或做针线活儿的女人。大多数情况下，她们对经过窗户边的人视若无睹，不会抬头看上一眼。前来寻欢猎艳的男人

1　火奴鲁鲁（Honolulu）是美国夏威夷州首府和港口城市，华人称之为檀香山，位于北太平洋夏威夷群岛中瓦胡岛的东南角，延伸于滨河平原上。

from the ships in port, enlisted men off the gunboats, **somberly**① drunk, and soldiers from the **regiments**②, white and black, quartered on the island; there were Japanese, walking in twos and threes; Hawaiians, Chinese in long robes, and Filipinos in **preposterous**③ hats. They were silent and as it were oppressed. Desire is sad.

"It was the most crying scandal of the Pacific," exclaimed Davidson **vehemently**④. "The missionaries had been agitating against it for years, and at last the local press took it up. The police refused to stir. You know their argument. They say that **vice**⑤ is inevitable and consequently the best thing is to localise and control it. The truth is, they were paid. Paid. They were paid by the saloon-keepers, paid by the bullies, paid by the women themselves. At last they were forced to move."

"I read about it in the papers that came on board in Honolulu," said Dr. Macphail.

"Iwelei, with its sin and shame, ceased to exist on the very day we arrived. The whole population was brought before the justices. I don't know why I didn't understand at once what that woman was."

"Now you come to speak of it," said Mrs. Macphail, "I remember seeing her come on board only a few minutes before the boat sailed. I remember thinking at the time she was cutting it rather fine."

"How dare she come here!" cried Davidson indignantly. "I'm not going to allow it."

He strode towards the door.

"What are you going to?" asked Macphail.

"What do you expect me to do? I'm going to stop it. I'm not going to have this house turned into—into . . . "

He sought for a word that should not offend the ladies' ears. His eyes were flashing and his pale face was paler still in his emotion.

"It sounds as though there were three or four men down there," said the

像那些女人们一样，来自不同的国度。有美国人、那些船只停泊在港湾的水手、从炮舰上下来喝得酩酊大醉的列兵，还有驻岛兵团的士兵，白人黑人都有。有日本人，三三两两地漫步着。有夏威夷人，有身穿长袍的中国人，还有戴着古怪帽子的菲律宾人。他们沉默不语，好像受到了压抑，欲望得不到满足。

“这可是太平洋区域最为臭名昭著的地方啊，”戴维森情绪激动地大声说，“多少年来，传教士们情绪激愤，纷纷对其声讨，最后，当地的报纸给予了声援。但警方拒绝采取行动，您知道他们的理由。他们说，丑恶现象不可避免，因此，最有效的办法就是，划定专门区域，实施控制。实际情况是，他们被买通了，被买通了。他们收了酒吧老板的钱，收了妓院皮条客们的钱，还收了那些女人们的钱。最后，他们迫于压力才采取了行动。”

“船停泊在火奴鲁鲁时，我从送到船上来的报纸上看到这个情况。”麦克费尔医生说。

“我们抵达的那天，充满了罪恶和耻辱的伊韦雷不复存在了。那儿的所有人都要受到审判。我不知道，自己为何没有立刻明白过来，那女人是何货色。”

“您现在说起这事啊，”麦克费尔夫人说，“我记得，仅仅在船起航的前几分钟，看到那个女的登船。我记得，当时自己在想，她把时间卡得真准啊。”

“她胆子真大，竟敢到这儿来！”戴维森大声说着，义愤填膺，“我不能容忍这样的事情。”

他大步走向门口。

“您打算去干什么？”麦克费尔问了一声。

“您希望我去干什么呢？我去制止。我决不能让这幢住宅变成——变成……”

他在寻找一个恰当的词，不至于让两位夫人听后觉得刺耳。情绪激动之中，他双眼闪着亮光，苍白的脸庞变得更加苍白了。

“听声音楼下好像有三四个男人，”医生说，“现在

① somberly ['sɔmbəli] *ad.* 阴沉沉地
② regiment ['redʒimənt] *n.* 【军事】团
③ preposterous [pri'pɔstərəs] *a.* 十分荒谬的
④ vehemently ['viːiməntli] *ad.* 激烈地
⑤ vice [vais] *n.* 恶习

doctor. "Don't you think it's rather rash to go in just now?"

The missionary gave him a **contemptuous**① look and without a word flung out of the room.

"You know Mr. Davidson very little if you think the fear of personal danger can stop him in the performance of his duty," said his wife.

She sat with her hands nervously clasped, a spot of colour on her high cheekbones, listening to what was about to happen below. They all listened. They heard him **clatter**② down the wooden stairs and throw open the door. The singing stopped suddenly, but the gramophone continued to bray out its vulgar tune. They heard Davidson's voice and then the noise of something heavy falling. The music stopped. He had **hurled**③ the gramophone on the floor. Then again they heard Davidson's voice, they could not make out the words, then Miss Thompson's, loud and shrill, then a confused **clamour**④ as though several people were shouting together at the top of their lungs. Mrs. Davidson gave a little gasp, and she **clenched**⑤ her hands more tightly. Dr. Macphail looked uncertainly from her to his wife. He did not want to go down, but he wondered if they expected him to. Then there was something that sounded like a **scuffle**⑥. The noise now was more distinct. It might be that Davidson was being thrown out of the room. The door was slammed. There was a moment's silence and they heard Davidson come up the stairs again. He went to his room.

"I think I'll go to him," said Mrs. Davidson.

She got up and went out.

"If you want me, just call," said Mrs. Macphail, and then when the other was gone: "I hope he isn't hurt."

"Why couldn't he mind his own business?" said Dr. Macphail.

They sat in silence for a minute or two and then they both started, for the gramophone began to play once more, defiantly, and mocking voices shouted hoarsely the words of an **obscene**⑦ song.

Next day Mrs. Davidson was pale and tired. She complained of headache, and she looked old and **wizened**⑧. She told Mrs. Macphail that the missionary

闯入那个房间，您不觉得会显得有点鲁莽吗？”

传教士轻蔑地瞥了他一眼，一声没吭，冲出了房间。

“您若是认为戴维森先生在履行自己的职责时，他会因为担心个人的安危而止步不前，那说明您太不了解他了。”戴维森夫人说。

她坐在那儿，心神不宁，两只手扣在一块儿，高高的颧骨上泛起了一块红晕，倾听着楼下将要出现的情况。他们全都倾听着。他们听见他蹬蹬走下木楼梯，用力敲开门。唱歌的声音戛然而止，但留声机还在继续播放那俗不可耐的曲调。他们听见了戴维森说话的声音，接着是什么笨重的东西掉下的声音。音乐声停止了。他把留声机扔在了地上。他们随即又听见了戴维森说话的声音，但听不清他说什么。然后是汤普森小姐说话的声音，高亢尖细，然后是一片嘈杂的声音，好像有几个人在声嘶力竭地大喊大叫着。戴维森夫人倒吸了一口凉气，两只手握得更紧了。麦克费尔医生心里没有底，一会儿看看戴维森夫人，一会儿看看自己夫人。他不想下楼去，但不知道她们是否希望他下去。这时候，传来了一阵像是打斗的声响。喧闹声此时更加清晰了。很有可能，他们把戴维森先生扔到房间外面了，因为房门砰地一声关上了。出现了片刻安静，他们听见戴维森返回楼上的脚步声。他进了自己的房间。

“我看，我得到他身边去。”戴维森夫人说。

她站起身，走出了房间。

“若是需要我们，喊一声就行。”麦克费尔夫人说。等到另外这一位出去了之后，她又说：“但愿他没有受伤啊。”

“他管好自己的事情不就得了吗？”麦克费尔医生说。

他们坐了片刻，沉默不语。然后，两个人都怔了一下，因为留声机再次开始播放音乐了，挑衅似的，用嘲笑的声音沙哑地吼着一首低俗的歌曲。

翌日，戴维森夫人显得脸色苍白，精疲力竭。她说自己患了头痛症，显得苍老而又憔悴。她告诉麦克费尔夫人，传教士彻夜未眠，整个晚上都诚惶诚恐，情绪激

① contemptuous [kən'temptjuəs] *a.* 轻视的

② clatter ['klætə] *v.* 咔哒地迅速移动

③ hurl [hə:l] *v.* 用力掷

④ clamour ['klæmə] *n.* 吵嚷

⑤ clench [klentʃ] *v.* 握紧

⑥ scuffle ['skʌfl] *n.* 混战

⑦ obscene [əb'si:n] *a.* 粗俗的

⑧ wizened ['wizənd] *a.* 枯槁的

had not slept at all; he had passed the night in a state of frightful **agitation**① and at five had got up and gone out. A glass of beer had been thrown over him and his clothes were **stained**② and **stinking**③. But a sombre fire glowed in Mrs. Davidson's eyes when she spoke of Miss Thompson.

"She'll bitterly **rue**④ the day when she **flouted**⑤ Mr. Davidson," she said. "Mr. Davidson has a wonderful heart and no one who is in trouble has ever gone to him without being comforted, but he has no mercy for sin, and when his **righteous**⑥ **wrath**⑦ is excited he's terrible."

"Why, what will he do?" asked Mrs. Macphail.

"I don't know, but I wouldn't stand in that creature's shoes for anything in the world."

Mrs. Macphail **shuddered**⑧. There was something positively alarming in the triumphant assurance of the little woman's manner. They were going out together that morning, and they went down the stairs side by side. Miss Thompson's door was open, and they saw her in a **bedraggled**⑨ dressing-gown, cooking something in a **chafing-dish**⑩.

"Good morning," she called. "Is Mrs. Davidson better this morning?"

They passed her in silence, with their noses in the air, as if she did not exist. They flushed, however, when she burst into a shout of **derisive**⑪ laughter. Mrs. Davidson turned on her suddenly.

"Don't you dare to speak to me," she screamed. "If you insult me I shall have you turned out of here."

"Say, did I ask Mr. Davidson to visit with me?"

"Don't answer her," whispered Mrs. Macphail hurriedly.

They walked on till they were out of earshot.

"She's **brazen**⑫, brazen," burst from Mrs. Davidson.

Her anger almost **suffocated**⑬ her.

And on their way home they met her strolling towards the quay. She had all

动，五点钟就起床，之后便外出了。那伙人当时把一杯啤酒泼了他一身，衣服弄脏了，一股酒味。但是，戴维森夫人一提到汤普森小姐时，眼睛里面闪烁着怒火。

“她用轻蔑简慢的态度对待戴维森先生，将来会后悔莫及的，”她说，“戴维森先生拥有博大的胸怀，但凡有人遇到困难去找他，没有得不到安慰的。但是，他对罪恶行为毫不留情，一旦激发起了他的义愤，那情形着实可怕。”

“啊，他会干什么呢？”麦克费尔夫人问了一声。

“我不知道，但是，不管怎么说，我是不会设身处地站在那个货色的立场上说话的。”

麦克费尔夫人身子颤抖一下。眼前这个小个子女人的态度中充满了得意和自信，确实令人感到惊恐。当天早上，两位夫人一块儿出门了。她们并排下楼。汤普森小姐的房门敞开着。她们看见她披着一件脏兮兮的的晨衣[1]，用火锅在做什么吃的。

“早上好，”她招呼了一声，“戴维森夫人今天早上好些了吗？”

她们没吭一声，昂首挺胸，走了过去，好像对方压根儿就不存在似的。不过，当汤普森小姐爆发出一阵讥讽的哈哈大笑声时，她们满脸绯红。戴维森夫人猛然间转过身对着她。

“你竟然敢对我说话，”她大声叫喊着，“你若是侮辱我，我一定让你从这儿滚出去。”

“喂，难道是我要求戴维森先生去我房间里的不成？”

“别理会她。”麦克费尔夫人急忙低声说。

她们继续朝前走，最后听不见那声音了。

“她简直厚颜无耻，厚颜无耻，”戴维森夫人脱口说出。她怒不可遏，都感觉快要窒息了。

她们返回住处的途中，遇见汤普森小姐悠闲地朝着

① agitation [ˌædʒiˈteiʃən] *n.* 焦虑

② stained [steind] *a.* 弄脏的

③ stinking [ˈstiŋkiŋ] *a.* 恶臭的

④ rue [ruː] *v.* 对…感到悔恨

⑤ flout [ˈflaut] *v.* 侮辱

⑥ righteous [ˈraitʃəs] *a.* 正义的

⑦ wrath [ræθ] *n.* 愤怒

⑧ shudder [ˈʃʌdə] *v.* 哆嗦

⑨ bedraggled [biˈdrægld] *a.* 破旧的

⑩ chafing-dish [ˈtʃeifiŋ ˌdiʃ] *n.* 火锅

⑪ derisive [diˈraisiv] *a.* 嘲笑的

⑫ brazen [ˈbreizən] *a.* 厚颜无耻的

⑬ suffocate [ˈsʌfəkeit] *v.* 使窒息

1　晨衣（dressing-gown）是指梳妆、休息等时候罩在睡衣外面的衣服，“晨衣”和“睡衣”（pajamas, sleepcoat, nightgown, nighty, bathrobe, jams, nightclothes, nightdress）并不是同一个东西。

her finery on. Her great white hat with its vulgar, showy flowers was an **affront**[①]. She called out cheerily to them as she went by, and a couple of American sailors who were standing there grinned as the ladies set their faces to an icy stare. They got in just before the rain began to fall again.

"I guess she'll get her fine clothes spoilt," said Mrs. Davidson with a bitter **sneer**[②].

Davidson did not come in till they were half-way through dinner. He was wet through, but he would not change. He sat, morose and silent, refusing to eat more than a mouthful, and he stared at the **slanting**[③] rain. When Mrs. Davidson told him of their two encounters with Miss Thompson he did not answer. His deepening frown alone showed that he had heard.

"Don't you think we ought to make Mr. Horn turn her out of here?" asked Mrs. Davidson. "We can't allow her to insult us."

"There doesn't seem to be any other place for her to go," said Macphail.

"She can live with one of the natives."

"In weather like this a native hut must be a rather uncomfortable place to live in."

"I lived in one for years," said the missionary.

When the little native girl brought in the fried bananas which formed the sweet they had every day, Davidson turned to her.

"Ask Miss Thompson when it would be convenient for me to see her," he said.

The girl nodded shyly and went out.

"What do you want to see her for, Alfred?" asked his wife.

"It's my duty to see her. I won't act till I've given her every chance."

"You don't know what she is. She'll insult you."

"Let her insult me. Let her spit on me. She has an **immortal**[④] soul, and I must do all that is in my power to save it."

① affront [ə'frʌnt] *n.* 公开侮辱

② sneer [sniə] *n.* 冷笑

③ slanting ['slɑːntiŋ] *a.* 斜向的

④ immortal [i'mɔːtəl] *a.* 不朽的

码头走去。她衣着艳丽，大白帽子上缀着庸俗扎眼的花朵，简直是公然挑衅。她一边走一边兴致勃勃地同她们打招呼。两位夫人一副冷若冰霜的态度，眼睛盯着她看，惹得站立在一旁的几位美国水手咧着嘴笑。她们刚一进门，天又开始下雨了。

“我估计，她的那些漂亮衣服这下可糟蹋啦。”戴维森夫人说着，语气尖酸而轻蔑。

他们的午餐用到了一半，戴维森先生才进来。他衣服湿透了，但执意不肯去换。他坐了下来，神情忧郁，沉默不语，吃了一点点便不再吃了，眼睛盯着外面斜落下的雨水。戴维森夫人告诉他，她们两次同汤普森小姐照面的情况，但他没有回话。他皱眉蹙眼，眉宇间的蹙纹加深了。仅凭这一点就说明他已经听见了。

“你不觉得，我们应该给霍恩先生施加压力，要他把她从这儿赶走吗？”戴维森夫人问了一声，“我们不能容许她侮辱我们啊。”

“她看起来也没有别的什么地方可去呀。”麦克费尔医生说。

“她可以住到某位土著居民家里去。”

“遇上这样的天气，住在土著居民的棚屋里一定很不舒服的。”

“我曾经在一间棚屋住了很多年呢。”传教士说。

他们每天都用煎香蕉当甜点。当那位土著小姑娘端上煎香蕉来时，戴维森转身对着她。

“问一声汤普森小姐，我什么时候去见她方便，”他说。

小姑娘点了点头，显得很羞怯，然后出去了。

“你去见她想要干什么，阿尔弗雷德？”他夫人问了一声。

“去见她是我的责任。我一定要先给她机会，做到仁至义尽，然后才会采取行动的。”

“你不知道她是什么货色，她会侮辱你的。”

“那就让她来侮辱我吧，让她来对着我吐唾沫吧。她也拥有不朽的灵魂，我一定要尽我所能，拯救她的灵魂。”

Mrs. Davidson's ears rang still with the **harlot's**[1] mocking laughter.

"She's gone too far."

"Too far for the mercy of God?" His eyes lit up suddenly and his voice grew **mellow**[2] and soft.

"Never. The sinner may be deeper in sin than the depth of hell itself, but the love of the Lord Jesus can reach him still."

The girl came back with the message.

"Miss Thompson's compliments and as long as Rev. Davidson don't come in business hours she'll be glad to see him any time."

The party received it in **stony**[3] silence, and Dr. Macphail quickly **effaced**[4] from his lips the smile which had come upon them. He knew his wife would be **vexed**[5] with him if he found Miss Thompson's **effrontery**[6] amusing.

They finished the meal in silence. When it was over the two ladies got up and took their work, Mrs. Macphail was making another of the innumerable **comforters**[7] which she had turned out since the beginning of the war, and the doctor lit his pipe. But Davidson remained in his chair and with abstracted eyes stared at the table. At last he got up and without a word went out of the room. They heard him go down and they heard Miss Thompson's defiant "Come in" when he knocked at the door. He remained with her for an hour. And Dr. Macphail watched the rain. It was beginning to get on his nerves. It was not like soft English rain that drops gently on the earth; it was unmerciful and somehow terrible; you felt in it the **malignancy**[8] of the primitive powers of nature. It did not pour, it flowed. It was like a **deluge**[9] from heaven, and it **rattled**[10] on the roof of corrugated iron with a steady persistence that was maddening. It seemed to have a fury of its own. And sometimes you felt that you must scream if it did not stop, and then suddenly you felt powerless, as

① harlot ['hɑːlət] *n.* 妓女

② mellow ['meləu] *a.*（声音）圆润的

③ stony ['stəuni] *a.* 面无表情的

④ efface [i'feis] *v.* 抹去

⑤ vexed [vekst] *a.* 烦恼的

⑥ effrontery [i'frʌntəri] *n.* 厚颜无耻（的行为）

⑦ comforter ['kʌmfətə] *n.* 羊毛围巾

⑧ malignancy [mə'lignənsi] *n.* 恶意

⑨ deluge ['deljuːdʒ] *n.* 洪水

⑩ rattle ['rætl] *v.* 发出嘎嘎声

戴维森夫人的耳畔仍然回响着那个娼妓讥讽的哈哈大笑声。

"她已经走得太远了。"

"远到无法得到上帝的宽恕吗？"他的眼睛突然闪亮起来，声音温柔和蔼了起来。"绝不可能。有罪的人所犯罪行可能比地狱本身更深重，但是，主耶稣的爱照样可以到达他们的身边。"

小姑娘把消息带回来了。

"汤普森小姐带来问候。只要戴维森神父不在她做生意的时间里去，她什么时间都乐于同他见面。"

一拨人听到这个回音后，态度冰冷，沉默不语。麦克费尔医生急忙把已经挂在了嘴边的微笑抹去。他知道，他若是觉得汤普森小姐厚颜无耻的行径很好玩，他夫人会跟他急的。

他们在沉默中用完了午餐。用过午餐后，两位夫人站起身，拿起了她们的手工活儿。麦克费尔夫人正在编织一条新的围巾。自从战争[1]爆发后，她编织了不知多少条这样的围巾。医生开始抽起了烟斗。但是，戴维森先生坐在椅子上一动不动，眼睛出神地盯着餐桌上看。最后，他站起身，一声不吭地走出了房间。他们听见了他下楼的脚步声。他们还听见，当他敲门时，汤普森小姐语气简慢地说了声"进来"。戴维森先生同她在一块儿待了一个小时。麦克费尔医生注视着外面下雨的情形。连绵的雨水让他心里开始感到不安起来。这儿下雨和英国的情况不一样。英国的雨水淅淅沥沥，轻柔地落在大地上。这儿的雨水残酷无情，多少有点让人恐惧。您从中可以感受到，大自然邪恶的原始力量。这儿的雨水不是倾盆而下，而是犹如滔滔江水。雨水犹如来自天上的洪流，倾泻在瓦楞铁皮的房顶上，一刻不停，疯狂不羁。看起来，雨水也有自己的怒气。有时候，您会感觉到，雨水若是再不停下，便会尖叫起来。紧接着，您会感觉

1 毛姆的这篇作品创作于1920年，所以，此处是指第一次世界大战。

though your bones had suddenly become soft; and you were miserable and hopeless.

Macphail turned his head when the missionary came back. The two women looked up.

"I've given her every chance. I have **exhorted**[①] her to **repent**[②]. She is an evil woman."

He paused, and Dr. Macphail saw his eyes darken and his pale face grow hard and **stern**[③].

"Now I shall take the whips with which the Lord Jesus drove the **usurers**[④] and the money changers out of the Temple of the Most High."

He walked up and down the room. His mouth was close set, and his black brows were frowning.

"If she fled to the uttermost parts of the earth I should pursue her."

With a sudden movement he turned round and strode out of the room. They heard him go downstairs again.

"What is he going to do?" asked Mrs. Macphail.

"I don't know." Mrs. Davidson took off her pince-nez and wiped them. "When he is on the Lord's work I never ask him questions."

She sighed a little.

"What is the matter?"

"He'll wear himself out. He doesn't know what it is to spare himself."

Dr. Macphail learnt the first results of the missionary's activity from the half-caste trader in whose house they lodged. He stopped the doctor when he passed the store and came out to speak to him on the **stoop**[⑤]. His fat face was worried.

"The Rev. Davidson has been at me for letting Miss Thompson have a room here," he said, "but I didn't know what she was when I rented it to her. When people come and ask if I can rent them a room all I want to know is if they've the money to pay for it. And she paid me for hers a week in advance."

Dr. Macphail did not want to commit himself.

"When all's said and done it's your house. We're very much obliged to you

到无能为力，好像感觉您骨架都酥软了似的。您会感到痛苦和绝望。

传教士返回时，麦克费尔医生扭过头看着。两位女士也抬头看了看。

“我已经给了她所有机会，规劝她悔过自新，但她是个邪恶的女人。”

他打住了。麦克费尔医生看见他的眼睛阴沉了下来，苍白的面孔绷得紧紧的，神色严厉。

“主耶稣曾经用鞭子把放高利贷者和货币兑换者驱赶出了至上神殿，我现在要接过那些鞭子。”

他在房间里来回走着，双唇紧闭，浓眉紧锁。

“她即便逃到天涯海角，我也要追上她。”

他猛然一动，转过身来，大步走出了房间。他们听见了他再次下楼的脚步声。

“他这是要去干什么啊？”麦克费尔夫人问了一声。

“我不知道，”戴维森夫人取下鼻梁上的眼镜，擦拭一番，“每当他在按照上帝的旨意行事时，我是不会问他问题的。”

她微微叹息了一声。

“怎么回事？”

“他会把自己弄得精疲力竭的，就是不知道如何爱惜自己。”

关于传教士第一次采取行动后的结果，麦克费尔医生是从他们的房东老板那儿听到的。医生路过店铺时，老板叫住了他，从店里出来在门廊处同他说话。老板脸上的表情显得很忧虑。

“戴维森神父找到我，说我不该把在这儿把房间租给汤普森小姐住，”他说，“但是，我把房间租给她时，我不知道她是干什么的。若是有人上门来打听是否有房间出租，我需要知道的就是，他们是否付得起租金。而她预交了一个星期的房租呢。”

麦克费尔医生不愿意给自己惹麻烦。

“不管怎么说，房子总归是您的。您能够让我们大

① exhort [ig'zɔ:t] v. 劝告
② repent [ri'pent] v. 悔改
③ stern [stə:n] a. 严肃的
④ usurer ['ju:ʒərə] n. 高利贷者
⑤ stoop [stu:p] n. 小门廊

for taking us in at all."

Horn looked at him doubtfully. He was not certain yet how definitely Macphail stood on the missionary's side.

"The missionaries are in with one another," he said, hesitatingly. "If they get it in for a trader he may just as well shut up his store and quit."

"Did he want you to turn her out?"

"No, he said so long as she behaved herself he couldn't ask me to do that. He said he wanted to be just to me. I promised she shouldn't have no more visitors. I've just been and told her.

"How did she take it?"

"She gave me Hell."

The trader **squirmed**① in his old **ducks**②. He had found Miss Thompson a rough customer.

"Oh, well, I daresay she'll get out. I don't suppose she wants to stay here if she can't have anyone in."

"There's nowhere she can go, only a native house, and no native'll take her now, not now that the missionaries have got their knife in her."

Dr. Macphail looked at the falling rain.

"Well, I don't suppose it's any good waiting for it to clear up."

In the evening when they sat in the parlour Davidson talked to them of his early days at college. He had had no **means**③ and had worked his way through by doing odd jobs during the vacations. There was silence downstairs. Miss Thompson was sitting in her little room alone. But suddenly the gramophone began to play. She had set it on in defiance, to cheat her loneliness, but there was no one to sing, and it had a melancholy note. It was like a cry for help Davidson took no notice. He was in the middle of a long anecdote and without change of expression went on. The gramophone continued. Miss Thompson put on one **reel**④ after another. It looked as though the silence of the night were getting on her nerves. It was breathless and **sultry**⑤. When the Macphails went to bed they could not sleep. They lay side by side with their eyes wide open, listening to the

家住下来，我们已经感激不尽。”

霍恩满腹狐疑地打量着对方。他心里没有底，不知道麦克费尔医生多大程度上支持传教士。

“传教士会一个接着一个到这儿来，”霍恩说，态度显得犹豫，“倘若他们都来干涉一位生意人的事情，那他还不得关门走人呀。”

“他想要您赶她走吗？”

“没有，他说了，只要她检点自己的行为，他便不会要求我做那样的事情。他说，他会公平对待我。我承诺了，要求她不要再接待客人。我刚刚去对她说了。”

“她是个什么态度呢？”

“她数落了我一番。”

店老板穿着一条旧帆布裤子，扭动着身子。他发现，汤普森小姐不是个善主。

“噢，是啊，我肯定，她会离开的。我认为，只要她招揽不到客人，她就不会想要待在这儿的。”

“她没有地方可去的，只有住到某个土著居民家里去，现在土著居民中也没有哪个会收留她，毕竟传教士们已经对她耿耿于怀了。”

麦克费尔医生看着外面落下的雨水。

“是啊，我觉得吧，要等到雨过天晴，这样也无济于事。”

傍晚，他们坐在客厅里时，戴维森先生给他们讲述自己早年在大学的岁月。他没有经济来源，只能通过假期打零工来支撑学业。楼下悄无声息。汤普森小姐独自一人坐在自己的房间里。但是，突然间，留声机开始播放起音乐来了。她公然播放留声机，以便掩饰自己的孤独，但没有唱歌，留声机播放的是一支哀婉忧伤的曲调。声音像是在呼喊着求助，但戴维森毫不理会。他漫长的人生趣事才讲述到中间部分。他表情毫无变化，继续讲述下去。留声机继续播放着。汤普森小姐把唱片放了一张又一张。看起来，寂静的漫漫长夜令她心惊胆战。天气炎热，让人透不过气来。麦克费尔夫妇上床后，无法入眠。他们并排躺着，睁大着眼睛，倾听着蚊帐外面蚊

① squirm [skwəːm] *v.* 扭动
② duck [dʌk] *n.* 紧身弹力薄棉衫
③ means [miːnz] *n.* 收入
④ reel [riːl] *n.*（磁带等的）一盘
⑤ sultry [sʌltri] *a.* 闷热的

cruel singing of the mosquitoes outside their curtain.

"What's that?" whispered Mrs. Macphail at last.

They heard a voice, Davidson's voice, through the wooden **partition**①. It went on with a **monotonous**②, earnest insistence. He was praying aloud. He was praying for the soul of Miss Thompson.

Two or three days went by. Now when they passed Miss Thompson on the road she did not greet them with ironic **cordiality**③ or smile; she passed with her nose in the air, a **sulky**④ look on her painted face, frowning, as though she did not see them. The trader told Macphail that she had tried to get lodging elsewhere, but had failed. In the evening she played through the various reels of her gramophone, but the pretence of **mirth**⑤ was obvious now. The ragtime had a cracked, heart-broken rhythm as though it were a one-step of despair. When she began to play on Sunday Davidson sent Horn to beg her to stop at once since it was the Lord's day. The reel was taken off and the house was silent except for the steady **pattering**⑥ of the rain on the iron roof.

"I think she's getting a bit worked up," said the trader next day to Macphail. "She don't know what Mr. Davidson's up to and it makes her scared."

Macphail had caught a glimpse of her that morning and it struck him that her arrogant expression had changed. There was in her face a **hunted**⑦ look. The half-caste gave him a sidelong glance.

"I suppose you don't know what Mr. Davidson is doing about it?" he **hazarded**⑧.

"No, I don't."

It was **singular**⑨ that Horn should ask him that question, for he also had the idea that the misssionary was mysteriously at work. He had an impression that he was weaving a net around the woman, carefully, systematically, and

① partition [pɑ:'tiʃən] *n.* 隔墙
② monotonous [mə'nɔtənəs] *a.* 单调的
③ cordiality [ˌkɔ:di'æliti] *n.* 热诚
④ sulky ['sʌlki] *a.* 阴郁的
⑤ mirth [mə:θ] *n.* 高兴
⑥ pattering ['pætəriŋ] *n.* 嗒嗒声
⑦ hunted ['hʌntid] *a.* 惊恐万状的
⑧ hazard ['hæzəd] *v.* 斗胆提出
⑨ singular ['siŋgjulə] *a.* 异常的

子无情的嗡嗡声。

“怎么回事？”麦克费尔夫人最后小声说。

他们听见了一个声音，是戴维森先生说话的声音。声音是从木板墙隔壁的房间里传过来的。声音单调，但诚恳，而且持续不断。他是在大声祈祷来着。他是在替汤普森小姐的灵魂祈祷。

两三天过去了。他们现在在路上遇见汤普森小姐时，她不会用讥讽而又热情的口吻同他们打招呼，或者冲着他们微笑。她会昂首挺胸地走过去，浓妆艳抹的脸上挂着阴郁的表情，眉头紧锁，好像没有看见他们似的。店老板告诉了麦克费尔医生，她已经想方设法在别处寻找住处，但没有找到。到了夜晚，她便打开留声机播放各种唱片，但是，这种假装开心的情形已经显而易见了。传出来的雷格泰姆音乐[1]犹如绝望的一步舞曲[2]，节奏破碎，旋律忧伤。她在星期天播放留声机时，戴维森便会打发霍恩去恳请她立刻停止播放，因为这是安息日。唱片取下来了，整幢房子里一片寂静，只有雨水不停地打在铁皮房顶上啪啪的声音。

“我觉得，她有点醒悟了，”翌日，店老板对麦克费尔说，“她不知道戴维森先生将会采取什么措施，她对此感到害怕。”

当天早上，麦克费尔曾见过她一面。他突然发现，她那种傲气十足的表情有了变化了，一副惊恐不安的样子。店老板斜睨着眼睛瞥了他一眼。

“我估计，您也不知道戴维森先生如何处理这件事情吧？”他壮起胆子问了一声。

“对啊，不知道呢。”

非同寻常的是，霍恩竟然会在他面前提出这么个问题，因为医生也在寻思着，传教士处事神秘兮兮的。他有一种感觉，认为传教士在那个女人周围织起了一张

1　雷格泰姆音乐（ragtime）是一种多用切分音法的早起爵士乐，19世纪末20世纪初流行于美国。

2　一步舞曲（one-step）是一种快速的两拍狐步舞。

suddenly, when everything was ready, would pull the strings tight.

"He told me to tell her," said the trader, "that if at any time she wanted him she only had to send and he'd come."

"What did she say when you told her that?"

"She didn't say nothing. I didn't stop. I just said what he said I was to and then I beat it. I thought she might be going to start weepin'."

"I have no doubt the loneliness is getting on her nerves," said the doctor. "And the rain—that's enough to make anyone **jumpy**①," he continued irritably. "Doesn't it ever stop in this confounded place?"

"It goes on pretty steady in the rainy season. We have three hundred inches in the year. You see, it's the shape of the bay. It seems to attract the rain from all over the Pacific."

"Damn the shape of the bay," said the doctor.

He scratched his mosquito bites. He felt very short-tempered. When the rain stopped and the sun shone, it was like a hot-house, **seething**②, humid, sultry, breathless, and you had a strange feeling that everything was growing with a savage violence. The natives, **blithe**③ and childlike by reputation, seemed then, with their **tattooing**④ and their dyed hair, to have something **sinister**⑤ in their appearance; and when they pattered along at your heels with their naked feet you looked back instinctively. You felt they might at any moment come behind you swiftly and **thrust**⑥ long knife between your shoulder-blades. You could not tell what dark thoughts **lurked**⑦ behind their wide-set eyes. They had a little the look of ancient Egyptians painted on a temple wall, and there was about them the terror of what is immeasurably old.

The missionary came and went. He was busy, but the Macphails did not know what he was doing. Horn told the doctor that he saw the governor every day, and once Davidson mentioned him.

"He looks as if he had plenty of determination," he said, "but when you **come down to brass tacks**⑧ he has no backbone."

网，小心翼翼，周密系统。等到一切都水到渠成时，他便会突然收网。

“他吩咐我告诉她，”店老板说，“无论何时，她若是想要见他，她只需要打发人来说一声，他就会到。”

“您把这个意思告诉她时，她怎么说的呢？”

“她什么也没说。我没有逗留，只是把传教士吩咐我说的话转达了，接着便赶紧离开了。我当时觉得，她可能立刻要哭出来了。”

“毫无疑问，我认为，她受不了眼下的寂寞，”医生说。“还有这雨——这已经够让人心烦的了，”他接着说，显得很恼火，“这么个鬼地方，难道雨就不会停了吗？”

“雨季当中，雨下起来是持续不断的。年降雨量达到三百英寸。您看吧，这是海湾地势的原因。看起来，它似乎把整个太平洋区域的雨水都吸引过来了。”

“该死的海湾地势啊。”医生说。

他抓挠着蚊虫叮咬过的地方，焦躁不安。雨过天晴之后，这儿就像个暖房，炎热潮湿，令人透不过气来。您会有一种奇怪的感觉，认为万物生长都会带有一种野蛮的暴力。土著居民们虽然以率真快乐、充满孩子气闻名，但是，凭着他们满身刺着图案，还有染过的头发，他们身上似乎有种邪恶的东西。当他们光着脚啪嗒啪嗒地跟随在您身后时，您会不由自主地回头看上一眼。您会觉得，他们可能随时都会急速到达您的身后，用长刀架到您两肩中间的脖子上。您无法弄清楚，他们睁大着的眼睛后面潜藏着什么歹意。他们那副模样有点儿像画在神庙墙壁上的古埃及人，浑身透着年代久远的古老的恐怖气息。

传教士进来又出去了。他很忙碌，但麦克费尔夫妇不知道，他在忙碌些什么。霍恩告诉医生，说他每天都去见总督。戴维森有一次还提到过他。

“他看起来好像很有决心的样子，”戴维森先生说，“但是，当触及到实质性的问题时，他的脊梁骨便硬不起来了。”

① jumpy ['dʒʌmpi] *a.* 紧张不安的

② seething ['si:ðiŋ] *a.* 火热的

③ blithe [blaið] *a.* 无忧无虑的

④ tattooing [tə'tu:iŋ] *n.* 纹身

⑤ sinister ['sinistə] *a.* 邪恶的

⑥ thrust [θrʌst] *v.* 刺入

⑦ lurk [lə:k] *v.* 潜伏

⑧ come down to brass tacks 讨论实质性问题

"I suppose that means he won't do exactly what you want," suggested the doctor **facetiously**①.

The missionary did not smile.

"I want him to do what's right. It shouldn't be necessary to persuade a man to do that."

"But there may be differences of opinion about what is right."

"If a man had a **gangrenous**② foot would you have patience with anyone who hesitated to **amputate**③ it?"

"Gangrene is a matter of fact."

"And Evil?"

What Davidson had done soon appeared. The four of them had just finished their midday meal, and they had not yet separated for the **siesta**④ which the heat imposed on the ladies and on the doctor. Davidson had little patience with the slothful habit. The door was suddenly flung open and Miss Thompson came in. She looked round the room and then went up to Davidson.

"You **low-down**⑤ **skunk**⑥, what have you been saying about me to the governor?"

She was **spluttering**⑦ with rage. There was a moment's pause. Then the missionary drew forward a chair.

"Won't you be seated, Miss Thompson? I've been hoping to have another talk with you."

"You poor low-life bastard."

She burst into a torrent of insult, **foul**⑧ and **insolent**⑨. Davidson kept his grave eyes on her.

"I'm indifferent to the abuse you think fit to **heap**⑩ on me, Miss Thompson," he said, "but I must beg you to remember that ladies are present."

Tears by now were struggling with her anger. Her face was red and swollen as though she were choking.

"What has happened?" asked Dr. Macphail.

"A feller's just been in here and he says I gotter beat it on the next boat."

“我估计，这意味着，他不会完全按照您的意思去做啊。”医生提示着说，语气诙谐。

传教士的脸上没有笑容。

“我想要他做正确的事情，本来是不需要说服一个人去这样做的。”

“但是，关于何为正确的事情，不同的人可能有不同的看法啊。”

“倘若一个人的脚上生了坏疽病，但他态度犹豫，不知道是否该把它切除，这时候，您还会有耐性等他吗？”

“坏疽病是个事实。”

“那么罪恶呢？”

戴维森已经采取了什么措施很快就明晰了。他们四个人刚刚用完了午餐，但还没有各自分开去午睡，这是炎热的天气迫使两位夫人和医生必须要进行的活动。戴维森对这种懒散的习惯缺少耐性。房门突然摔开了，汤普森小姐走了进来。她先环顾了一番房间四周，然后走向戴维森。

“你这个卑鄙的小人，你在总督面前说我什么了？”

她怒不可遏，唾沫飞溅。出现了片刻停顿。传教士随后拖过来一把椅子。

“请坐下来吧，汤普森小姐。我想要和您再谈一谈。”

“你这个臭不要脸的杂种。”

她破口大骂起来，污言秽语，不堪入耳。戴维森目光严峻，盯着她看。

“您对我破口大骂，我不会理会的，汤普森小姐，”他说，“但是，我请求您别忘了，有两位夫人在场呢。”

这时候，她怀着满腔的怒火，泪水在眼睛里打转，脸色通红，双颊肿胀，好像哽咽哭泣了。

“发生什么事情啦？”麦克费尔医生问了一声。

“刚才有个家伙来找了我。他说，我必须乘下一班船走人。”

① facetiously [fə'si:ʃəsli] *ad.* 滑稽地

② gangrenous ['gæŋgrinəs] *a.* 生坏疽的

③ amputate ['æmpjuteit] *v.* 截（肢）

④ siesta [si'estə] *n.* 午休

⑤ low-down ['ləuˌdaun] *a.* 下等的

⑥ skunk [skʌŋk] *n.* 卑鄙小人

⑦ splutter ['splʌtə] *v.* 语无伦次

⑧ foul [faul] *a.* 亵渎的

⑨ insolent ['insələnt] *a.* 侮辱的

⑩ heap [hi:p] *v.* 拼命添加

Was there a gleam in the missionary's eyes? His face remained impassive.

"You could hardly expect the governor to let you stay here under the circumstances."

"You done it," she shrieked. "You can't kid me. You done it."

"I don't want to deceive you. I urged the governor to take the only possible step consistent with his obligations."

"Why couldn't you leave me be? I wasn't doin' you no harm."

"You may be sure that if you had I should be the last man to resent it."

"Do you think I want to stay on in this poor imitation of a **burg**①? I don't look no busher, do I?"

"In that case I don't see what cause of complaint you have," he answered.

She gave an inarticulate cry of rage and flung out of the room. There was a short silence.

"It's a relief to know that the governor has acted at last," said Davidson finally. "He's a weak man and he **shilly-shallied**②. He said she was only here for a fortnight anyway, and if she went on to Apia, that was under British **jurisdiction**③ and had nothing to do with him."

The missionary sprang to his feet and strode across the room.

"It's terrible the way the men who are in authority seek to evade their responsibility. They speak as though evil that was out of sight ceased to be evil. The very existence of that woman is a **scandal**④ and it does not help matters to shift it to another of the islands. In the end I had to speak **straight from the shoulder**⑤."

Davidson's brow lowered, and he **protruded**⑥ his firm chin. He looked fierce and determined.

"What do you mean by that?"

"Our mission is not entirely without influence at Washington. I pointed out to the governor that it wouldn't do him any good if there was a complaint about

传教士的眼中是否闪过一束亮光？他的脸上仍然毫无表情。

“面对这样的情况，您不可能指望着总督会同意您待在此地。”

“是你干的好事，”她尖声尖气地说，“你骗不了我，是你干的好事。”

“我不想骗您。我敦促总督采取了这个唯一可行的措施，因为这是他的职责所在。”

“你为何不可以不管我的事情呢？我并没有伤害到你呀。”

“您尽管放心好啦，您即便伤害到了我，我也绝不会有什么怨恨的。”

“你以为我愿意待在这么个巴掌大的鬼地方吗？我看起来可不像个乡巴佬吧？”

“既然如此，我看您就没有什么好抱怨的。”他回答说。

她气得说不出话来，愤怒地大叫了一声，然后冲出了房间。现场出现了短暂沉默。

“得知总督终于采取措施了，令人松了一口气啊，”戴维森最后说，“总督是个软弱的人，行事优柔寡断。他说了，不管怎么说，汤普森小姐只在此地待两个星期，她若是继续行程，到阿皮亚去，那儿属英国管辖，那就不关他的什么事了。”

传教士一跃身子站立起来，大步走过房间。

“当权者逃避责任的方式真可是耸人听闻啊。按照他们的说法，没有出现在眼前的罪恶就不再是罪恶了。那个女人的存在是一件丑恶事情，把责任推到另外一个岛上去无济于事。到了最后，我还是得实话实说来着。”

戴维森紧锁着眉头，前突着下颚。他表情凶狠，态度坚决。

“您这话是什么意思啊？”

“我们在海外的传教会在华盛顿并非毫无影响力的。我向总督指出了，他若是在处理此地的事务时，出

① burg [bə:g] *n.* 小村

② shilly-shally ['ʃiliˌʃæli] *v.* 优柔寡断

③ jurisdiction [ˌdʒuəris'dikʃən] *n.* 管辖范围

④ scandal ['skændəl] *n.* 耻辱

⑤ straight from the shoulder 直截了当地

⑥ protrude [prəu'tru:d] *v.* 使突出

the way he managed things here."

"When has she got to go?" asked the doctor, after a pause.

"The San Francisco boat is due here from Sydney next Tuesday. She's to sail on that."

That was in five days' time. It was next day, when he was coming back from the hospital where for want of something better to do Macphail spent most of his mornings, that the half-caste stopped him as he was going upstairs.

"Excuse me, Dr. Macphail, Miss Thompson's sick. Will you have a look at her."

"Certainly."

Horn led him to her room. She was sitting in a chair idly, neither reading nor sewing, staring in front of her. She wore her white dress and the large hat with the flowers on it. Macphail noticed that her skin was yellow and **muddy**① under her powder, and her eyes were heavy.

"I'm sorry to hear you're not well," he said.

"Oh, I ain't sick really. I just said that, because I just had to see you. I've got to clear on a boat that's going to 'Frisco."

She looked at him and he saw that her eyes were suddenly startled. She opened and clenched her hands **spasmodically**②. The trader stood at the door, listening.

"So I understand," said the doctor.

She gave a little **gulp**③.

"I guess it ain't very convenient for me to go to 'Frisco just now. I went to see the governor yesterday afternoon, but I couldn't get to him. I saw the secretary, and he told me I'd got to take that boat and that was all there was to it. I just had to see the governor, so I waited outside his house this morning, and when he come out I spoke to him. He didn't want to speak to me, I'll say, but I wouldn't let him shake me off, and at last he said he hadn't no objection to my staying here till the next boat to Sydney if the Rev. Davidson will stand for it."

She stopped and looked at Dr. Macphail anxiously.

现了民怨，对他是没有好处的。”

“她必须什么时候离开？”一阵停顿之后，医生问了一声。

“从悉尼驶向旧金山的船下星期二到达这儿。她到时就上那条船。”

那还有五天时间。翌日，麦克费尔医生从医院返回时，店老板在楼梯上拦住了他。医生每天上午大部分时间都会在医院度过，医院里有他觉得更好的事情可做。

“对不起，麦克费尔医生，汤普森小姐生病了，您可以去看看她吗？”

“当然可以。”

霍恩领着他进了她的房间。她坐在一把椅子上，百无聊赖的样子，没有看书，也没有干针线活儿，眼睛盯着自己前面看。她身穿白色衣裙，头戴着上面缀了花朵的大帽子。医生注意到，她施了脂粉的脸颊上暗淡泛黄，目光显得呆滞。

“很遗憾，听说您身体不舒服。”他说。

“噢，我并没有真的生病。我这样说，只是想要见到您，因为我必须搭乘下一班船前往旧金山了。”

她看了看他。他注意到，她突然流露出惊愕的神情。她时而放开双手，时而握住双手。店老板站立在门口，倾听着。

“我明白了。”医生说。

她微微吸了口气。

“我觉得，我此时不方便去旧金山。我昨天下午去找总督，但没有见到他。我见了那位秘书。他告诉我说，我必须要搭乘那艘船，别无其他选择。我就是想要见到总督，于是，今天上午在他的官邸外面等待来着。他出门后，我便找他说话。我知道，他是不想跟我说话的，但是，我紧紧跟随着，不让他摆脱我。最后，他说，戴维森神父若是同意的话，他不反对我在此地带着，一直等到下一班船前往悉尼。”

她停下不说了，心急火燎地看着麦克费尔医生。

① muddy ['mʌdi] *a.* 暗淡的

② spasmodically [spæz'mɔdikli] *ad.* 痉挛性地

③ gulp [gʌlp] *n.* 大口大口地吸（气）

"I don't know exactly what I can do," he said.

"Well, I thought maybe you wouldn't mind asking him. I swear to God I won't start anything here if he'll just only let me stay. I won't go out of the house if that'll suit him. It's no more'n a fortnight."

"I'll ask him."

"He won't stand for it," said Horn. "He'll have you out on Tuesday, so you may as well make up your mind to it."

"Tell him I can get work in Sydney, straight stuff, I mean. 'Tain't asking very much."

"I'll do what I can."

"And come and tell me right away, will you? I can't set down to a thing till I get the **dope**① one way or the other."

It was not an **errand**② that much pleased the doctor, and, characteristically perhaps, he went about it indirectly. He told his wife what Miss Thompson had said to him and asked her to speak to Mrs. Davidson. The missionary's attitude seemed rather arbitrary and it could do no harm if the girl were allowed to stay in Pago-Pago another fortnight. But he was not prepared for the result of his diplomacy. The missionary came to him straightway.

"Mrs. Davidson tells me that Thompson has been speaking to you."

Dr. Macphail, thus directly tackled, had the shy man's resentment at being forced out into the open. He felt his temper rising, and he flushed.

"I don't see that it can make any difference if she goes to Sydney rather than to San Francisco, and so long as she promises to behave while she's here it's dashed hard to **persecute**③ her."

The missionary fixed him with his stern eyes. "Why is she unwilling to go back to San Francisco?"

"I didn't inquire," answered the doctor with some **asperity**④. "And I think one does better to mind one's own business."

Perhaps it was not a very tactful answer.

"The governor has ordered her to be **deported**⑤ by the first boat that leaves

“我实际上并不知道，自己能够干什么。”他说。

“啊，我寻思着，您不会介意去问问他吧。我向上帝起誓，只要他允许我在这儿留下来，我不会干任何事情的。他若是觉得合适，我就会成天待在室内。也就不超过两个星期的时间。”

“我会去问问他。”

“他不会同意的，”霍恩说，“他会要求你下星期二离开，你还是面对现实吧。”

“请告诉他，我会到悉尼找份事做的，正儿八经的工作，我指的是这个意思。我没有过高的要求。”

“我尽我的能力吧。”

“有了结果尽快告诉我，好吗？事情不定下来，我内心安定不下来。”

医生并不是很乐意去完成这样一件差事，或许由于性格方面的原因，他会拐弯抹角地去处理这件事情。他把汤普森小姐对他说的话告诉夫人，请她再去对戴维森夫人说。传教士的态度显得过于专横，其实允许那姑娘在帕果帕果再待上两个星期也不会有什么害处。但是，他并没有预料到自己的斡旋行动所取得的结果。传教士直截了当找他来了。

“戴维森夫人告诉我说，汤普森已经找您谈过了。”

麦克费尔医生生性羞怯，但现如今却如此这般地要直面他人，不得不敞开自己的心扉，这未免有点强人所难，心生怨恨。他觉得自己火气上升，脸上通红。

“她若是不去旧金山，而是去悉尼，我觉得，这并没有多大的差别，况且她已经承诺了，待在这儿期间会规规矩矩行事，现在这样强逼着她，未免过于苛刻啊。”

传教士盯着他看，目光严厉。“她为何就不愿意返回旧金山呢？”

“我没有问，”医生回答说，语气有点生硬，“我觉得，一个人最好还是管好自己的事情为妙。”

这或许不是一个很有技巧的回答。

“总督已经下令要把她驱逐出去，搭乘最先离岛的

① dope [dəup] *n.* 消息
② errand ['erənd] *n.* 差事
③ persecute ['pə:sikju:t] *v.* 为难
④ asperity [æ'sperəti] *n.* 严厉
⑤ deport [di'pɔ:t] *v.* 带走

the island. He's only done his duty and I will not interfere. Her presence is a **peril**① here."

"I think you're very harsh and **tyrannical**②."

The two ladies looked up at the doctor with some alarm, but they need not have feared a quarrel, for the missionary smiled gently.

"I'm terribly sorry you should think that of me, Dr. Macphail. Believe me, my heart bleeds for that unfortunate woman, but I'm only trying to do my duty."

The doctor made no answer. He looked out of the window **sullenly**③. For once it was not raining and across the bay you saw **nestling**④ among the trees the huts of a native village.

"I think I'll take advantage of the rain stopping to go out," he said.

"Please don't **bear me malice**⑤ because I can't **accede to**⑥ your wish," said Davidson, with a melancholy smile. "I respect you very much, doctor, and I should be sorry if you thought ill of me."

"I have no doubt you have a sufficiently good opinion of yourself to bear mine with **equanimity**⑦," he retorted.

"That's one on me," chuckled Davidson.

When Dr. Macphail, vexed with himself because he had been uncivil **to no purpose**⑧, went downstairs, Miss Thompson was waiting for him with her door **ajar**⑨.

"Well," she said, "have you spoken to him?"

"Yes, I'm sorry, he won't do anything," he answered, not looking at her in his embarrassment.

But then he gave her a quick glance, for a sob broke from her. He saw that her face was white with fear. It gave him a shock of dismay. And suddenly he had an idea.

"But don't give up hope yet. I think it's a shame the way they're treating you and I'm going to see the governor myself."

"Now?"

He nodded. Her face brightened.

船只离开。他只是在履行自己的职责，我不会加以干预的。她在此地抛头露面，很危险。”

“我觉得，您过于苛刻和强悍了。”

两位夫人抬头看着医生，显得有点震惊。但是，她们用不着担心会吵起来，因为传教士微笑着，态度和蔼。

“我感到十分遗憾，您竟然会这样看我啊，麦克费尔医生。请相信我，我的内心在替那个不幸的女人滴血呢，但我必须要尽力履行好自己的职责。”

医生没有接话。他朝着窗户外面看，一脸不高兴的样子。难得不在下雨，远眺着海湾，您便看见某一座土著居民村庄的棚屋在树丛间若隐若现。

“我想要利用雨停的功夫出去走走。”他说。

“请不要因为我没有遵从您的意愿而记恨我，”戴维森说，脸上露出了苦笑，“我十分敬重您，医生，您若是往坏里去想我，我会很难过的。”

“我可以肯定，您对自己感觉良好，能够坦然容忍我的看法。”医生回驳了一句。

“这一点算是说对啦。”戴维森咯咯笑了起来。

麦克费尔医生由于失了礼而且还没办成事情，对自己挺窝火的。他下楼时，汤普森小姐的房门半开着，正等着他。

“对啦，”她说，“您对他说过了吗？”

“说了，但很遗憾，他不会管的。”他回答说，感到很尴尬，没有抬头看她一眼。

但是，他随即很快瞥了她一眼，因为她突然抽泣了起来。他看到，她因惧怕而脸色苍白。他很沮丧，心里一怔，然后突然有了主意。

“但还不要抛弃希望。我认为，他们这样对待您，很令人遗憾。我准备亲自去见总督。”

“现在吗？”

他点了点头。她的表情亮堂了起来。

“哎呀，您真是太好啦。您若是出面替我说话，我肯定，总督一定会让我待着的。我待在这儿期间，一定

① peril ['peril] *n.* 危险

② tyrannical [ti'rænikəl] *a.* 专横的

③ sullenly ['sʌlənli] *ad.* 阴沉地

④ nestle ['nesl] *v.* 半隐半现

⑤ bear sb malice 怀恨（某人）

⑥ accede to 同意

⑦ equanimity [ˌiːkwə'niməti] *n.* 沉着

⑧ to no purpose 完全徒劳无益

⑨ ajar [ə'dʒɑː] *a.* 半开着（的）

"Say, that's real good of you. I'm sure he'll let me stay if you speak for me. I just won't do a thing I didn't ought all the time I'm here."

Dr. Macphail hardly knew why he had made up his mind to appeal to the governor. He was perfectly indifferent to Miss Thompson's affairs, the missionary had irritated him, and with him temper was a **smouldering**① thing. He found the governor at home. He was a large, handsome man, a sailor, with a grey toothbrush moustache; and he wore a spotless uniform of white **drill**②.

"I've come to see you about a woman who's lodging in the same house as we are," he said. "Her name's Thompson."

"I guess I've heard nearly enough about her, Dr. Macphail," said the governor, smiling. "I've given her the order to get out next Tuesday and that's all I can do."

"I wanted to ask you if you couldn't **stretch a point**③ and let her stay here till the boat comes in from San Francisco so that she can go to Sydney. I will guarantee her good behaviour."

The governor continued to smile, but his eyes grew small and serious.

"I'd be very glad to oblige you, Dr. Macphail, but I've given the order and it must stand."

The doctor put the case as reasonably as he could, but now the governor ceased to smile at all. He listened sullenly, with **averted**④ gaze. Macphail saw that he was making no impression.

"I'm sorry to cause any lady inconvenience, but she'll have to sail on Tuesday and that's all there is to it."

"But what difference can it make?"

"Pardon me, doctor, but I don't feel called upon to explain my official actions except to the proper authorities."

Macphail looked at him shrewdly. He remembered Davidson's **hint**⑤ that he had used threats, and in the governor's attitude he read a singular embarrassment.

"Davidson's a damned busybody," he said hotly.

"Between ourselves, Dr. Macphail, I don't say that I have formed a very favourable opinion of Mr. Davidson, but I am bound to confess that he was

① smouldering ['sməuldəriŋ] a. 闷在心里的

② drill [dril] n.【纺织业】粗斜纹布

③ stretch a point 破例让步

④ averted [ə'vəːtid] a.（尤指目光）移开的

⑤ hint [hint] n. 暗示

不会做不该做的事情的。”

麦克费尔医生不太清楚，自己为何要打定主意去向总督求情。他本来对于汤普森小姐的事情漠不关心，但传教士的表情惹恼了他，而他又是个有火憋在心里的人。他在总督官邸找到了总督。总督身材魁梧，仪表堂堂，曾经当过水手，留着一口牙刷似的灰色胡子，身穿着一尘不染的白色斜纹制服。

“我来找您，想要和您谈谈关于与我们同住在一幢房子里面一位女士的事情，”医生说，“她姓汤普森。”

“关于她的事情，我想，我已经听得够多了，麦克费尔医生，”总督说，脸上露着微笑，“我已经下过命令了，她下星期二必须离开。我能够做到的就是这个。”

“我想要请求您，能否变通变通，让她待在这儿，直到旧金山开出的船到达这儿，她可以搭乘去悉尼。我保证，她一定会规规矩矩的。”

总督持续微笑着，但眼睛眯着变小了，神情严肃。

“我很乐意照着您的意思办，麦克费尔医生，但是，我已经下达了命令，必须生效了。”

医生据理力争，但医生此时脸上已经完全没有了笑容。他闷闷不乐地听着，凝视对方时目光游离。麦克费尔看出来了，自己的话并没有起作用。

“给那位女士带来了不便，我感到很遗憾，但她必须星期二乘船离开，事情就这样了。”

“但这件事有什么区别吗？”

“对不起，医生，除了对有关上司之外，我觉得没有必要向任何人解释自己的行政行为。”

麦克费尔机敏地看了看他。他记得戴维森暗示过自己使用了威胁手段。他从总督的态度中看到一种奇特的尴尬模样。

“戴维森真是个该死的爱管闲事者。”他说，一肚子火气。

“也就我们两个人之间说说，麦克费尔医生，我可以说，自己对戴维森先生并没有特别的好感。但是，我必须

within his rights in pointing out to me the danger that the presence of a woman of Miss Thompson's character was to a place like this where a number of enlisted men are stationed among a native population."

He got up and Dr. Macphail was obliged to do so too.

"I must ask you to excuse me. I have an engagement. Please give my respects to Mrs. Macphail."

The doctor left him **crestfallen**[1]. He knew that Miss Thompson would be waiting for him, and unwilling to tell her himself that he had failed, he went into the house by the back door and **sneaked**[2] up the stairs as though he had something to hide.

At supper he was silent and ill-at-ease, but the missionary was **jovial**[3] and animated. Dr. Macphail thought his eyes rested on him now and then with **triumphant**[4] good-humour. It struck him suddenly that Davidson knew of his visit to the governor and of its ill success. But how on earth could he have heard of it? There was something sinister about the power of that man. After supper he saw Horn on the verandah and, as though to have a casual word with him, went out.

"She wants to know if you've seen the governor," the trader whispered.

"Yes. He wouldn't do anything. I'm awfully sorry, I can't do anything more."

"I knew he wouldn't. They daren't go against the missionaries."

"What are you talking about?" said Davidson **affably**[5], coming out to join them.

"I was just saying there was no chance of your getting over to Apia for at least another week," said the trader **glibly**[6].

He left them, and the two men returned into the parlour. Mr. Davidson devoted one hour after each meal to recreation. Presently a timid knock was heard at the door.

"Come in," said Mrs. Davidson, in her sharp voice.

The door was not opened. She got up and opened it. They saw Miss

得实话实说，这个地方的土著居民中间驻扎着大量的现役军人，有汤普森小姐这样品性的女人抛头露面，存在危险。而戴维森先生向我指出这一点属于他的职权范围。”

总督站起身，麦克费尔医生也只好跟着站立起来。

“我必须请求您原谅我。我有个约会，请代我向麦克费尔夫人问好。”

医生一脸沮丧地离开了总督。他知道，汤普森小姐一直在等着他，但他不愿意亲口告诉她自己没有把事情办成。他走后门进入了住处，悄然溜上了楼，好像有什么东西要藏着掖着似的。

晚餐时，麦克费尔医生沉默不语，局促不安，但传教士却兴高采烈，眉飞色舞。麦克费尔医生感觉到，传教士的目光时不时地落在自己身上，透着一种得意洋洋的神情。他突然想到，戴维森一定知道自己去找过总督了，而且没有把事情办成。但是，他到底是通过什么途径听说的呢？这个人身上具有某种邪恶的力量啊。晚餐过后，他在露台上看见了霍恩，好像有事情要跟他聊一聊，然后出去了。

“她想要知道您是否已经见过总督了。”店老板笑声说。

“见过了，但他不肯帮忙。我十分抱歉，我只能做到这一步了。”

“我知道，他是不会帮忙的。他们不敢与传教士对着干。”

“你们在说什么呢？”戴维森态度和蔼地说，一边出来走到他们身边。

“我刚才在说，你们至少一个星期之内不可能去阿皮亚。”店老板机智地说。

店老板离开了，他们两位返回客厅。戴维森先生每一顿饭之后花费一个小时时间娱乐。随即，门口传来轻微的敲门声。

“进来。”戴维森夫人说，声音很尖细。

房门没有开，她起身去开门。他们看见汤普森小姐

① crestfallen ['krestˌfɔːlən] *a.* 沮丧的

② sneak [sniːk] *v.* 溜走

③ jovial ['dʒəuviəl] *a.* 愉快的

④ triumphant [trai'ʌmfənt] *a.* 胜利的

⑤ affably ['æfəbli] *ad.* 殷勤地

⑥ glibly [glibli] *ad.* 油嘴滑舌地

Thompson standing at the **threshold**[①]. But the change in her appearance was extraordinary. This was no longer the flaunting **hussy**[②] who had **jeered at**[③] them in the road, but a broken, frightened woman. Her hair, as a rule so **elaborately**[④] arranged, was tumbling untidily over her neck. She wore bedroom slippers and a shirt and blouse. They were unfresh and bedraggled. She stood at the door with the tears streaming down her face and did not dare to enter.

"What do you want?" said Mrs. Davidson harshly.

"May I speak to Mr. Davidson?" she said in a choking voice.

The missionary rose and went towards her.

"Come right in, Miss Thompson," he said in cordial tones. "What can I do for you?"

She entered the room.

"Say, I'm sorry for what I said to you the other day an' for—for everythin' else. I guess I **was** a bit **lit up**[⑤]. I beg pardon."

"Oh, it was nothing. I guess my back's broad enough to bear a few hard words."

She stepped towards him with a movement that was horribly **cringing**[⑥].

"You've got me beat. I'm all in. You won't make me go back to 'Frisco?"

His genial manner vanished and his voice grew on a sudden hard and stern.

"Why don't you want to go back there?"

She cowered before him.

"I guess my people live there. I don't want them to see me like this. I'll go anywhere else you say."

"Why don't you want to go back to San Francisco?"

"I've told you."

He leaned forward, staring at her, and his great, shining eyes seemed to try to bore into her soul. He gave a sudden gasp.

"The penitentiary."

① threshold ['θreʃhəuld] *n.* 门口
② hussy ['hʌsi] *n.* 荡妇
③ jeer at 嘲弄
④ elaborately [i'læbərətli] *ad.* 精巧地
⑤ be lit up［美国俚语］喝醉了
⑥ cringing [krindʒiŋ] *a.* 谄媚（的）

站在门口。不过，她外表相貌上的变化不同寻常。眼前站立着的已不再是那位在大路上对他们冷嘲热讽的轻佻招摇的女子，而是一位失魂落魄、诚惶诚恐的妇人。她一贯精心梳理好的头发现在蓬乱地垂落在颈部。她脚上趿拉着卧室里用的拖鞋，身上穿着短衫长裙，肮脏打皱。她伫立在门口，泪流满面，不敢跨进房门。

“您想要干什么？”戴维森夫人问了一声，声音粗声粗气。

“我可以和戴维森先生谈一谈吗？”她压低着嗓子说。

传教士站起身，走向她。

“直接进来吧，汤普森小姐，”他说，声音热情洋溢，“我能够帮您什么忙呢？”

她走进了房间。

“是啊，我很对不起，那天不该那样对您说话——还有其他的事情。我觉得，自己当时有点喝醉了。我请求原谅。”

“噢，没什么。我想自己的心胸还是挺宽的，能够容忍得了几句难听的话的。”

她朝着他身边走去，一副十足的卑躬屈膝的模样。

“您把我击垮了，我已经精疲力竭了。您不会要求我返回旧金山，对吧？”

他亲切和蔼的态度顿时消失，说话的声音变得生硬而又严厉。

“您为何就不愿意回那儿去呢？”

她战战兢兢地站在他面前。

“我想，我的亲朋好友都住在那儿，我不想让他们看见我这副模样。别的地方您说哪儿我都愿意去。”

“您为何不想返回到旧金山去呢？”

“我已经告诉您了。”

他前倾着身子，盯着她看。他那双硕大闪亮的眼睛似乎想要看透她的灵魂。他突然喘息了一声。

“收容所[1]。”

1　此处的收容所（penitentiary）是指专门收容妓女的所在，源于19世纪的英国。

She screamed, and then she fell at his feet, clasping his legs.

"Don't send me back there. I swear to you before God I'll be a good woman. I'll give all this up."

She burst into a torrent of confused **supplication**① and the tears coursed down her painted cheeks. He leaned over her and, lifting her face, forced her to look at him.

"Is that it, the penitentiary?"

"I beat it before they could get me, she gasped. "If the **bulls**② grab me it's three years for mine."

He let go his hold of her and she **fell in a heap**③ on the floor, sobbing bitterly. Dr. Macphail stood up.

"This alters the whole thing," he said. "You can't make her go back when you know this. Give her another chance. She wants to turn over a new leaf."

"I'm going to give her the finest chance she's ever had. If she **repents**④ let her accept her punishment."

She misunderstood the words and looked up. There was a gleam of hope in her heavy eyes.

"You'll let me go?"

"No. You shall sail for San Francisco on Tuesday."

She gave a **groan**⑤ of horror and then burst into low, hoarse shrieks which sounded hardly human, and she beat her head passionately on the ground. Dr. Macphail sprang to her and lifted her up:

"Come on, you mustn't do that. You'd better go to your room and lie down. I'll get you something."

He raised her to her feet and partly dragging her, partly carrying her, got her downstairs. He was furious with Mrs. Davidson and with his wife because they made no effort to help. The half-caste was standing on the landing and with his assistance he managed to get her on the bed. She was **moaning**⑥ and crying. She was almost insensible. He gave her a **hypodermic**⑦ injection. He was hot and exhausted when he went upstairs again.

她尖叫了起来，紧接着跪在他跟前，紧紧抱住他的双腿。

“不要把我送回到那儿去。我在上帝面前向您起誓，一定要做一个规规矩矩的女人。我要痛改前非。”

① supplication [ˌsʌpliˈkeiʃən] n. 哀求

她不停地苦苦哀求，语无伦次，眼泪从涂脂抹粉的脸颊上流淌了下来。他俯身对着她，抬起她的面孔，迫使她看着自己。

“是那儿吗，收容所？”

② bull [bul] n. 警察

“我逃跑了，他们未能抓住我，”她气喘吁吁地说，“警察若是抓住了我，我得待上三年。”

③ fall in a heap 瘫倒

他松开了手。她瘫倒在地上，痛苦地哭泣着。麦克费尔医生站起身。

“这样一来改变了整个事态了，”他说，“您既然知道了这个情况，那就不应该把她送回哪儿去。再给她一个机会，她想要获得新生啊。”

④ repent [riˈpent] v. 忏悔

“我要给他一辈子都最难得到的机会。她若是想要改过自新，那就让她接受对自己的惩罚。”

她误解了上面这话的意思，抬头看了看。她目光呆滞的眼中闪过了一束希望之光。

“您愿意放了我？”

“不，下星期二得去旧金山。”

⑤ groan [grəun] n. 呻吟

她发出了恐惧的呻吟声，然后突然低沉、沙哑地尖叫起来，听起来不像是人发出的声音。她情绪激动地把脑袋往地上磕。麦克费尔医生一跃身子冲到她身边，把她搀扶起来：

“起来吧，您不能这样。您最好还是回到自己房间去躺一躺。我给您拿点药。”

他搀扶着她站立起来，半拽半抱着，把她弄到了楼下。他对戴维森夫人和自己夫人大为光火，因为她们无动于衷，都不过来帮一把。店老板站在楼梯下面的过道上，助了一臂之力，医生这才设法把她搀扶到了床上。她呻吟着，哭泣着，几乎失去知觉了。他给她做了皮下注射。等他返回到楼上之后，感到又热又疲倦。

⑥ moan [məun] v. 呜咽

⑦ hypodermic [ˌhaipəuˈdəːmik] a. 皮下的

"I've got her to lie down."

The two women and Davidson were in the same positions as when he had left them. They could not have moved or spoken since he went.

"I was waiting for you," said Davidson, in a strange, distant voice. "I want you all to pray with me for the soul of our erring sister."

He took the Bible off a shelf, and sat down at the table at which they had **supped**①. It had not been cleared, and he pushed the tea-pot out of the way. In a powerful voice, **resonant**② and deep, he read to them the chapter in which is narrated the meeting of Jesus Christ with the woman taken in adultery.

"Now kneel with me and let us pray for the soul of our dear sister, Sadie Thompson."

He burst into a long, passionate prayer in which he implored God to have mercy on the sinful woman. Mrs. Macphail and Mrs. Davidson knelt with covered eyes. The doctor, taken by surprise, awkward and sheepish, knelt too. The missionary's prayer had a savage eloquence. He was extraordinarily moved, and as he spoke the tears ran down his cheeks. Outside, the pitiless rain fell, fell steadily, with a fierce malignity that was all too human.

At last he stopped. He paused for a moment and said:

"We will now repeat the Lord's prayer."

They said it and then, following him, they rose from their knees. Mrs. Davidson's face was pale and restful. She was comforted and at peace, but the Macphails felt suddenly **bashful**③. They did not know which way to look.

"I'll just go down and see how she is now," said Dr. Macphail.

When he knocked at her door it was opened for him by Horn. Miss Thompson was in a rocking-chair, sobbing quietly.

"What are you doing there?" exclaimed Macphail. "I told you to lie down."

"I can't lie down. I want to see Mr. Davidson."

"My poor child, what do you think is the good of it? You'll never move him."

① sup [sʌp] v. 吃晚饭
② resonant ['rezənənt] a. 洪亮的
③ bashful ['bæʃful] a. 局促不安的

“我让她躺下了。”

医生离开后，两位夫人和戴维森一直待在原先的位置上。自从他离开后，他们既没有动，也没有说话。

“我一直在等着您呢，”戴维森说，语气显得怪异而又疏远，“我想要你们大家和我一块儿祈祷，为了拯救我们犯了过错的姐妹的灵魂。”

他从书架上取下《圣经》，在他们用过晚餐的桌子边坐了下来。餐桌尚未收拾。他把桌上的茶壶推到一旁。他给他们朗读叙述耶稣基督同那位与人通奸的女人会面的那一章，声音高亢有力，洪亮而又深沉。

“现在和我一道跪下吧，让我们为拯救我们亲爱的姐妹——萨迪·汤普森——的灵魂而祈祷。”

他突然充满激情地念出了一串冗长的祈祷词，恳请上帝怜悯宽恕那位犯了罪的女人。麦克费尔夫人和戴维森夫人跪了下来，双目紧闭。医生惊诧不已，局促不安，也跟着跪了下来。传教士的祈祷激情飞扬，滔滔不绝。他自己异乎寻常地受到了感动，边说眼泪边从脸颊上往下流。室外，雨无情地下着，一刻不停地下着，显露着人间从未见识过的凶狠和恶毒。

他最后祈祷结束，停顿了片刻，然后说：

“我们现在重复一遍对上帝的祈祷。”

他们重复过祈祷词之后，跟随着他站立了起来。戴维森夫人脸色苍白，神态安宁。她感到慰藉，内心平静，但是，麦克费尔夫妇突然感到羞愧不已。他们不知道眼睛该朝哪个方向看。

“我这就下楼去，看看她现在情况如何。”麦克费尔医生说。

他敲了她的房门，是霍恩替他开的门。汤普森小姐坐在一把摇椅上，小声哭泣着。

“您坐在这儿干什么啊？”麦克费尔激动地大声说，“我不是吩咐您躺下的吗？”

“我不能躺着，我想要见戴维森先生。”

“可怜的姑娘啊，您觉得去见他有什么用吗？您绝

"He said he'd come if I sent for him."

Macphail motioned to the trader.

"Go and fetch him."

He waited with her in silence while the trader went upstairs. Davidson came in.

"Excuse me for asking you to come here," she said, looking at him sombrely.

"I was expecting you to send for me. I knew the Lord would answer my prayer."

They stared at one another for a moment and then she looked away. She kept her eyes averted when she spoke.

"I've been a bad woman. I want to repent."

"Thank God! thank God! He has heard our prayers."

He turned to the two men.

"Leave me alone with her. Tell Mrs. Davidson that our prayers have been answered."

They went out and closed the door behind them.

"Gee whizz," said the trader.

That night Dr. Macphail could not get to sleep till late, and when he heard the missionary come upstairs he looked at his watch. It was two o'clock. But even then he did not go to bed at once, for through the wooden partition that separated their rooms he heard him praying aloud, till he himself, exhausted, fell asleep.

When he saw him next morning he was surprised at his appearance. He was paler than ever, tired, but his eyes shone with inhuman fire. It looked as though he were filled with an overwhelming joy.

"I want you to go down presently and see Sadie," he said. "I can't hope that her body is better, but her soul—her soul is transformed."

The doctor was feeling **wan**[①] and nervous.

"You were with her very late last night," he said.

不可能打动他的。”

“他说过了，如果去叫他，他就会来的。”

医生示意了一下店老板。

“去把他叫来吧。”

店老板上楼期间，医生和汤普森小姐默不作声地等待着。戴维森来了。

“对不起，把您叫到这儿来。”她说，神情忧郁地看着他。

“我一直期待着您来找我呢。我知道，上帝会回应我的祈祷的。”

他们相互对视了片刻，随后，她目光移向别处。她说话时眼睛一直看着别处。

“我一直就是个坏女人，现在想要改过自新。”

“感谢上帝！感谢上帝啊！他听见我们的祈祷了。”

他转身对着两个男人。

“让我单独同她待一会儿吧，告诉戴维森夫人，我们的祈祷有回应了。”

他们出去了，关上了房门。

“我的天哪。”店老板说。

当晚，麦克费尔医生很晚才睡觉。当他听见传教士上楼的脚步声时，他看了看自己的表，时间是两点钟。但即便到了这个时候，传教士也还是没有立刻上床睡觉，因为透过将他们的房间分隔开来的木板墙，他听见了他在大声祈祷，直到最后，医生自己精疲力竭了，这才入睡了。

翌日早晨，医生看见传教士时，对方的脸令他大吃了一惊。传教士比平常脸色更加苍白了，满脸倦容，但眼睛里闪烁着一团烈火。他看起来像是洋溢着一股抑制不住的欢乐之情。

“我想要您这就下楼去看看萨迪，”传教士说，“我不能指望她的身体好些了，但她的灵魂——她的灵魂转变了。”

医生感觉情绪阴郁，心神不宁。

“您昨晚同她在一块儿待到很晚啊。”医生说。

① wan [wɔn] *a.* 忧郁的

"Yes, she couldn't bear to have me leave her."

"You look as pleased as Punch," the doctor said irritably.

Davidson's eyes shone with ecstasy.

"A great mercy has been **vouchsafed**[①] me. Last night I was privileged to bring a lost soul to the loving arms of Jesus."

Miss Thompson was again in the rocking-chair. The bed had not been made. The room was in disorder. She had not troubled to dress herself, but wore a dirty dressing-gown, and her hair was tied in a **sluttish**[②] knot. She had given her face a dab with a wet towel, but it was all swollen and creased with crying. She looked a drab.

She raised her eyes dully when the doctor came in. She was cowed and broken.

"Where's Mr. Davidson?" she asked.

"He'll come presently if you want him," answered Macphail acidly. "I came here to see how you were."

"Oh, I guess I'm OK. You needn't worry about that."

"Have you had anything to eat?"

"Horn brought me some coffee."

She looked anxiously at the door.

"D'you think he'll come down soon? I feel as if it wasn't so terrible when he's with me."

"Are you still going on Tuesday?"

"Yes, he says I've got to go. Please tell him to come right along. You can't do me any good. He's the only one as can help me now."

"Very well," said Dr. Macphail.

During the next three days the missionary spent almost all his time with Sadie Thompson. He joined the others only to have his meals. Dr. Macphail noted that he hardly ate.

"He's wearing himself out," said Mrs. Davidson pitifully. "He'll have a breakdown if he doesn't take care, but he won't spare himself."

① vouchsafe [vautʃ'seif] *v.* 赐予

② sluttish ['slʌtiʃ] *a.* 邋遢的

"是啊，我要离开她，她会受不了。"

"您倒是看起来像潘趣[1]一样兴致勃勃嘛。"医生说，语气显得很烦躁。

戴维森的眼睛里透着欣喜若狂的神情。

"上帝已经把至上的宽恕怜悯之情托付给了我。我昨晚已经荣耀地把一颗失落的灵魂送到了主耶稣充满了爱的怀抱。"

汤普森小姐又坐在了摇椅上。床铺没有铺过，房间里凌乱不堪。她都没有费心整一整自己的装束，只是披了一件肮脏的晨衣，头发也只是随随便便地打了个结。她用毛巾抹了一把脸，但面部肿胀，仍然看得到泪痕。她看起来无精打采。

医生进入房间时，她抬起了眼睛，目光呆滞，她受到恐吓后整个人颓废不已。

"戴维森先生在哪儿呢？"她问了一声。

"您若是想要见他，他立刻就来，"麦克费尔回答说，语气显得尖酸，"我来这儿看看您情况怎么样。"

"噢，我想我还行吧。您用不着费心思。"

"您吃了东西吗？"

"霍恩给我送来了一些咖啡。"

她心急火燎地看着门口。

"您觉得他立刻会下楼来吗？他跟我待在一块儿时，我感觉事情不是那么可怕了。"

"您还是要星期二离开吗？"

"是啊，他说了，我必须离开。请告诉他立刻下来。您帮不了我什么忙。他现在是唯一能够帮上我的忙的人。"

"很好啊。"麦克费尔医生说。

随后三天期间，传教士大部分时间里都和萨迪·汤普森待在一块儿，只是吃饭时才加入到其他人的行列。麦克费尔医生注意到，他没怎么吃东西。

"他这是要把他自己拖垮啊，"戴维森夫人说，语气中充满怜惜，"他若是不加注意，一定会崩溃的，但就是不爱惜自己。"

1 潘趣源自英国传统滑稽木偶剧《潘趣和朱迪》(*Punch and Judy*)。

She herself was white and pale. She told Mrs. Macphail that she had no sleep. When the missionary came upstairs from Miss Thompson he prayed till he was exhausted, but even then he did not sleep for long. After an hour or two he got up and dressed himself, and went for a **tramp**① along the bay. He had strange dreams.

"This morning he told me that he'd been dreaming about the mountains of Nebraska," said Mrs. Davidson.

"That's curious," said Dr. Macphail.

He remembered seeing them from the windows of the train when he crossed America. They were like huge **mole-hills**②, rounded and smooth, and they rose from the plain abruptly. Dr. Macphail remembered how it struck him that they were like a woman's breasts.

Davidson's restlessness was intolerable even to himself. But he was buoyed up by a wonderful exhilaration. He was tearing out by the roots the last **vestiges**③ of sin that lurked in the hidden corners of that poor woman's heart. He read with her and prayed with her.

"It's wonderful," he said to them one day at supper. "It's a true rebirth. Her soul, which was black as night, is now pure and white like the new-fallen snow. I am humble and afraid. Her **remorse**④ for all her sins is beautiful. I am not worthy to touch the **hem**⑤ of her garment."

"Have you the heart to send her back to San Francisco?" said the doctor. "Three years in an American prison. I should have thought you might have saved her from that."

"Ah, but don't you see? It's necessary. Do you think my heart doesn't bleed for her? I love her as I love my wife and my sister. All the time that she is in prison I shall suffer all the pain that she suffers."

"**Bunkum**⑥," cried the doctor impatiently.

"You don't understand because you're blind. She's sinned, and she must suffer.

① tramp [træmp] *n.* 步行

② mole-hill 鼹鼠丘

③ vestige ['vestidʒ] *n.* 残留部分

④ remorse [ri'mɔ:s] *n.* 懊悔

⑤ hem [hem] *n.* 贴边

⑥ bunkum ['bʌŋkəm] *n.* 空话

夫人自己也脸色煞白。她告诉麦克费尔夫人说，她自己无法入眠。传教士从汤普森小姐的房间上楼来后，他就会一直祈祷，一直到精疲力竭，但是，即便到了这种时候，她也睡不了多大一会儿。他睡了一两个小时后便起床穿衣，到海湾边上去散步。他做了一些怪异的梦。

“今天早晨，他告诉我说，夜间梦见了内布拉斯加州[1]的群山。”戴维森夫人说。

“这真有意思啊。”麦克费尔医生说。

他记得，自己乘坐火车横过美国时，曾在窗口眺望过那些群山。起伏的群上犹如巨型的鼹鼠丘，又圆又光滑，从平原上突然耸立起来。麦克费尔医生记得，他当时突然想到，群山犹如女人的乳房。

戴维森焦虑不安的情绪连他自己都感到无法忍受了。但是，他心里怀着一样奇妙的兴奋感，精神振奋。潜藏在那个可怜女人内心深处某些角落里的最后那一点点罪恶残迹，他正在将其连根拔除。他同她一块儿诵读《圣经》，一块儿祈祷。

“真的是很奇妙啊，”某一天晚餐时，他对他们说，“这确实是重生呀。她的灵魂先前犹如黑夜一般漆黑，现在却是纯洁无暇，犹如新近飘落的雪一样洁白。我感到自己卑微渺小，充满恐惧。她对自己全部罪恶的悔悟之情美妙圆满。我都不配去触碰一下她的长裙边啊。”

“您还忍心把她遣送回旧金山去吗？”麦克费尔医生问，“可得在收容所里待上三年啊。我倒是觉得，您可以拯救她，让她免受监禁之苦。”

“啊，但难道您不明白吗？这是必需的。您难道以为我的心没有在替她滴血吗？我如同爱自己的妻子和姐妹一样爱她啊。她待在收容所期间，我会一直对她忍受的痛苦感同身受。”

“说得好听啊。”医生大声说，显得不耐烦。

“您不理解，那是因为您不想理解。她犯了罪，必

1　内布拉斯加州（Nebraska）是美国中西部的一个州，位于高平原中心。北接南达科他州，南邻堪萨斯州，西界怀俄明州，东隔密苏里河与艾奥瓦州相望，西南与科罗拉多州接壤。

I know what she'll endure. She'll be starved and tortured and humiliated. I want her to accept the punishment of man as a sacrifice to God. I want her to accept it joyfully. She has an opportunity which is offered to very few of us. God is very good and very merciful."

Davidson's voice trembled with excitement. He could hardly articulate the words that tumbled passionately from his lips.

"All day I pray with her and when I leave her I pray again, I pray **with all my might and main**①, so that Jesus may **grant**② her this great mercy. I want to put in her heart the passionate desire to be punished so that at the end, even if I offered to let her go, she would refuse. I want her to feel that the bitter punishment of prison is the thank-offering that she places at the feet of our Blessed Lord, who gave his life for her."

The days passed slowly. The whole household, intent on the **wretched**③, tortured woman downstairs, lived in a state of unnatural excitement. She was like a victim that was being prepared for the savage **rites**④ of a bloody idolatry. Her terror numbed her. She could not bear to let Davidson out of her sight; it was only when he was with her that she had courage, and she hung upon him with a **slavish**⑤ dependence. She cried a great deal, and she read the Bible, and prayed. Sometimes she was exhausted and **apathetic**⑥. Then she did indeed look forward to her **ordeal**⑦, for it seemed to offer an escape, direct and concrete, from the anguish she was enduring. She could not bear much longer the vague terrors which now **assailed**⑧ her. With her sins she had put aside all personal vanity, and she slopped about her room, **unkempt**⑨ and **dishevelled**⑩, in her **tawdry**⑪ dressing-gown. She had not taken off her night-dress for four days, nor put on stockings. Her room was littered and untidy. Meanwhile the rain fell with a cruel persistence. You felt that the heavens must at last be empty of water, but still it poured down, straight and heavy, with a maddening **iteration**⑫, on the iron roof. Everything was **damp**⑬ and **clammy**⑭. There was **mildew**⑮ on the walls and on the boots that stood on the floor. Through the sleepless nights the mosquitoes **droned**⑯ their angry **chant**⑰.

须要受苦。我知道她将要忍受些什么。她要忍饥挨饿，备受折磨，饱受凌辱。我想要她接受人类应该受到的惩罚，作为对上帝所做出的牺牲。我想要她兴高采烈地接受惩罚。她拥有我们中间极少有人能够获得的良机。上帝十分仁慈，充满悲悯情怀。”

戴维森情绪激动，声音颤抖。他说话含糊不清，话语从嘴里抖了出来。

“我整天和她一块儿祈祷。我离开她之后还要祈祷，全身心投入祈祷，恳求耶稣基督赐予她极大的宽恕。我想要让她内心深处甘愿受罚，到最后，即便我主动放过她，她也会拒绝。我想要让她感觉到，我们的主耶稣为了她奉献出了自己的生命，而她进入收容所接受痛苦的惩罚是她奉献在主面前的谢礼。”

日子缓慢地过去。住宅里的所有人全神贯注于楼下那位备受痛苦折磨的女人身上。他们生活在一种很反常的兴奋状态中。她就像是一件为了崇拜一位凶神举行的残暴祭祀活动准备的祭品。她因恐惧而变得麻木呆滞了。眼前没有戴维森的踪影，她便受不了。只有当他和她待在一块儿时，她才会有勇气。她对他如影随形，像奴隶一样百依百顺。她不停地痛哭，诵读《圣经》，做祈祷。她有时候精疲力竭，麻木不仁。她后来确实期待着迎接自己将要面临的苦难，因为看起来，这样她便可以直接而有效地逃脱自己眼下正在忍受的痛苦。现在，种种若隐若现的恐惧感正向她袭来，她再也忍受不了了。她背负着种种罪恶，把所有的个人虚荣都搁置在了一边，在自己的房间里不停地走来走去，身穿艳丽的晨衣，头发蓬乱，衣衫不整。她已经四天没有脱下睡衣了，也没有穿过袜子。她的房间里东西摆得到处都是，凌乱不堪。同时，外面雨还在无情地下着。您会感觉到，天上的水恐怕都已经全部倒空了，但却依然大雨滂沱，直流而下，疯狂地落在铁皮屋顶上。一切物品都变得潮湿和黏糊。四周的墙壁和摆放在地上的靴子上都出现了霉斑。漫漫无眠的长夜里，蚊虫愤怒地嗡嗡乱叫着。

① with might and main 竭尽全力地
② grant [grɑːnt] *v.* 授予
③ wretched ['retʃid] *a.* 可怜的
④ rite [rait] *n.* 庆典
⑤ slavish ['sleiviʃ] *a.* 奴隶般的
⑥ apathetic [ˌæpə'θetik] *a.* 冷漠的
⑦ ordeal [ɔː'diːl] *n.* 苦难的经历
⑧ assail [ə'seil] *v.* 困扰
⑨ unkempt [ˌʌn'kempt] *a.* 蓬乱的
⑩ disheveled [di'ʃevəld] *a.* 不整洁的
⑪ tawdry ['tɔːdri] *a.* 俗丽的
⑫ iteration [ˌitə'reiʃən] *n.* 重复
⑬ damp [dæmp] *a.* 潮湿的
⑭ clammy ['klæmi] *a.* 冷湿的
⑮ mildew ['mildjuː] *n.* 霉菌
⑯ drone ['drəun] *v.* 发嗡嗡声
⑰ chant [tʃɑːnt] *n.* 旋律

"If it would only stop raining for a single day it wouldn't be so bad," said Dr. Macphail.

They all looked forward to the Tuesday when the boat for San Francisco was to arrive from Sydney. The **strain**① was intolerable. So far as Dr. Macphail was concerned, his pity and his resentment were alike extinguished by his desire to be rid of the unfortunate woman. The inevitable must be accepted. He felt he would breathe more freely when the ship had sailed. Sadie Thompson was to be **escorted**② on board by a clerk in the governor's office. This person called on the Monday evening and told Miss Thompson to be prepared at eleven in the morning. Davidson was with her.

"I'll see that everything is ready. I mean to come on board with her myself."

Miss Thompson did not speak.

When Dr. Macphail blew out his candle and crawled cautiously under his mosquito curtains, he gave a sigh of relief.

"Well, thank God that's over. By this time tomorrow she'll be gone."

"Mrs. Davidson will be glad too. She says he's wearing himself to a shadow," said Mrs. Macphail. "She's a different woman."

"Who?"

"Sadie. I should never have thought it possible. It makes one humble."

Dr. Macphail did not answer, and presently he fell asleep. He was tired out, and he slept more soundly than usual.

He was awakened in the morning by a hand placed on his arm, and, starting up, saw Horn by the side of his bed. The trader put his finger on his mouth to prevent any exclamation from Dr. Macphail and **beckoned**③ him to come. As a rule he wore shabby ducks, but now he was barefoot and wore only the lava-lava of the natives. He looked suddenly savage, and Dr. Macphail, getting out of bed, saw that he was heavily tattooed. Horn made him a sign to come on to the

“这雨哪怕只是停一天，情况也不至于这么糟糕啊。”麦克费尔医生说。

他们都在等待着星期二那一天的到来，因为到时从悉尼驶向旧金山的船就到达了。紧张的气氛令人无法忍受。就麦克费尔医生而言，他渴望摆脱掉那个不幸的女人，这种欲望把他的怜悯之心和愤恨之意全都消耗殆尽了。面对无法避免的结果，人必须要接受。等到船只扬帆远去后，他便能够自由自在地呼吸。萨迪·汤普森拟由总督府的一位办事员护送上船。那人星期一傍晚上门来了，并且告知汤普森小姐，翌日上午十一点做好准备。戴维森当时陪同着她。

① strain [strein] *n.* 极度紧张

② escort ['eskɔːt] *v.* 陪同

“我会负责把一切都办妥贴的。我的意思是说，我自己亲自陪她上船。”

汤普森小姐没有吭声。

麦克费尔医生吹灭了蜡烛，小心翼翼地钻进蚊帐内。这时候，他叹了口气，如释重负。

“啊，感谢上帝，一切都过去了。到了明天这个时候，她就离开了。”

“戴维森夫人也会很高兴的。她说，戴维森先生自己身心疲惫，人都成了个影子了，”麦克费尔夫人说，“她是个不一样的女人了。”

“谁啊？”

“萨迪呀，我压根儿没有想到，竟然会有这样的结果，让一个人变得谦卑内敛。”

麦克费尔医生没有回答，很快便睡着了。他感觉很疲劳，所以比平常睡得更香。

③ beckon ['bekən] *v.* 示意；召唤

翌日早晨，他醒来时，感觉有一只手触碰他的胳膊。他霍地一下起来，看见霍恩在他床边。店老板用一根手指抵住自己的嘴，示意医生不要大声嚷嚷，同时示意他出去。平常情况下，他穿的是一条旧帆布裤，但他眼下光着脚，只围了一条土著人的短围裙，看上去突然变成一副很野蛮的样子。麦克费尔医生从床上下来，看见霍恩满身刺着纹身图案。霍恩示意他到外面的露台上去。

veranda. Dr. Macphail got out of bed and followed the trader out.

"Don't make a noise," he whispered. "You're wanted. Put on a coat and some shoes. Quick."

Dr. Macphail's first thought was that something had happened to Miss Thompson.

"What is it? Shall I bring my instruments?"

"Hurry, please, hurry."

Dr. Macphail crept back into the bedroom, put on a waterproof over his pyjamas, and a pair of rubber-soled shoes. He rejoined the trader, and together they tiptoed down the stairs. The door leading out to the road was open and at it were standing half a dozen natives.

"What is it?" repeated the doctor.

"Come along with me," said Horn.

He walked out and the doctor followed him. The natives came after them in a little bunch. They crossed the road and came on to the beach. The doctor saw a group of natives standing round some object at the water's edge. They hurried along, a couple of dozen yards perhaps, and the natives opened out as the doctor came up. The trader pushed him forwards. Then he saw, lying half in the water and half out, a dreadful object, the body of Davidson. Dr. Macphail bent down—he was not a man to lose his head in an emergency—and turned the body over. The throat was cut from ear to ear, and in the right hand was still the razor with which the deed was done.

"He's quite cold," said the doctor. "He must have been dead some time."

"One of the boys saw him lying there on his way to work just now and came and told me. Do you think he did it himself?"

"Yes. Someone ought to go for the police."

Horn said something in the native tongue, and two youths started off.

"We must leave him here till they come," said the doctor.

"They mustn't take him into my house. I won't have him in my house."

麦克费尔离开了床边，跟随着店老板到了外面。

“别弄出动静来，”他小声说，“找您呢，穿上外套，还有鞋子，快点。”

麦克费尔医生首先想到的就是，汤普森小姐有什么情况。

“发生了什么事情？我需要带医疗器械吗？”

“快点，求求您，快点。”

医生悄然返回了卧室，睡衣外面套着雨衣，穿上了胶皮套鞋。他返回到了店老板身边。紧接着，他们两个人一同蹑手蹑脚地下楼了。朝向外面大路的门开着，门口站着五六位土著居民。

“发生了什么事情？”医生又问了一声。

“跟我走吧。”霍恩说。

霍恩到了门外，医生跟随着他。那一小拨土著居民跟随在他们后面。他们横过了大路，到了海滩。医生看见一群土著居民围着水边的一个东西站立着。他们匆忙向前走，距离大概二十多码的样子。医生走近时，土著居民让开了一条道。店老板在后面推着他向前。这时，医生看到，一个可怕的东西一半在水中一半在岸上。那东西是戴维森的尸体。麦克费尔医生躬下身子——他不是那种面对紧急情况不知所措的人——把那具尸体翻了个个。两耳之间的颈脖处显现出刀口，右手上还握着形成刀口的剃刀片。

“尸体已经冰凉了，”医生说，“他死亡一定有一段时间了。”

“这些小伙子中有一位刚才去上工的途中看见他在那儿躺着，就赶紧告诉我。您认为他这是自己干的吗？”

“是啊，得有个人去报警啊。”

霍恩用土著人的语言说了些什么。两个年轻人立刻离开了。

“警察来之前，我们不能动他。”医生说。

“他们决不能把他抬到我住宅里去，我不想把他放进我家里。”

"You'll do what the authorities say," replied the doctor sharply. "In point of fact I expect they'll take him to the **mortuary**①."

They stood waiting where they were. The trader took a cigarette from a fold in his lava-lava and gave one to Dr. Macphail. They smoked while they stared at the corpse. Dr. Macphail could not understand.

"Why do you think he did it?" asked Horn.

The doctor shrugged his shoulders. In a little while native police came along, under the charge of a marine, with a **stretcher**②, and immediately afterwards a couple of naval officers and a naval doctor. They managed everything in a businesslike manner.

"What about the wife?" said one of the officers.

"Now that you've come I'll go back to the house and get some things on. I'll see that it's broken to her. She'd better not see him till he's been fixed up a little."

"I guess that's right," said the naval doctor. When Dr. Macphail went back he found his wife nearly dressed.

"Mrs. Davidson's in a dreadful state about her husband," she said to him as soon as he appeared. "He hasn't been to bed all night. She heard him leave Miss Thompson's room at two, but he went out. If he's been walking about since then he'll be absolutely dead."

Dr. Macphail told her what had happened and asked her to break the news to Mrs. Davidson.

"But why did he do it?" she asked, horror-stricken.

"I don't know."

"But I can't. I can't."

"You must."

She gave him a frightened look and went out. He heard her go into Mrs. Davidson's room. He waited a minute to gather himself together and then began to shave and wash. When he was dressed he sat down on the bed and waited for his wife. At last she came.

"She wants to see him," she said.

① mortuary ['mɔːtjuəri] *n.* 太平间

② stretcher ['stretʃə] *n.* 担架

“当局怎么说您就怎么办好啦，”医生回答说，语气严厉，“事实上，我估计他们会把他抬到停尸间去的。”

他们站立在原地等待着。店老板从自己短围裙的皱褶里掏出香烟，递了一支给麦克费尔医生。他们一边盯着尸体看，一边吸着烟。麦克费尔医生无法理解。

“您为何认为这是他自己干的呢？”霍恩问了一声。

医生耸了耸肩膀。一会儿过后，当地的警察到达了，是由一位海军陆战队的士兵领着来的。他们带了担架。很快，来了两位海军陆战队的军官和一位军医。他们按照常规惯例处理好了一切。

“那位夫人怎么办？”一位军官问。

“你们既然已经到场了，那我就回到住处去穿点衣服。我来负责把事情告诉她。最好等到你们把他收拾妥帖了一点，才让夫人见他。”

“我看这样妥当。”海军军医说。麦克费尔医生返回到住处时，他夫人已经差不多已经穿着好了。

“戴维森夫人对自己的丈夫很是担忧，”医生刚一出现，夫人便说，“他整夜都没有回来睡觉。她听见丈夫两点钟时离开汤普森小姐，但他出门了。他若是从那时开始一直四处走动，他一定是没命了。”

麦克费尔医生把发生了的情况告诉夫人，并请夫人把消息转告给戴维森夫人。

“但是，他为何要这样做啊？”她反问了医生，惊恐不安。

“我不知道。”

“但是，我不能去转告，我不能去。”

“你必须去。”

她惊恐地看了一眼丈夫，走出了房间。他听见她进了戴维森夫人的卧室。他稍等片刻定了定神，然后开始洗脸修面。他装束完毕后，在床上坐了下来，等待夫人回来。她最后回来了。

“她想去看他。”她说。

"They've taken him to the mortuary. We'd better go down with her. How did she take it?"

"I think she's stunned. She didn't cry. But she's trembling like a leaf."

"We'd better go at once."

When they knocked at her door Mrs. Davidson came out. She was very pale, but dry-eyed. To the doctor she seemed unnaturally **composed**[1]. No word was exchanged, and they set out in silence down the road. When they arrived at the mortuary Mrs. Davidson spoke.

"Let me go in and see him alone."

They stood aside. A native opened a door for her and closed it behind her. They sat down and waited. One or two white men came and talked to them in undertones. Dr. Macphail told them again what he knew of the tragedy. At last the door was quietly opened and Mrs. Davidson came out. Silence fell upon them.

"I'm ready to go back now," she said.

Her voice was hard and steady. Dr. Macphail could not understand the look in her eyes. Her pale face was very stern. They walked back slowly, never saying a word, and at last they came round the bend on the other side of which stood their house. Mrs. Davidson gave a gasp, and for a moment they stopped still. An incredible sound assaulted their ears. The gramophone which had been silent for so long was playing, playing ragtime loud and harsh.

"What's that?" cried Mrs. Macphail with horror.

"Let's go on," said Mrs. Davidson.

They walked up the steps and entered the hall. Miss Thompson was standing at her door, chatting with a sailor. A sudden change had taken place in her. She was no longer the cowed **drudge**[2] of the last days. She was dressed in all her finery, in her white dress, with the high shiny boots over which her fat legs bulged in their cotton stockings; her hair was elaborately arranged; and she wore that enormous hat covered with **gaudy**[3] flowers. Her face was painted, her eyebrows were **boldly**[4] black, and her lips were **scarlet**[5]. She held herself **erect**[6]. She

“他们已经把他抬到停尸间去了。我们最好陪同她一块儿去，她怎么接受得了这个事实啊？”

“我看她已经懵了，都没有哭出来。但她像一片树叶一样直哆嗦。”

“我们还是立刻去吧。”

他们敲门时，戴维森夫人出来了。她脸色煞白，但眼睛里没有泪水。医生看来，她似乎镇静得反常。他们之间没有言辞交流，而是默不作声地顺着大路走。他们到达停尸间时，戴维森夫人开始说话了。

“让我一个人进去看他吧。”

他们站立在一旁。一位土著人替她打开了一扇门，门接着在她身后关上了。他们坐下来等待。来了一两个白人，压低着嗓子同他们交谈起来。麦克费尔医生把他知道的悲剧情况对他们又说了一遍。最后，门悄然打开了，戴维森夫人走了出来。他们都缄口不言。

“我现在要回去了。”戴维森夫人说。

她说话的声音生硬而坚定。麦克费尔医生看不懂她眼神中的表情。她苍白的面孔十分冷峻。他们缓步往回走，没有吭一声。最后，他们走到了拐角处，对面就是他们居住的那幢住宅。戴维森夫人喘了口粗气，他们静静地驻足了片刻。耳畔突然传来令人难以置信的声响。沉寂了很长时间的留声机又开始播放起来了，雷格泰姆音乐高亢刺耳。

“什么声音？”麦克费尔夫人惊恐地大声问。

“往前走吧。”戴维森夫人说。

他们走上台阶，进入到了厅堂。汤普森小姐站立在她的房间门口，同一位水手闲聊着。她身上突然有了一种变化，一扫往日里那种失魂落魄的样子。她衣着华丽，一身白色，脚上是一双白铮亮的高跟靴子，上方露着两条套了长筒棉纱袜的粗腿，鼓鼓囊囊的。头发经过了精心梳理。头上戴着装饰了俗艳花朵的大帽子。脸上经过了涂脂抹粉，眉毛描得又浓又黑。双唇涂成了大红。她挺直了身子，摆出了他们初次见到她时的那副得意洋洋

① composed [kəm'pəuzd] *a.* 镇定的

② drudge [drʌdʒ] *n.* 做苦工的人

③ gaudy ['gɔ:di] *a.* 华丽而俗气的

④ boldly [bəuldli] *ad.* 浓密地

⑤ scarlet ['skɑ:lət] *a.* 猩红色的

⑥ erect [i'rekt] *a.* 挺直的

was the flaunting queen that they had known at first. As they came in she broke into a loud, jeering laugh; and then, when Mrs. Davidson involuntarily stopped, she collected the **spittle**① in her mouth and spat. Mrs. Davidson cowered back, and two red spots rose suddenly to her cheeks. Then, covering her face with her hands, she broke away and ran quickly up the stairs. Dr. Macphail was outraged. He pushed past the woman into her room.

"What the devil are you doing?" he cried. "Stop that damned machine."

He went up to it and tore the record off. She turned on him.

"Say, doc, you can stop that stuff with me. What the hell are you doin' in my room?"

"What do you mean?" he cried. "What d'you mean?"

She gathered herself together. No one could describe the scorn of her expression or the contemptuous hatred she put into her answer.

"You men! You **filthy**②, dirty pigs! You're all the same, all of you. Pigs! Pigs!"

Dr. Macphail gasped. He understood.

的女皇姿态。他们进门时，她爆发出了响亮嘲讽的哈哈笑声。随后，戴维森夫人不由自主地停下脚步时，她酝酿了一嘴口水并且吐了出来。戴维森夫人向后退缩，脸颊上突然出现了两块红色。她随即双手捂住脸，迅速冲上了楼梯。麦克费尔医生怒不可遏。他把面前的女人一把推进了她的房间。

“你到底要干什么啊?”他大声说，“关了那架该死的留声机。”

他走向留声机，把唱片取了下来。她转身对着他。

“啊，医生，您竟然对我这个态度。您到底想在我的房间里干什么啊？”

“你什么意思？”他大声问，“你什么意思？”

她镇定了一下，做出了回答，说话时显露出的轻蔑表情或者说憎恨的态度无法用言语形容。

“你们这些男人！你们这些污秽肮脏的猪猡！你们全是一丘之貉，全部都是。猪猡！猪猡！”

麦克费尔喘息了一声。他明白了。

① spittle ['spitl] *n.* 唾沫

② filthy ['filθi] *a.* 下流的

The Cabinet Minister

He received me in a long room **looking on to**① a sandy garden. The roses withered on the **stunted**② bushes and the great old trees **flagged**③ **forlorn**④. He sat me down on a square **stool**⑤ at a square table and took his seat in front of me. A servant brought cups of flowered tea and American cigarettes. He was a thin man, of the middle height, with thin, elegant hands; and through his gold-rimmed spectacles he looked at me with large, dark, and melancholy eyes. He had the look of a student or of a dreamer. His smile was very sweet. He wore a brown silk gown and over it a short black silk jacket, and on his head a **billy-cock**⑥ hat.

"Is it not strange," he said, with his charming smile, "that we Chinese wear this gown because three hundred years ago the Manchus were horsemen?"

"Not so strange," I retorted, "as that because the English won the battle of Waterloo Your Excellency should wear a bowler."

"Do you think that is why I wear it?"

"I could easily prove it."

Since I was afraid that his **exquisite**⑦ **courtesy**⑧ would prevent him from asking me how, I hastened in a few well-chosen words to do so.

内阁大臣

① look on to 面向，朝向
② stunted ['stʌntid] *a.* 生长不良的
③ flag [flæg] *v.*（草木等）凋谢
④ forlorn [fə'lɔːn] *a.* 孤苦伶仃的
⑤ stool [stuːl] *n.* 凳子
⑥ billy-cock ['bilikɔk] *n.* 圆顶硬礼帽
⑦ exquisite ['ekskwizit] *a.* 过分讲究的
⑧ courtesy ['kəːtisi] *n.* 谦恭

他在一间很长的房间里接待了我，室外是一座沙地花园。生长不良的玫瑰灌木丛上的花朵已经凋零了，参天的古树因缺水而萎垂萧疏。他让我在一张方桌旁边的一个方凳上坐了下来。仆人端上了两杯花茶，还拿来了美国香烟。他身材瘦削，个头中等，双手纤细精巧。他戴了一副金丝边框的眼镜，乌黑忧郁的大眼睛透过眼镜片看着我。他的神态像个学者或梦想家。他的微笑给人温馨的感觉。他身穿棕褐色的丝绸长衫，外面套了一件黑色的丝绸短上衣，头上戴了一顶圆顶硬礼帽。

"我们中国人之所以穿这种长衫，就是因为三百年前，满族人是马背上的民族，"他说，脸上露着迷人的微笑，"这难道不很奇怪吗？"

"没什么奇怪的，"我回应着说，"好比英国人赢得了滑铁卢战役[1]的胜利，阁下您应该戴圆顶高帽。"

"您觉得这是我戴这种帽子的原由吗？"

"我可以轻而易举地证明这一点。"

我担心，他保持着一副完美的谦谦君子风度，不至于开口问我如何证明，因此，我急忙字斟句酌，用寥寥

1 滑铁卢战役（Battle of Waterloo）是指1815年6月18日由法军对反法联军在比利时小镇滑铁卢进行的决战。战役结局是反法联军获得了决定性胜利。战役结束了拿破仑帝国。拿破仑战败后被放逐至圣赫勒拿岛，自此退出历史舞台。

He took off his hat and looked at it with the shadow of a sigh. I glanced round the room. It had a green Brussels carpet, with great flowers on it, and round the walls were highly carved blackwood chairs. From a picture rail hung scrolls on which were writings by the great masters of the past, and to vary these, in bright gold frames, were oil paintings which in the nineties might very well have been exhibited in the Royal Academy. The Minister did his work at an American roll-top desk.

He talked to me with melancholy of the state of China. A civilisation, the oldest the world had known, was now being **ruthlessly**① swept away. The students who came back from Europe and from America were tearing down what endless generations had built up, and they were placing nothing in its stead. They had no love of their country, no religion, no **reverence**②. The temples, deserted by worshipper and priest, were falling into decay and presently their beauty would be nothing but a memory.

But then, with a gesture of his thin, aristocratic hands, he put the subject aside. He asked me whether I would care to see some of his works of art. We walked round the room and he showed me priceless **porcelains**③, bronzes, and Tang figures. There was a horse from a grave in Honan which had the grace and the exquisite modelling of a Greek work. On a large table by the side of his desk was a number of rolls. He chose one and holding it at the top gave it to me to unroll. It was a picture, of some early dynasty, of mountains seen through **fleecy**④ clouds, and with smiling eyes he watched my pleasure as I looked. The picture was set aside and he showed me another and yet another. Presently I protested that I could not allow a busy man to waste his time on me, but he would not let me go. He brought out picture after picture. He was a **connoisseur**⑤. He was pleased to tell me the schools and periods to which they belonged and **neat**⑥ anecdotes about their painters.

"I wish I could think it was possible for you to appreciate my greatest

数语加以解释。

他摘下帽子，眼睛看着帽子，微微叹息了一声。我环顾了一番房间，地上铺上绿色布鲁塞尔地毯，地毯上面有巨大的鲜花图案。四周的墙壁边摆放着精雕细刻过的黑檀木椅子。挂镜线处挂着一个个卷轴，卷轴上有昔日大师们书写的文字。与这些东西不同的是，用一个个铮亮的镀金框子框着油画，若是在90年代，完全可以拿到英国皇家艺术院去展出。这位内阁大臣在一张美式卷盖书桌旁办公。

内阁大臣神情忧郁，同我谈起了中国。现在，世界上最古老的一种文明正在被无情地摧毁着。从欧洲和美洲回来的学者们正在拆除无数代人建立起来的东西。但他们没有在先前的地方放置进任何东西。他们对自己的国家毫无爱意，没有宗教信仰，没有敬畏之心。崇拜者和祭司离弃了一座座庙宇，庙宇正在圮废坍塌，其壮美的景观很快便不复存在了，只残存在人们的记忆之中。

但后来，他那双纤细而又富有贵族气派的手做了个动作，便把这个话题搁置到一旁了。他询问我是否愿意观赏一下他的艺术品。我们绕着房间走，他领着我观看价值连城的瓷器、青铜器，还有中国唐朝的塑像。有一尊从河南古墓中出土的马匹塑像，精致优雅，造型美观，足可以同古希腊的艺术品相媲美。书桌旁边的一张大桌子上摆放着大量卷轴。他选择了其中一个，抓住卷轴的顶部，展开给我看。上面是一幅出自早期某个朝代的群山图画，白云朵朵，环绕着山峦。我观赏着画作的当儿，他两眼洋溢着微笑，注视着我欣喜的表情。他把画作放到了一旁，把另外的画作一幅接着一幅展示给我看。我不一会儿便声称说，自己不能让一位工作繁忙的人士把时间浪费在我身上，但是，他执意不让我离开。他把画作一幅接着一幅地拿出来。他是位收藏家，乐此不疲地告诉我，画作属于哪个流派，哪个时代，还要讲述关于画家们的趣闻轶事。

“但愿我可以觉得您能够充分欣赏我的这些珍贵宝

① ruthlessly ['ruːθlisli] *ad.* 无情地

② reverence ['revərəns] *n.* 尊重

③ porcelain ['pɔːsəlin] *n.* 瓷器

④ fleecy [fliːsi] *a.* 柔软而轻的

⑤ connoisseur [ˌkɔnə'səː] *n.* 鉴赏家

⑥ neat [niːt] *a.* 简洁的

treasures," he said, pointing to the scrolls that adorned his walls. "Here you have examples of the most perfect **calligraphies**[1] of China."

"Do you like them better than paintings?" I asked.

"**Infinitely**[2]. Their beauty is more **chaste**[3]. There is nothing **meretricious**[4] in them. But I can quite understand that a European would have difficulty in appreciating so severe and so delicate an art. Your taste in Chinese things tends a little to the **grotesque**[5], I think."

He produced books of paintings and I turned their leaves. Beautiful things! With the dramatic instinct of the collector he kept to the last the book by which he set most store. It was a series of little pictures of birds and flowers, roughly done with a few **strokes**[6], but with such a power of suggestion, with so great a feeling for nature and such a playful tenderness, that it took your breath away. There were **sprigs**[7] of plum-blossom that held in their dainty freshness all the magic of the spring; there were sparrows in whose **ruffled**[8] **plumage**[9] were the beat and the tremor of life. It was the work of a great artist.

"Will these American students ever produce anything like this?" he asked with a **rueful**[10] smile.

But to me the most charming part of it was that I knew all the time that he was a **rascal**[11]. Corrupt, inefficient, and unscrupulous, he let nothing stand in his way. He was a master of the squeeze. He had acquired a large fortune by the most **abominable**[12] methods. He was dishonest, cruel, **vindictive**[13], and **venal**[14]. He had certainly had a share in reducing China to the desperate **plight**[15] which he so sincerely lamented. But when he held in his hand a little vase of the colour of **lapis lazuli**[16] his fingers seemed to curl about it with a charming tenderness, his melancholy eyes caressed it as they looked, and his lips were slightly parted as though with a sigh of desire.

贝，”他说，一边指着装饰他房间墙面的卷轴，“您在此看到了最完美的中国书法精品。”

“相对于那些画作，您更加喜欢这些书法作品吧？”我问了一声。

“可不是嘛。书法作品透出的美感更加纯正高雅。其中毫无华而不实的东西。但是，我很清楚，面对这样一种十分严苛而又精美绝伦的艺术，欧洲人很难欣赏。您对中国艺术的欣赏品味有点倾向于奇异怪诞的东西。我是这么认为的。”

他拿出了一本本绘画集，我翻看着。多么美妙的作品啊！凭着收藏家不同凡响的直觉，他把这本绘画放到了最后。这是一本小幅的花鸟画集，全是用寥寥数笔粗略勾勒而成的，但是，其中充满着丰富的联想力，对大自然的深厚情感，还有嬉戏玩耍的志趣，所以，画集会让您惊羡得喘不过气来。有挂满枝头的李子花，鲜嫩欲滴的花蕾上，承载着春天里的所有魔力。有怒竖羽毛的麻雀，展示着生命的节拍与律动。这是一位伟大艺术家的作品。

“那些美国的学者能够创作出类似于这样的作品吗？”他反问了一声，脸上露着悲切的微笑。

但是，在我看来，其中最有意思的一部分便是，我一直都知道，他是个流氓恶棍。他贪污腐败，慵懒无能，肆无忌惮，扫除妨碍自己的一切障碍。他是搜刮民脂民膏的高手。他利用极不正当的手段积敛了大量钱财。他为人不厚道，手段残忍，充满恶意，贪赃枉法。毫无疑问，把中国拖入绝望的困境的行动，有他一份，但他却对此表露出了由衷的悲切之情。但是，当他的一只手握着一个天青石色的小花瓶时，他的手指似乎成了缠绕的着花瓶的装饰，美丽柔和。他忧郁的眼睛看着花瓶时，洋溢着宠爱。他的双唇稍稍张开着，好像要发出一声充满欲望的叹息。

① calligraphy [kə'ligrəfi] *n.* 书法
② infinitely ['infinətli] *ad.* 极其
③ chaste [tʃeist] *a.* 高雅的
④ meretricious [ˌmeri'triʃəs] *a.* 华而不实的
⑤ grotesque [grəu'tesk] *n.* 奇异风格的艺术作品
⑥ stroke [strəuk] *n.* 笔画
⑦ sprig [sprig] *n.* 小枝
⑧ ruffle ['rʌfl] *v.* 鸟受惊时羽毛竖起
⑨ plumage ['plu:midʒ] *n.* 羽毛
⑩ rueful ['ru:ful] *a.* 悲伤的
⑪ rascal ['rɑ:skəl] *n.* 恶棍
⑫ abominable [ə'bɔminəbl] *a.* 可鄙的
⑬ vindictive [vin'diktiv] *a.* 恶意的
⑭ venal ['vi:nəl] *a.* 贪污的
⑮ plight [plait] *n.* 困境
⑯ lapis lazuli [ˌlæpis'læzjulai] *n.* 天青石

The Consul

Mr. Pete was in a state of the liveliest **exasperation**①. He had been in the consular service for more than twenty years and he had had to deal with all manner of **vexatious**② people, officials who would not listen to reason, merchants who took the British Government for a debt-collecting agency, missionaries who resented as gross injustice any attempt at fair play; but he never recollected a case which had left him more completely at a loss. He was a mild-mannered man, but for no reason he flew into a passion with his writer and he very nearly **sacked**③ the Eurasian clerk because he had wrongly spelt two words in a letter placed before him for his official signature. He was a conscientious man and he could not persuade himself to leave his office before the clock struck four, but the moment it did he jumped up and called for his hat and stick. Because his boy did not bring them at once he abused him roundly. They say that the consuls all grow a little odd; and the merchants who can live for thirty-five years in China without learning enough of the language to ask their way in the street say that it is because they have to study Chinese; and there was no doubt that Mr. Pete was decidedly odd. He was a bachelor and on that account had been sent to a series of posts which by reason of their isolation were thought unsuited to married men. He had lived so much alone that his natural tendency to **eccentricity**④ had developed to an extravagant degree, and he had habits which surprised the stranger. He was very absent-minded.

领事

① exasperation [ɪgˌzæspəˈreiʃən] *n.* 愤怒

② vexatious [vekˈseiʃəs] *a.* 令人烦恼的

③ sack [sæk] *v.* 开除

④ eccentricity [ˌeksenˈtrisəti] *n.* 古怪

皮特先生情绪激动，怒不可遏。他在领事的职位上已经待了二十多年，跟什么形形色色的人都打过交道，有令人伤尽脑筋的普通人，有蛮不讲理的官员，有把英国政府当成是收债代理的商人，有对在按照规矩开展的活动中公然爆出明显的不公正企图表示愤怒的海外传教团成员。但是，在他的记忆中，还没有哪一件事情比这让他更加不知所措的。他本来是个态度温和的人，但是，他却无故冲着自己的书记员大发雷霆。他差一点把那位欧亚混血的职员给解雇了，因为后者在一封信函中拼写错了两个词，信函呈交到他面前需要他正式签署。他是个一丝不苟的人，下午四点钟之前，决不会离开自己的办公室。但眼下，他一跃身子站立起来，嚷嚷着要人给他拿来帽子和手杖。因为替他跑腿的男仆没有立刻把他需要的东西拿来，他便劈头盖脑地痛骂了人家一顿。人们说，领事们全都变得有点性情古怪了。商人们在中国可以生活上三十五年，而无需掌握够多中文以便在大街上问路。于是他们说，因为领事们必须要学习中文。毫无疑问，皮特先生铁定性情古怪。他是个单身汉，基于这个理由，当局派遣他到了一系列岗位去履职，因为需要远离家庭，对于有家室的人而言，那些岗位不适宜他们。他长期独自一人生活，从而大大滋长了他的怪癖性

He paid no attention to his house, which was always in great disorder, nor to his food; his boys gave him to eat what they liked and for everything he had, made him **pay through the nose**①. He was untiring in his efforts to suppress the opium traffic, but he was the only person in the city who did not know that his servants kept opium in the **consulate**② itself, and a busy traffic in the drug was openly conducted at the back door of the compound. He was an ardent collector and the house provided for him by the Government was filled with the various things which he had collected one after the other, **pewter**③, brass, carved wood; these were his more legitimate enterprises; but he also collected stamps, birds' eggs, hotel labels, and postmarks: he boasted that he had a collection of postmarks which was unequalled in the Empire. During his long **sojourning**④ in lonely places he had read a great deal, and though he was no **sinologue**⑤ he had a greater knowledge of China, its history, literature, and people, than most of his colleagues; but from his wide reading he had acquired not toleration but vanity. He was a man of a singular appearance. His body was small and frail and when he walked he gave you the idea of a dead leaf dancing before the wind; and then there was something extraordinarily odd in the small Tyrolese hat, with a cock's feather in it, very old and shabby, which he wore perched **rakishly**⑥ on the side of his large head. He was exceedingly bald. You saw that his eyes, blue and pale, were weak behind the spectacles, and a drooping, ragged, dingy moustache did not hide the **peevishness**⑦ of his mouth. And now, turning out of the street in which was the consulate, he made his way on to the city wall, for there only in the **multitudinous**⑧ city was it possible to walk with comfort.

He was a man who took his work hardly, worrying himself to death over every trifle, but as a rule a walk on the wall **soothed**⑨ and rested him. The city stood in the midst of a great plain and often at sundown from the wall you could see in the distance the snow-capped mountains, the mountains of Tibet; but now he walked quickly, looking neither to the right nor to the left, and his fat spaniel frisked about him unobserved. He talked to himself rapidly in a low monotone. The cause of his irritation was a visit that he had that

情。他的种种行为习惯往往会让不明就里的陌生人惊讶不已。他会心不在焉，对自己的住处毫不在意，所以一直都是乱成一团。他对自己的饮食也毫不在意，几位男仆乐意提供给他什么，他就吃什么。他购买每一样东西时，都得支付过高的费用。他竭尽全力打击鸦片贸易，而且乐此不疲。但是，他的仆人们在领事馆内私藏鸦片，大院的后门处公开有鸦片买卖，而且生意兴隆。关于这个情况，整座城市里唯有他一个人蒙在鼓里。他是位充满热情的收藏家，政府提供给他住处到处摆放着他一件一件收集起来的物品，有白镴器皿、黄铜器、雕花木。收藏这类物品是他更加正当的事业，但他也收集邮票、鸟蛋、旅馆标记，还有邮戳。他曾经夸下海口说，他收集到的邮戳整个帝国无以伦比。他在长期独居一隅期间，博览群书，尽管他不懂中文，但比起他的绝大多数同僚，他掌握了更加丰富的中国知识，包括中国的历史、文学和人民。但是，他从广泛的阅读当中获取到的不是宽容忍让，而是虚荣自负。他是位有着奇特外表的人，身材矮小，身体虚弱。他走路时让您联想到枯叶迎风抖动的样子。此外，那顶小型号的蒂罗尔[1]帽子显得与众不同，怪模怪样，上面饰有公鸡羽毛。帽子非常老旧破烂，戴在他的大脑袋上，故意歪向一边。他头上秃顶很严重。您会看到，他眼镜片后面淡蓝色的眼睛视力很弱。胡子下垂着，蓬乱而色泽暗淡，却掩盖不住挂在他嘴边的怒气。他此时从领事馆所在的街道转了出来，向着城墙上走去，因为在这座人口众多的城市中，只有那儿才能悠闲舒适地散步。

他是个对待工作很严格的人，对待每一件小事情都往往会极度担忧犯愁，但通常情况下，在城墙上散步，他会感到舒心和安宁。城市坐落在大平原的中心地带，日落余晖下，伫立在城墙上，您往往可以看见远处白雪皑皑的群山——西藏的群山。但此刻，他快步行走，没有左顾右盼，他的肥胖猎犬自顾自地跟随在他身边，蹦蹦

① pay through the nose 被勒索

② consulate [ˈkɔnsjuleit] *v.* 领事馆

③ pewter [ˈpjuːtə] *n.* 白镴器皿

④ sojourning [ˈsɔdʒəːniŋ] *n.* 逗留

⑤ sinologue [ˈsinəlg] *n.* 汉学家

⑥ rakishly [ˈreikiʃli] *ad.* 灵巧地

⑦ peevishness [ˈpiːviʃnis] *n.* 脾气不好

⑧ multitudinous [ˌmʌltiˈtjuːdinəs] *a.* 人数众多的

⑨ soothe [suːð] *v.* 安慰

1 蒂罗尔（Tirol）是南部欧洲的一个地区，在奥地利西部和意大利北部。

day received from a lady who called herself Mrs. Yü and whom he with a consular passion for precision insisted on calling Miss Lambert. This in itself **sufficed**① to deprive their intercourse of **amenity**②. She was an Englishwoman married to a Chinese. She had arrived two years before with her husband from England where he had been studying at the University of London; he had made her believe that he was a great personage in his own country and she had imagined herself to be coming to a gorgeous palace and a position of consequence. It was a bitter surprise when she found herself brought to a shabby Chinese house crowded with people; there was not even a foreign bed in it, nor a knife and fork; everything seemed to her very dirty and smelly. It was a shock to find that she had to live with her husband's father and mother and he told her that she must do exactly what his mother bade her; but in her complete ignorance of Chinese it was not till she had been two or three days in the house that she realised that she was not her husband's only wife. He had been married as a boy before he left his native city to acquire the knowledge of the barbarians. When she bitterly **upbraided**③ him for deceiving her he shrugged his shoulders. There was nothing to prevent a Chinese from having two wives if he wanted them and, he added with some disregard to truth, no Chinese woman looked upon it as a hardship. It was upon making this discovery that she paid her first visit to the consul. He had already heard of her arrival—in China everyone knows everything about everyone—and he received her without surprise. Nor had he much sympathy to show her. That a foreign woman should marry a Chinese at all filled him with indignation, but that she should do so without making proper inquiries vexed him like a personal affront. She was not at all the sort of woman whose appearance led you to imagine that she would be guilty of such a folly. She was a solid, thick-set, young person, short, plain, and matter-of-fact. She was cheaply dressed in a tailor-made suit and she wore a tam-o'-shanter. She had bad teeth and a muddy skin. Her hands were large and red and ill cared for. You could tell that

① suffice [sə'fais] v. 足够
② amenity [ə'mi:nəti] n. 愉快
③ upbraid [ʌp'breid] v. 责备

跳跳。他小声地自言自语，语速很快。当天，有位女士上门来了，她称自己是俞夫人。而他——怀着一股领事要追求精准的热情——坚持称她为兰伯特小姐。他之所以恼羞成怒，就是因为有了夫人来访的事情。这件事情本身就足以弄得他们之间的会面很不愉快。她是位英国妇女，嫁给了一位中国人。两年前，她随同丈夫离开英国来到中国。她丈夫先前一直在伦敦大学读书。丈夫让她相信了，他在他自己的国家是个了不起的人物。她曾经想象着，自己将要进入一座富丽堂皇的宫殿，拥有显赫的地位。当她被领进一幢挤满了人的破旧中国民宅时，感到痛苦而又惊讶。那儿连一张外国的床铺都没有，也没有刀叉。她觉得，每一样东西都是脏兮兮的，散发着臭味。令她感到震惊的是，她必须得同丈夫的父母住在一块儿。丈夫还告诉她说，她必须要完全按照他母亲吩咐她的去做。但是，由于她完全不懂中文，她在那幢住宅里生活了两三天之后，才发现，自己并不是丈夫唯一的妻子。少年时代，他离开自己故乡的城市前去"师夷长技"之前，已经有了妻室。当她愤怒地指责他，说他欺骗了自己时，他耸了耸肩膀。中国男人若是打算要娶两房妻室，那是没有什么东西可以阻挠的。他还罔顾事实地补充说，任何中国妇女都不会把这是看作是一种苦难。正是有了这个发现之后，她第一次拜访了领事大人。他已经听说了她来中国的事情——在中国，关于每个人的事情，每个人都知晓——所以，他接待她时，并没有感到惊讶。他也没有对她表达多少同情。一位外国女士竟然嫁给一位中国人，他对此义愤填膺。但是，她竟然不打听清楚底细，就这么嫁了，更是像一件对个人侮辱的事情，令他大为恼火。有种女人从外表上来判断，您想象得到，她会对自己的愚蠢行为感到很内疚，但她绝对不属于那种女人。她年纪轻轻，体型粗壮结实，个头不高，相貌平平，直来直去。她身穿一套由裁缝缝制的廉价衣服，头戴一顶苏格兰式的便帽。她牙齿不美观，肤色灰暗。一双大手，通红的，疏于保养。您可以看出，她习惯于干重活。她

she was not unused to hard work. She spoke English with a Cockney **whine**①.

"How did you meet Mr. Yü?" asked the consul **frigidly**②.

"Well, you see, it's like this," she answered. "Dad was in a very good position, and when he died mother said: 'Well, it seems a sinful waste to keep all these rooms empty, I'll put a card in the window.'"

The consul interrupted her.

"He had lodgings with you?"

"Well, they weren't exactly lodgings," she said.

"Shall we say apartments then?" replied the consul, with his thin, slightly vain smile.

That was generally the explanation of these marriages. Then because he thought her a very foolish vulgar woman he explained **bluntly**③ that according to English law she was not married to Yü and that the best thing she could do was to go back to England at once. She began to cry and his heart softened a little to her. He promised to put her in charge of some missionary ladies who would look after her on the long journey, and indeed, if she liked, he would see if meanwhile she could not live in one of the missions. But while he talked Miss Lambert dried her tears.

"What's the good of going back to England?" she said at last. "I 'aven't got nowhere to go to."

"You can go to your mother."

"She was all against my marrying Mr. Yü. I should never hear the last of it if I was to go back now."

The consul began to argue with her, but the more he argued the more determined she became, and at last he lost his temper.

"If you like to stay here with a man who isn't your husband, it's your own look out, but I wash my hands of all responsibility."

Her retort had often **rankled**④.

"Then you've got no cause to worry," she said, and the look on her face returned to him whenever he thought of her.

① whine [wain] *n.* 发哀声
② frigidly ['fridʒidli] *ad.* 冷淡地
③ bluntly [blʌntli] *ad.* 坦率地
④ rankle ['ræŋkl] *v.* 使生气

说英语时会像伦敦东区人那样哼哼唧唧。

“您是如何认识俞先生的？”领事问了一声，语气冷淡。

“是啊，您看吧，情况是这么回事，”她回答说，“我父亲拥有很体面的社会地位。他去世后，母亲说：‘唉，让这些房子空着真是太浪费了，我在窗户开口放一个招租的牌子了。’”

领事打断了她的话。

“他租住你们家的公寓了吗？”

“对啦，那不是严格意义上的公寓。”她说。

“那我们就称之为居室怎么样？”领事回答说，脸上露出了难看的、有点华而不实的微笑。

有关这一类婚姻，人们大都会做出这样的解释。这么说来，由于领事觉得她是个愚蠢而又俗气的女人，他便直言不讳地解释说，依照英国的法律，她并没有嫁给姓俞的人。她能够做的最明智的事情就是立刻返回英国去。她开始哭了起来，他的心对她稍稍软了一点儿。他承诺把她托付给一些担任传教工作的女士们，她们会在慢慢旅途当中照顾好她的。实际上，他在考虑，她若是愿意的话，是否可以到一所慈善会堂去。但是，他在说着话的当儿，兰伯特小姐擦干了眼泪。

“返回到英国去有什么好呢？”她最后说，“我没有任何地方可去了。”

“您可以回到您母亲身边去呀。”

“她极力反对我嫁给俞先生。我若是现在回去，真不知道结果会是什么样的。”

领事开始对她讲道理，但是，他越讲道理，她的态度反而更加坚决。最后，他发火了。

“您若是愿意同一个不是您丈夫的男人待在这儿，那是您自己找的，但我不会负任何责任的。”

她的回应往往会激起他的怨恨。

“这么说来，您就没有理由担忧啦。”她说，而每当他想起她时，他的脑海里就会浮现出她当时脸上的表情。

That was two years ago and he had seen her once or twice since then. It appeared that she got on very badly both with her mother-in-law and with her husband's other wife, and she had come to the consul with **preposterous**① questions about her rights according to Chinese law. He repeated his offer to get her away, but she remained **steadfast**② in her refusal to go, and their interview always ended in the consul's flying into a passion. He was almost inclined to pity the **rascally**③ Yü, who had to keep the peace between three **warring**④ women. According to his English wife's account he was not unkind to her. He tried to act fairly by both his wives. Miss Lambert did not improve. The consul knew that ordinarily she wore Chinese clothes, but when she came to see him she put on European dress. She has become extremely **blowsy**⑤. Her health suffered from the Chinese food she ate and she was beginning to look wretchedly ill. But really he was shocked when she had been shown into his office that day. She wore no hat and her hair was dishevelled. She was in a highly hysterical state.

"They're trying to poison me," she screamed and she put before him a bowl of some foul-smelling food. "It's poisoned," she said. "I've been ill for the last ten days, it's only by a miracle I've escaped."

She gave him a long story, circumstantial and probable enough to convince him: after all nothing was more likely than that the Chinese women should use familiar methods to get rid of an intruder who was hateful to them.

"Do they know you've come here?"

"Of course they do; I told them I was going to **show** them **up**⑥."

Now at last was the moment for decisive action. The consul looked at her in his most official manner.

"Well, you must never go back there. I refuse to put up with your nonsense any longer. I insist on your leaving this man who isn't your husband."

But he found himself helpless against the woman's insane **obstinacy**⑦. He repeated all the arguments he had used so often, but she would not listen, and as

① preposterous [pri'pɔstərəs] *a.* 愚蠢的

② steadfast ['stedfɑːst] *a.* 不动摇的

③ rascally ['rɑːskəli] *a.* 无赖的

④ warring ['wɔriŋ] *a.* 敌对的

⑤ blowsy ['blauzi] *a.* 蓬乱的

⑥ show sb up 使人难堪

⑦ obstinacy ['ɔbstinəsi] *n.* 固执

这是两年前的事情。他后来还见过她两三次。看起来，她同她的婆婆和她丈夫的另外那个妻子相处得很糟糕。她来找领事，问了一些荒谬透顶的问题，说是对照中国法律，她自己有些什么权利。他重申了曾经向她承诺过的，帮助她离开，但是，她还是一如既往地态度坚决，执意不肯走。领事一直不停地大发雷霆，他们的会面结束了。领事都几乎要同情起那位恶棍品性的俞姓男子了，因为他必须要让三个相互敌视的女人保持相安无事。按照他的英国妻子的陈述，他对她说不上不体贴仁慈。面对两位妻子，他必须要做到一碗水端平。兰伯特小姐并无改进。领事知道，她通常都穿中国服装，但她来见他时，则穿欧洲服装。她变得极度粗俗邋遢了。她的身体适应不了中国的饮食，看上去面黄肌瘦，一脸病态了。但是，确实，当天仆人领着她进入他的办公室时，他感到很震惊。她没有戴帽子，头发蓬乱，一副歇斯底里的状态。

"她们想要毒死我。"她尖着嗓子大声说。她把一碗变质发臭的食物端到他的面前。"这有毒的，"她说，"最近十天以来，我一直生病来着。出现了奇迹我才得以死里逃生啊。"

她把冗长的经过一五一十地讲述给了他听，或许足以令他坚信不疑。毕竟，说中国女人采用人们熟悉的手段清除仇视她们的闯入者，这种可能性再大不过了。

"她们知道您来过这儿吗？"

"她们当然知道。我已经告诉过她们，一定要让她们难堪。"

现在终于到了要采取断然行动的时刻了。领事看着她，摆出一副官架子。

"好啦，您决不能在回到那儿去了。我不会再耐着性子来听您的这些毫无意义的话了。我坚持要求您离开那个并不是您丈夫的男人。"

但是，眼前的女人精神状态不正常，执拗任性。他发现自己对此束手无策。他重复着他常常讲的那些道理，

usual he lost his temper. It was then, in answer to his final, desperate question, that she had made the remark which had entirely robbed him of his calm.

"But what on earth makes you stay with the man?" he cried.

She hesitated for a moment and a curious look came into her eyes.

"There's something in the way his hair grows on his forehead that I can't help liking," she answered.

The consul had never heard anything so **outrageous**[①]. It really was the last straw. And now while he strode along, trying to walk off his anger, though he was not a man who often used bad language he really could not restrain himself, and he said fiercely:

"Women are simply **bloody**[②]."

但她充耳不闻，结果还是和平常一样，他火冒三丈。正是在这最后时刻回答他绝望的问题时，她说出的话让他完全无法冷静对待。

“但到底是什么原因，您非要同那个男人待在一块儿呢？”他大声问着。

她迟疑了片刻，目光中流露出奇特的神情。

“他额头上发型的式样，我无法不喜欢啊。”她回答说。

领事从未听说过如此荒唐透顶的事情。这确实是最后一根稻草。而此时此刻，他信步向前走着的当儿，企图想要通过散步来消消气，尽管他并不是个常常使用恶毒语言的人，但他事实上还是忍不住了，于是气急败坏地说：

“女人简直令人厌恶透顶。”

① outrageous [aut'reidʒəs] *a.* 令人吃惊的

② bloody ['blʌdi] *a.* 讨厌的

The Philosopher

It was surprising to find so vast a city in a spot that seemed to me so remote. From its **battlemented**[1] gate towards sunset you could see the snowy mountains of Tibet. It was so populous that you could walk at ease only on the walls and it took a rapid walker three hours to complete their circuit. There was no railway within a thousand miles and the river on which it stood was so shallow that only **junks**[2] of light burden could safely navigate it. Five days in a **sampan**[3] were needed to reach the Upper Yangtze. For an uneasy moment you asked yourself whether trains and steamships were as necessary to the conduct of life as we who use them every day consider; for here a million persons throve, married, begat their kind, and died; here a million persons were busily occupied with commerce, art, and thought.

哲学家 [1]

① battlemented ['bætl,mentid] *a.* 有城垛的

② junk [dʒʌŋk] *n.* 帆船

③ sampan ['sæmpæn] *n.* 舢板

如此偏远的一隅之地竟然还可以找到偌大的一座城市，我觉得这真是不可思议啊。夕阳西下时分，登上有雉堞的城门远远望去，您便可以看到西藏那白雪皑皑的群山。城市人口十分稠密，只有在城墙上才可以悠闲自得地散步。快步行走都得花费三个小时才能顺着城墙走完一圈。方圆一千英里之内都不通铁路。流经城市的那条河，水很浅，只有载重量很轻的船只才能安全航行。乘坐舢板船需要五天才能抵达扬子江上游。处在如此不方便的时刻，您会问一问自己，我们这些每天都乘坐火车和汽船的人，是否会觉得这些交通工具是人生进程中必不可少的？而正是在此，数以百万计的人们出生成长，结婚成家，繁衍后代，最后离开人世。正是在此，数以百万计的人们忙忙碌碌，经商挣钱，创造艺术，思索问题。

---

1 此处指辜鸿铭（1856—1928），字汤生，号立诚，自称慵人、东西南北人，祖籍福建省同安县，生于南洋英属马来西亚槟榔屿。学博中西，号称“清末怪杰”，精通英、法、德、拉丁、希腊、马来亚等九种语言，获十三个博士学位，是满清时代精通西洋科学、语言兼及东方华学的中国第一人。他翻译了中国“四书”中的三部——《论语》、《中庸》和《大学》，并著有《中国的牛津运动》（原名《清流传》）和《中国人的精神》（原名《春秋大义》）等英文书，热衷向西方人宣传东方的文化和精神，并产生了重大的影响，西方人曾流传一句话：到中国可以不看三大殿，不可不看辜鸿铭。毛姆曾在 20 世纪 20 年代拜访了辜鸿铭。

And here lived a philosopher of repute the desire to see whom had been to me one of the incentives of a somewhat arduous journey. He was the greatest authority in China on the Confucian learning. He was said to speak English and German with facility. He had been for many years secretary to one of the **Empress Dowager's**① greatest **viceroys**②, but he lived now in retirement. On certain days in the week, however, all through the year he opened his doors to such as sought after knowledge, and **discoursed**③ on the teaching of Confucius. He had a body of **disciples**④, but it was small, since the students for the most part preferred to his modest dwelling and his severe **exhortations**⑤ the **sumptuous**⑥ buildings of the foreign university and the useful science of the barbarians: with him this was mentioned only to be scornfully dismissed. From all I heard of him I concluded that he was a man of character.

When I announced my wish to meet this distinguished person my host immediately offered to arrange a meeting; but the days passed and nothing happened. I made enquiries and my host shrugged his shoulders.

"I sent him a **chit**⑦ and told him to come along," he said. "I don't know why he hasn't turned up. He's a **cross-grained**⑧ old fellow."

I did not think it was proper to approach a philosopher in so **cavalier**⑨ a fashion and I was hardly surprised that he had ignored a summons such as this. I caused a letter to be sent asking in the politest terms I could **devise**⑩ whether he would allow me to call upon him and within two hours received an answer making an appointment for the following morning at ten o'clock.

I was carried in a chair. The way seemed **interminable**⑪. I went through crowded streets and through streets deserted till I came at last to one, silent and empty, in which at a small door in a long white wall my bearers set down my chair. One of them knocked, and after a considerable time a **judas**⑫ was opened; dark eyes looked through; there was a brief **colloquy**⑬; and finally I was admitted. A youth, **pallid**⑭ of face, wizened, and poorly dressed, motioned me to follow him. I did not know if he was a servant or a pupil of the great man. I passed through a shabby yard and was led into a long low room sparsely

在这样一座城市里，还生活着一位著名的哲学家。对我而言，正是怀着想要拜会这样一位哲学家的愿望，我才进行了这次不辞辛劳的长途跋涉之旅。他是中国儒学最了不起的权威。据说，他精通英语和德语。他曾多年担任皇太后的一位重臣的秘书，但现在已经退休赋闲在家了。不过，一年四季当中，每个星期有几天时间，他的大门一直向求知问学的人敞开着，他向这些人讲授儒学。他拥有一群门徒，但数量不大。绝大多数学生都喜欢他那朴实无华的住所，还有他对国外大学奢华建筑和蛮夷实用科学的严苛批判。若是有人在他面前提起这个话题，只会招致他冷嘲热讽的斥责。根据我所听到的有关他的情况，我断定，他是一位很有个性的人。

我表达了想去拜会这位出类拔萃的人物的愿望后，接待我的主人立刻安排了一次会面。但是，日子一天天过去了，却没有见到什么动静。我再三打听了解，主人却耸了耸肩膀。

“我打发人给他送去了一封便函，告诉他来一趟，”主人说，“我不知道，他为何迟迟没有出现，他可是位倔强任性的老头呢。”

我以为，以如此简慢的方式去接近一位哲学家并不合适，所以，他对这一种召唤不予理睬，我并不感到奇怪。我用自己能够想到的最为恭谦有礼的言辞给他写了一封信，询问他是否首肯我前去登门拜访他。信送出去不到两个小时，我便收到了回复，约定翌日上午十点钟见面。

我是被人用轿子抬着去的。上他家去的路似乎没有尽头。我们经过了熙来攘往的大街，也经过了人迹罕至的小巷。最后，我们抵达了一条街道，寂静无声，空无一人。街上的一道长长的白墙壁处有一扇小门，抬我的轿夫把我放了下来。其中一位敲了敲门，过了好一阵，门上的小窥视窗打开了。一双黑眼睛透过窥视窗张望着。简短的一番对话后，对方最后允许我进入。有个年轻人示意我跟着他。只见他脸色苍白，形容枯槁，衣着寒酸。

① Empress Dowager 皇太后
② viceroy ['vaisrɔi] n. 总督
③ discourse ['diskɔːs] v. 演讲
④ disciple [di'saipl] n. 门徒
⑤ exhortation [ˌegzɔː'teiʃən] n. 训诫
⑥ sumptuous ['sʌmptjuəs] a. 豪华的
⑦ chit [tʃit] n. 便函
⑧ cross-grained ['krɔːs'greind] a. 倔强的
⑨ cavalier [ˌkævə'liə] a. 漫不经心的
⑩ devise [di'vaiz] v. 想出
⑪ interminable [in'təːminəbl] a. 无休止的
⑫ judas ['dʒuːdəs] n. 窥视孔
⑬ colloquy ['kɔləkwi] n. 交谈
⑭ pallid ['pælid] a. 苍白的

furnished with an American roll-top desk, a couple of blackwood chairs and two little Chinese tables. Against the walls were shelves on which were a great number of books: most of them, of course, were Chinese, but there were many, philosophical and scientific works, in English, French and German; and there were hundreds of unbound copies of learned reviews. Where books did not take up the wall space hung scrolls on which in various calligraphies were written, I suppose, Confucian quotations. There was no carpet on the floor. It was a cold, bare, and comfortless chamber. Its sombreness was relieved only by a yellow **chrysanthemum**[①] which stood by itself on the desk in a long vase.

I waited for some time and the youth who had shown me in brought a pot of tea, two cups, and a tin of Virginian cigarettes. As he went out the philosopher entered. I hastened to express my sense of the honour he did me in allowing me to visit him. He waved me to a chair and poured out the tea.

"I am flattered that you wished to see me," he returned. "Your countrymen deal only with **coolies**[②] and with **compradores**[③]; they think every Chinese must be one or the other."

I ventured to protest. But I had not caught his point. He leaned back in his chair and looked at me with an expression of mockery.

"They think they have but to beckon and we must come."

I saw then that my friend's unfortunate communication still rankled. I did not quite know how to reply. I murmured something complimentary.

He was an old man, tall, with a thin grey **queue**[④], and bright, large eyes under which were heavy bags. His teeth were broken and discoloured. He was exceedingly thin, and his hands, fine and small, were withered and claw-like. I had been told that he was an opium-smoker. He was very shabbily dressed in a black gown, a little black cap, both much the worse for wear, and dark-grey trousers **gartered**[⑤] at the ankle. He was watching. He did not quite know what attitude to take up, and he had the manner of a man who was on his guard. Of course the philosopher occupies a royal place among those who concern themselves with the things of the spirit and we have the authority of Benjamin

我不知道，年轻人是大哲学家的仆人还是弟子。我走过一座萧疏杂乱的院落，然后被领进了一个进身很长、天花板很低的房间，里面放着几件简陋的家具：一张美式卷盖书桌，几把黑檀木椅子，两张中式小桌子。靠墙立着的是一排排书架，里面摆放着数量众多的书籍。其中大部分当然是中文书，但也有许多英文、法文和德文的哲学和科学著作。此外，还有几百种尚未装订的学术杂志。墙壁处没有被书架占去地方挂着卷轴，上面是各种书法作品，我估计是儒家格言。地上没有铺地毯。这是一个阴冷、简陋、很不舒服的房间。只有立在书桌上的一个长花瓶插着的黄色菊花才打破了房间里阴郁单调的氛围。

我等了一会儿，把我领进来的那个年轻人拿来了一壶茶，两个茶杯，还有一听弗吉尼亚产的烟卷。年轻人出去时，哲学家进来了。我急忙表达说，他允许我拜访他，我深感荣幸。他示意我在一把椅子上坐下，然后倒茶。

“您有意要来见我，我不胜荣幸之至啊，”他回应着说，“您的国人只与苦力和买办们打交道。他们认为，每一位中国人不是苦力就是买办。”

我斗胆提出异议，但是，没有弄明白他说话的意图。他仰靠在椅子上，看着我，一副嘲讽的表情。

“他们以为，他们只需要召唤一声，我们就必须到。”

我此时才明白，我朋友那种糟糕的交流方式仍然令他耿耿于怀呢。我真不知道该如何回答他。我喃喃地说了几句恭维的话。

他是位老者，身材很高，留着一条细长的灰白辫子，一双大眼睛炯炯有神，眼睛下面现出了厚厚的眼袋。牙齿参差不齐，而且有了污渍。他体型格外瘦削，一双手纤细小巧，显得干瘪，形同爪子。我听人家说了，他吸食鸦片。他衣着寒酸，穿着一件黑色长衫，头戴一顶很小的黑色帽子，长衫和帽子都破旧不堪。深灰色的长裤在脚踝处用袜带扎着。他一直注视着我，不怎么清楚该以什么态度对待我，但他的行为举止显得很警觉。当然，

① chrysanthemum [kri'sænθəməm] *n.* 菊

② coolie ['kuːli] *n.* 苦力

③ compradore [ˌkɔmprə'dɔː] *n.* 买办

④ queue [kjuː] *n.* 辫子

⑤ garter ['gɑːtə] *v.* 用（吊）袜带吊住

Disraeli that royalty must be treated with abundant flattery. I seized my **trowel**[1]. Presently I was conscious of a certain relaxation in his **demeanour**[2]. He was like a man who was all set and rigid to have his photograph taken, but hearing the shutter click lets himself go and eases into his natural self. He showed me his books.

"I took the Ph.D. in Berlin, you know," he said. "And afterwards I studied for some time in Oxford. But the English, if you will allow me to say so, have no great aptitude for philosophy."

Though he put the remark apologetically it was evident that he was not displeased to say a slightly disagreeable thing.

"We have had philosophers who have not been without influence in the world of thought," I suggested.

"Hume and Berkeley? The philosophers who taught at Oxford when I was there were anxious not to offend their theological colleagues. They would not follow their thought to its logical consequences in case they should **jeopardise**[3] their position in university society."

"Have you studied the modern developments of philosophy in America?" I asked.

"Are you speaking of Pragmatism? It is the last refuge of those who want to believe the incredible. I have more use for American petroleum than for American philosophy."

His judgments were **tart**[4]. We sat down once more and drank another

① trowel ['trauəl] *n.* 泥刀
② demeanour [di'mi:nə] *n.* 态度
③ jeopardise ['dʒepədaiz] *v.* 危及
④ tart [tɑ:t] *a.* 尖刻的

这位哲学家在关注精神事物的人们当中拥有至尊地位。我们国家的权威人物本杰明·迪斯累里[1]说过，享有至尊地位的人应该受到充分的恭维。我不失时机地说了很多恭维话。不一会儿，我便意识到，他的态度有所放松了。他如同一个等着人家来拍照的人，摆好了姿势，表情僵硬，等到听见按快门时的咔嚓声响过后，这才轻松了起来，恢复到了自己正常的状态。他领着我参观他的书籍。

“您知道，我在柏林获得博士学位，”他说，“后来，又在牛津大学学习了一段时间。但是，恕我说一句，英国人对哲学缺乏卓越的天赋。”

虽说他做出这个评价时表达了歉意，但很显然，他并非不喜欢说稍显逆耳的话。

“我们国家的哲学家中也不是没有对世界思想产生影响的啊。”我提示说。

“您是指休谟[2]和贝克莱[3]吗？但我在牛津时发现，那儿教书的哲学家们迫切想要做到的是，不要冒犯他们从事神学研究的同事。他们并不从心所欲，追求合乎逻辑的结果，以免危及到他们在大学社会中的地位。”

“您研究过现代哲学在美国的进展吗？”我问了一声。

“您指的是实用主义哲学思想[4]吗？实用主义哲学是那些想要信奉不可信之物的人们最后的避难所。比起美国的哲学来，我更加需要美国的石油。”

他的这些评价很尖刻。我们再次坐了下来，又喝了一

1 本杰明·迪斯累里（Benjamin Disraeli, 1804—1881）是英国首相（1868, 1874—1880）、保守党领袖和作家，写过小说和政论作品，其政府殖民主义扩张政策。

2 休谟（David Hume, 1711—1776）是英国哲学家、经济学家、历史学家，不可知论的代表人物，认为知觉是认识的唯一对象，否认感觉是外部世界的反映，主要著作有《人性论》、《人类理智研究》等。

3 贝克莱（George Berkeley, 1685—1753）是爱尔兰基督教新教主教、唯心主义哲学家，认为“存在即被感知”，存在的只是我的感觉和自我，著有《视觉新论》、《人类和知识原理》等。

4 实用主义（Pragmatism）是19世纪末产生于美国的现代唯心主义哲学思潮。到了20世纪初，成为一种主流思潮，对法律、政治、教育、社会、宗教和艺术的研究产生了很大的影响。

cup of tea. He began to talk with fluency. He spoke a somewhat formal but an idiomatic English. Now and then he helped himself out with a German phrase. So far as it was possible for a man of that stubborn character to be influenced he had been influenced by Germany. The method and the industry of the Germans had deeply impressed him and their philosophical **acumen**① was patent to him when a laborious professor published in a learned magazine an essay on one of his own writings.

"I have written twenty books," he said. "And that is the only notice that has ever been taken of me in a European publication."

But his study of Western philosophy had only served in the end to satisfy him that wisdom after all was to be found within the limits of the Confucian **canon**②. He accepted its philosophy with conviction. It answered the needs of his spirit with a completeness which made all foreign learning seem vain. I was interested in this because it **bore out**③ an opinion of mine that philosophy is an affair of character rather than of logic: the philosopher believes not according to evidence, but according to his own temperament; and his thinking merely serves to make reasonable what his instinct regards as true. If Confucianism gained so firm a hold on the Chinese it is because it explained and expressed them as no other system of thought could do.

My host lit a cigarette. His voice at first had been thin and tired, but as he grew interested in what he said it gained volume. He talked vehemently. There was in him none of the repose of the sage. He was a **polemist**④ and a fighter. He loathed the modern cry for individualism. For him society was the unit, and the family the foundation of society. He upheld the old China and the old school, monarchy, and the rigid canon of Confucius. He grew violent and bitter as he spoke of the students, fresh from foreign universities, who with **sacrilegious**⑤ hands tore down the oldest civilisation in the world.

"But you, do you know what you are doing?" he exclaimed. "What is the reason for which you deem yourselves our betters? Have you excelled us in arts or letters? Have our thinkers been less profound than yours? Has our civilisation

杯茶。他开始侃侃而谈起来。他说的是一口多少有点拘泥形式但却是很地道的英文，时不时地会忍不住冒出一个德语短语来。就一位性格固执的人可能受到的影响的程度而言，他还是受到了德国的影响。德国人处事方式和勤奋努力的精神对他留下了深刻的印象。有位勤奋的教授就哲学家本人著作中的一部在一家学术刊物上发表了一篇论文，这时候，哲学家看到了德国人敏锐的哲学才智。

“我写了二十部书，”他说，“那是欧洲的出版物对我的唯一关注点。”

但是，他研究哲学的唯一目的就是要证明：西方智慧全部都可在儒家学说中寻找到。他全盘接受儒家哲学，而且深信不疑。儒家哲学完全满足了他自己的精神需求，这一点令西方学说黯然失色。我对这一点很有兴趣，因为这佐证了我的一个观点，即哲学与其说是关于逻辑的学说，不如说是关于性格的学说。这位哲学家的信仰不是依据证据，而是依据他自己的性情。他所思所想只是要解释他凭着直觉认为是正确的东西合情合理。如果说儒家学说能够牢固地扎根于中国人的心中，那是因为，它向他们解释和表达的，其他任何思想体系都无法做到。

接待我的主人点燃了一支烟。他刚开始说话时，声音很细，也显得很疲倦，但是，随着他对讲述的东西兴趣加强，说话声音也洪亮了起来。他说话时充满了激情。此时的他一扫智者特有的平和性情，成了一位善辩者和斗士。他对现代哲学家鼓吹个人主义的行为深恶痛绝。在他看来，社会是世界的一个单元，而家庭则是社会的基础。他捍卫古老的中国，古老的学派、帝制，还有儒教中严厉的教条。他说到了学者们新近从国外的大学回国，大逆不道地亲手撕碎了这个世界上最古老的文明。这时候，他情绪暴躁，表情痛苦。

“但是你们，你们知道自己在干什么吗？”他激动地大声说，“你们凭什么认为你们的东西比我们更加优秀？你们在艺术或者文学上超越过了我们吗？我们的思

① acumen [əˌkjuːmen] *n.* 敏锐

② canon ['kænən] *n.* 准则

③ bear out 证实

④ polemist ['pɔləmist] *n.* 善辩论者

⑤ sacrilegious [ˌsækri'lidʒəs] *a.* 渎圣的

been less **elaborate**[1], less complicated, less refined than yours? Why, when you lived in caves and clothed yourselves with skins we were a cultured people. Do you know that we tried an experiment which is unique in the history of the world? We sought to rule this great country not by force, but by wisdom. And for centuries we succeeded. Then why does the white man despise the yellow? Shall I tell you? Because he has invented the machine-gun. That is your superiority. We are a defenceless **horde**[2] and you can blow us into eternity. You have shattered the dream of our philosophers that the world could be governed by the power of law and order. And now you are teaching our young men your secret. You have thrust your hideous inventions upon us. Do you not know that we have a genius for mechanics? Do you not know that there are in this country four hundred millions of the most practical and industrious people in the world? Do you think it will take us long to learn? And what will become of your superiority when the yellow man can make as good guns as the white and fire them as straight? You have appealed to the machine-gun and by the machine-gun shall you be judged."

But at that moment we were interrupted. A little girl came softly in and nestled close up to the old gentleman. She stared at me with curious eyes. He told me that she was his youngest child. He put his arms round her and with a murmur of caressing words kissed her fondly. She wore a black coat and trousers that barely reached her ankles, and she had a long pig-tail hanging down her back. She was born on the day the revolution was brought to a successful issue by the **abdication**[3] of the Emperor.

"I thought she **heralded**[4] the Spring of a new era," he said. "She was but the last flower of this great nation's Fall."

From a drawer in his roll-top desk he took a few cash, and handing them to

想家不如你们的思想家思想深邃吗？我们的文明不如你们的精湛、完善和卓越吗？是啊，你们还在住山洞，穿着兽皮时，我们已经是一个文明的民族啦。你们是否知道，我们曾经进行过世界历史上独一无二的实验？我们一直求索，探寻用智慧而非武力来统治这个伟大国家的途径。而多少个世纪以来，我们取得了成功。那么，白种人为何看不起黄种人呢？需要我告诉你们吗？因为白种人发明了机枪。这就是你们的优势。我们是一个不设防的民族，而你们能够攻打我们，让我们种族灭绝。我们的哲学家们憧憬着，世界将通过法律和秩序的力量来治理，但你们击碎了他们的梦想。而现如今，你们把你们的秘诀传授给了我们的年轻一代。你们把你们充满了邪恶的发明物强加给我们。你们难道不知道吗？我们是一个有机械天赋的民族啊。你们难道不知道吗？这个国家可是拥有四万万世界上最讲究实际和最勤劳的人民啊。你们以为我们需要花费很长的时间才能学会吗？等到黄种人能够像白种人一样制造出精良的枪炮并且直接向他们开火时，你们的优势从何说起呢？你们诉诸于机枪，但你们最后会因为机枪受到审判。”

但这时刻，我们的交谈打断了。一个小女孩动作轻柔地进来了，依偎在老先生的身边。她盯着我看，目光中充满了好奇。他告诉我说，她是他最年幼的孩子。他双臂搂着住她，一边喃喃细语，一边亲吻她。女孩身穿一件黑色外套，一条黑色裤子刚及脚踝处。一条长辫子拖到了背后。女孩是在辛亥革命成功那一天出生的。那场革命废除了帝制。

“我认为，她预示了一个新时代的春天[1]的到来，”他说，“她是我们这个伟大民族秋天里的最后一枝花。”

他从自己卷盖式书桌的抽屉里拿出了一点零钱，递

① elaborate [i'læbərət] *a.* 精密的

② horde [hɔːd] *n.*（人）群

③ abdication [ˌæbdi'keiʃən] *n.* 退位

④ herald ['herəld] *v.* 引领

1 由于所处地理环境的差异，中国人和英国人对春天的感受其实不尽相同。中国人认为春天是一年当中最美好的季节，万物复苏，是欣欣向荣的征兆，但英国的春天依旧寒冷刺骨，英国人认为一年当中最美好的季节是夏天，莎士比亚曾在自己的十四行诗中感叹说“我能否将你比作夏天？ 你比夏天更美丽温婉。”

her, sent her away.

"You see that I wear a queue," he said, taking it in his hands. "It is a symbol. I am the last representative of the old China."

He talked to me, more gently now, of how philosophers in long past days wandered from state to state with their disciples, teaching all who were worthy to learn. Kings called them to their councils and made them rulers of cities. His **erudition**① was great and his eloquent phrases gave a multi-coloured vitality to the incidents he related to me of the history of his country. I could not help thinking him a somewhat pathetic figure. He felt in himself the capacity to administer the state, but there was no king to entrust him with office; he had vast stores of learning which he was eager to impart to the great band of students that his soul **hankered after**②, and there came to listen but a few, wretched, half-starved, and **obtuse**③ **provincials**④.

Once or twice **discretion**⑤ had made me suggest that I should take my leave, but he had been unwilling to let me go. Now at last I was obliged to. I rose. He held my hand.

"I should like to give you something as a recollection of your visit to the last philosopher in China, but I am a poor man and I do not know what I can give you that would be worthy of your acceptance."

I protested that the recollection of my visit was in itself a priceless gift. He smiled.

"Men have short memories in these **degenerate**⑥ days, and I should like to give you something more substantial. I would give you one of my books, but you cannot read Chinese."

He looked at me with an **amicable**⑦ **perplexity**⑧. I had an inspiration.

"Give me a sample of your calligraphy," I said.

"Would you like that?" He smiled. "In my youth I was considered to wield the brush in a manner that was not entirely **despicable**⑨."

He sat down at his desk, took a fair sheet of paper, and placed it before him. He poured a few drops of water on a stone, rubbed the ink stick in it, and took his

给了她，打发她离开了。

“您看，我留着一条辫子，”他说，一边用双手抓住辫子，“它是一个象征，因为我是这个古老中国的最后代表。”

他现在用更加平和的语气对我谈到，昔日久远的年代里，哲学家们如何领着他们的弟子周游列国，向可以启蒙的人们传授知识。帝王们请他们入仕朝廷，任命他们为地方官吏。他学问渊博，能言善辩，绘声绘色地向我讲述着他的国家的一个个历史掌故。我不禁觉得，他是个多么值得悲悯的人物。他觉得自己有能力治理好这个国家，只是怀才不遇，不受任何帝王的青睐。他学富五车，热切地想要向他心仪的广大弟子们传授，但是，前来听讲者寥寥，而且还是一些穷困潦倒、忍饥挨饿而又愚笨迟钝的外乡人。

有一两次，我意识到，自己应该起身告辞了，但他执意不让我走。最后，我必须要告辞。我站起身，他握住了我的一只手。

“您来看望最后一位中国哲学家，我应该给您点什么东西可兹纪念才是啊，但我是个穷困的人，不知道该给您什么才值得您笑纳。”

我语气坚决地说，此次拜访本身就值得纪念，弥足珍贵。他微笑着。

“这样一个堕落的年代里，人们容易健忘啊。我还是应该给您点实实在在的东西。我本想送给一本拙作，但您看不懂中文。”

他看着我，目光中透着友善而又困惑的神情。我突然萌生了一个想法。

“送我一幅您的书法作品吧。”我说。

“您喜欢这个吗？”他微笑着说，“我年轻时的书法还算不得完全糟糕透顶啊。”

他在自己的书桌边坐了下来，拿出了一张宣纸，展开在面前。他在一口石砚上滴了几滴水，用墨条在砚台上磨了起来，然后拿出毛笔。随着手臂的自由移动，

① erudition [ˌeru:'diʃən] *n.* 学识

② hanker after 渴望

③ obtuse [əb'tju:s] *a.* 愚钝的

④ provincial [prəu'vinʃəl] *n.* 乡下人

⑤ discretion [dis'kreʃən] *n.* 谨慎

⑥ degenerate [di'dʒenəreit] *a.* 变坏的

⑦ amicable ['æmikəbl] *a.* 友好的

⑧ perplexity [pə'pleksiti] *n.* 困惑

⑨ despicable ['despikəbl] *a.* 可鄙的

brush. With a free movement of the arm he began to write. And as I watched him I remembered with not a little amusement something else which had been told me of him. It appeared that the old gentleman, whenever he could scrape a little money together, spent it **wantonly**① in the streets inhabited by ladies to describe whom a **euphemism**② is generally used. His eldest son, a person of standing in the city, was vexed and humiliated by the scandal of this behaviour; and only his strong sense of **filial**③ duty prevented him from reproaching the **libertine**④ with severity. I dare say that to a son such looseness would be **disconcerting**⑤, but the student of human nature could look upon it with equanimity. Philosophers are apt to elaborate their theories in the study, forming conclusions upon life which they know only at second hand, and it has seemed to me often that their works would have a more definite significance if they had exposed themselves to the **vicissitudes**⑥ which befall the common run of men. I was prepared to regard the old gentleman's **dalliance**⑦ in hidden places with leniency. Perhaps he sought but to **elucidate**⑧ the most **inscrutable**⑨ of human illusions.

He finished. To dry the ink he scattered a little ash on the paper and rising handed it to me.

"What have you written?" I asked.

I thought there was a slightly malicious gleam in his eyes.

"I have ventured to offer you two little poems of my own."

"I did not know you were a poet."

"When China was still an uncivilised country," he retorted with sarcasm, "all educated men could write verse at least with elegance."

I took the paper and looked at the Chinese characters. They made an agreeable pattern upon it.

"Won't you also give me a translation?"

"*Traduttore—traditore*," he answered. "You cannot expect me to betray myself. Ask one of your English friends. Those who know most about China

他开始书写了起来。趁着盯着他看的当儿，我饶有兴趣地回想起了人们告诉我的有关他的另外一些事情。据说，眼前这位老先生，只要积攒起了几个钱，便会把钱挥霍在烟花柳巷的女人身上——中国人一般用这个委婉词来表述。他的长子是城里的一位有头有脸的人物，但因为父亲的这种丑陋行为而倍感痛苦和羞辱。只是出于自己强烈的孝顺之心，他才没有对父亲进行严厉的斥责。我可以说，对于一个儿子来说，这种不检点的行为羞于启齿。但是，研究人性的学者们却能够坦然地对待此事。哲学家们善于在研究中详尽阐述自己的种种理论，只是依据间接经验来得出关于人生的种种结论。我常常觉得，哲学家们若是能够亲历普通人经历的种种事情，他们写出的著作肯定会更加有意义。我拟以宽容之心来对待这位老先生在隐秘之处的不检点行为。他或许只是企图阐述人类幻想中最不可思议的事情。

他书写完毕。他在纸张上面撒了些灰，以便让墨迹干了，站起身，交给我。

“您写的是什么内容呢？”我问了一声。

我感觉到，他的眼睛里掠过一丝幸灾乐祸的亮光。

“我不揣谫陋，把自己的两首小诗奉献给您。”

“我不知道您还是位诗人呢。”

“当中国还是个未开化的蛮邦时，”他回应着说，语气充满了揶揄，“但凡受过教育的人至少都能够写出优美的诗行。”

我拿起那张纸，看着上面的中国字。文字在上面排列得工整匀称，富有美感。

“您不打算同时给我译文吗？”

“*Traduttore—traditore*[1]，”他回答说，“您不要指望我背叛自己。请您的某位英国朋友翻译吧。那些最知道

① wantonly ['wɔntənli] *ad.* 放纵地

② euphemism ['ju:fimizəm] *n.* 委婉说法

③ filial ['filjəl] *a.* 孝顺的

④ libertine ['libəti:n] *n.* 放荡的人

⑤ disconcerting [ˌdiskən'sə:tiŋ] *a.* 令人不安的

⑥ vicissitude [vi'sisitju:d] *n.*（人生的）盛衰

⑦ dalliance ['dæliəns] *n.* 闲混

⑧ elucidate [i'l(j)u:sideit] *v.* 阐明

⑨ inscrutable [in'skru:təbl] *a.* 不可理解的

---

1 此处原文为意大利语，这是有关翻译问题的一句妙语，意为“翻译者，背叛者”。用英语表述则为“The translator, a traitor”或“The translator is a betrayer”，“The translator is a traitor”。

know nothing, but you will at least find one who is competent to give you a rendering of a few rough and simple lines."

I bade him farewell, and with great politeness he showed me to my chair. When I had the opportunity I gave the poems to a sinologue of my acquaintance, and here is the version he made.* I confess that, doubtless unreasonably, I was somewhat taken aback when I read it.

You loved me not: your voice was sweet;
Your eyes were full of laughter; your hands were tender.
And then you loved me: your voice was bitter;
Your eyes were full of tears; your hands were cruel.
Sad, sad that love should make you
Unlovable.

I craved the years would quickly pass
That you might lose
The brightness of your eyes, the peach-bloom of your skin,
And all the cruel splendour of your youth.
Then I alone would love you
And you at last would care.

The envious years have passed full soon
And you have lost
The brightness of your eyes, the peach-bloom of your skin,
And all the charming splendour of your youth.
Alas, I do not love you
And I care not if you care.

---

* I owe it to the kindness of my friend Mr. P. W. Davidson

中国的人实际上一无所知，但您至少可找到能够给您解释这几句粗简诗行的人。”

我向他告辞了，他彬彬有礼地把我送到我的轿子边。我后来找到了机会，把两首诗给了一位通晓汉学的熟人，以下是他的译文[1]。我得承认，每当我看到这个内容时，我总会莫名地感到震惊。

你当时不爱我了：你的声音很甜美。
你的双眼充满了笑意，你的双手很纤细。
你后来爱我了：你的声音很苦涩。
你的双眼充满了泪水，你的双手令人痛苦。
悲伤啊悲伤，爱竟然让你变得
不可爱。

我渴望着岁月匆匆逝去
　　那样你就可能失去
你明亮的双眸，桃花般的肌肤，
还有你全部残忍而又壮丽的青春。
　　然后我独自一人爱你
　　你最后才会在意。

令人羡慕的岁月匆匆逝去
　　而你也已经失去了
你明亮的双眸，桃花般的肌肤，
还有你全部迷人而又壮丽的青春。
　　哎呀，我不爱你了
　　即便你在意，我也不在意。

1　蒙我的朋友 P. W. 戴维森先生热心帮助，谨致谢意——作者注。

The Princess and the Nightingale

First the King of Siam had two daughters and he called them Night and Day. Then he had two more, so he changed the names of the first ones and called the four of them after the seasons, Spring and Autumn, Winter and Summer. But in course of time he had three others and he changed their names again and called all seven by the days of the week. But when his eighth daughter was born he did not know what to do till he suddenly thought of the months of the year. The Queen said there were only twelve and it confused her to have to remember so many new names, but the King had a **methodical**① mind and when he made it up he never could change it if he tried. He changed the names of all his daughters and called them January, February, March (though of course in Siamese) till he came to the youngest who was called August, and the next one was called September.

"That only leaves October, November, and December," said the Queen. "And after that we shall have to begin all over again."

"No, we shan't," said the King, "because I think twelve daughters are enough for any man and after the birth of dear little December I shall be reluctantly compelled to cut off your head."

He cried bitterly when he said this, for he was extremely fond of the Queen.

公主与夜莺

遥罗国[1]的国王刚开始时有两个女儿。他给她们取名为“黑夜”和“白天”。后来，他又添了两个女儿，于是，把前面两个女儿的名字给改了，按照一年四季给四个女儿取名为:“春天”和“秋天”,“冬天”和“夏天”。但是，久而久之，他又有了另外三个女儿。于是，他再次给他们改了名字，按照一个星期的日子来给七个女儿命名。但是，他第八个女儿出生后，他一时间不知该如何是好，后来，他突然灵机一动，想到了一年当中的月份。王后说，虽说只有十二个月，但要她记住这么多新名字，她会觉得容易搞混。然而，国王的头脑却条理清晰。当他把这件事情决定下来了之后，他便绝对不会改变。他给女儿们改了名字，给她们分别取名为:“一月”、“二月”、“三月”(不过是用的当然是暹罗语言)，最后，轮到最小的女儿叫“八月”，接下来的一个叫“九月”。

“这就只剩下‘十月’、‘十一月’和‘十二月’了，”王后说，“到时候，我们又得重新开始啊。”

“不，不会的，”国王说，“因为我认为，任何男人，有十二个女儿便足够了。等到亲爱的小‘十二月’出生后，尽管不愿意，但还是不得不砍掉你的脑袋。”

他说出这话时，伤心痛苦地大哭了起来，因为他无

① methodical [mi'θɔdikəl] *a.* 有条理的

1　暹罗国是泰国的旧称。

Of course it made the Queen very uneasy because she knew that it would distress the King very much if he had to cut off her head. And it would not be very nice for her. But it so happened that there was no need for either of them to worry because September was the last daughter they ever had. The Queen only had sons after that and they were called by the letters of the alphabet, so there was no cause for anxiety there for a long time, since she only reached the letter J.

Now the King of Siam's daughters had had their characters permanently **embittered**① by having to change their names in this way, and the older ones whose names of course had been changed oftener than the others had their characters more permanently embittered. But September who had never known what it was to be called anything but September (except of course by her sisters who because their characters were embittered called her all sorts of names) had a very sweet and charming nature.

The King of Siam had a habit which I think might be usefully imitated in Europe. Instead of receiving presents on his birthday he gave them and it looks as though he liked it, for he used often to say he was sorry he had only been born on one day and so only had one birthday in the year. But in this way he managed in course of time to give away all his wedding presents and the loyal addresses which the mayors of the cities in Siam presented him with and all his old crowns which had gone out of fashion. One year on his birthday, not having anything else handy, he gave each of his daughters a beautiful green parrot in a beautiful golden cage. There were nine of them and on each cage was written the name of the month which was the name of the Princess it belonged to. The nine Princesses were very proud of their parrots and they spent an hour every day (for like their father they were of a methodical turn of mind) in teaching them to talk. Presently all the parrots could say God Save the King (in Siamese, which is very difficult) and some of them could say Pretty Polly in no less than seven oriental languages. But one day when the Princess September went to say good-morning to her parrot she found it lying dead at the bottom of its golden cage. She burst into a flood of tears, and nothing that her Maids of Honour could

比宠爱王后。当然，王后听后感到很不安，因为她知道，国王若是不得不砍掉她的脑袋时，他会感到很痛苦的。对她而言，这也不是一件很好的事情。但是，很巧的是，他们两个人都没有必要担心受怕，因为“九月”是他们拥有的最后一个女儿。从那之后，王后只生儿子。儿子们的取名是根据字母顺序来的，因此，很长时间内，没有理由担心忧虑，因为她只生到了字母“J”。

如今，暹罗国国王的女儿们由于不得不以这样的方式改变她们的名字，所以她们的性格已经永久性地打上了愤懑的烙印。年龄稍大的那几位的名字当然比另外几位的更改得更加频繁，所以她们的性格打上了更加永久的愤懑烙印。不过，“九月”除了名叫“九月”之外，从未尝过被人叫别的什么名字的滋味（当然除了她的姐姐们之外，她们由于性格中打上了愤懑的烙印，常常会叫她形形色色的名字）。她有十分温婉迷人的性格。

① embitter [im'bitə] *v.* 使怨愤

暹罗国的国王有个习惯，我觉得该习惯可以在欧洲有效地加以模仿。他过生日时不是收别人的礼物，而是给人赠送礼物。他好像乐此不疲，因为他往往会说，他很遗憾，自己只是在一天当中出生的，所以一年当中只有一个生日。但是，久而久之，他设法以这样的方式赠送出了他全部的结婚礼物、暹罗国各个城市的市长们向他效忠的呈文、还有全部不合时尚的旧王冠。有一年他过生日时，由于手边没有什么别的东西了，他便给自己的女儿们每人一只美丽的绿羽毛鹦鹉，用一只精致美丽的金鸟笼装着。她们一共九个，每个鸟笼上都写着月份的名称，也就是鸟笼要归属的公主名字。九个公主很替她们的鹦鹉感到自豪。她们每天花费一个小时时间（因为她们像自己的父王一样，头脑天生条理清晰）教鹦鹉说话。没过多久，所有鹦鹉都会说“上帝拯救国王”（这话若是用暹罗语来说，很难表达），而且还能用不少于七种东方语言说“漂亮的鹦哥”。但是，有一天，“九月”公主去向自己的鹦鹉说早安时，发现鹦鹉躺在金鸟笼底部，死了。她突然泪

say comforted her. She cried so much that the Maids of Honour, not knowing what to do, told the Queen, and the Queen said it was stuff and nonsense and the child had better go to bed without any supper. The Maids of Honour wanted to go to a party, so they put the Princess September to bed as quickly as they could and left her by herself. And while she lay in her bed, crying still even though she felt rather hungry, she saw a little bird hop into her room. She took her thumb out of her mouth and sat up. Then the little bird began to sing and he sang a beautiful song all about the lake in the King's garden and the willow-trees that looked at themselves in the still water and the gold fish that **glided**① in and out of the branches that were reflected in it. When he had finished the Princess was not crying any more and she quite forgot that she had had no supper.

"That was a very nice song," she said.

The little bird gave her a bow, for artists have naturally good manners, and they like to be appreciated.

"Would you care to have me instead of your parrot?" said the little bird. "It's true that I'm not so pretty to look at, but on the other hand I have a much better voice."

The Princess September clapped her hands with delight and then the little bird hopped on to the end of her bed and sang her to sleep.

When she awoke next day the little bird was still sitting there, and as she opened her eyes he said good-morning. The Maids of Honour brought in her breakfast, and he ate rice out of her hand and he had his bath in her **saucer**②. He drank out of it too. The Maids of Honour said they didn't think it was very polite to drink one's bath water, but the Princess September said that was the artistic temperament. When he had finished his breakfast he began to sing again so beautifully that the Maids of Honour were quite surprised, for they had never heard anything like it, and the Princess September was very proud and happy.

"Now I want to show you to my eight sisters," said the Princess.

She stretched out the first finger of her right hand so that it served as a perch and the little bird flew down and sat on it. Then, followed by her Maids of Honour,

流满面痛哭了起来，公主的那些侍女们说什么也宽不了她的心。她不停地哭着，侍女们不知道该如何是好，只得去禀报王后。王后说，这简直是瞎胡闹，那孩子最好不要吃晚饭就上床睡觉去。侍女们想去参加一个晚会，所以她们把“九月”公主尽快安排上床睡觉去了，让她独自一人待着。公主躺在床上，虽然感到很饥饿，但仍然在痛哭。这时候，她看见一只小鸟齐足跳跃着进入了她的房间。她把拇指从嘴巴里抽出来，坐了起来。紧接着，小鸟开始鸣唱，唱起了一支美妙动听的歌曲，内容关于国王花园里那座湖泊，树枝倒影在平静的水中的柳树，还有游曳在水中树影枝椏间的金鱼。鸟儿唱完歌之后，公主不再痛哭了，她差不多已经忘记，自己还没有吃晚饭呢。

“这真是一支美妙的歌曲啊。”她说。

小鸟儿给她鞠了一躬，因为艺术家天生具有得体的举止。艺术家喜欢被人欣赏。

“您没有了鹦鹉，愿意收留我吗？”小鸟问，“我看起来不很漂亮，这是事实，但是，从另一方面来说，我的嗓音更加美妙。”

“九月”公主高兴地鼓起掌来，紧接着，小鸟一路齐足跳跃接近她的床头，唱着歌让她入睡了。

翌日，公主醒来时，小鸟儿仍然坐在那儿。她睁开眼睛时，小鸟说了声“早上好”。侍女们把她的早餐端进了她房间。小鸟从她的一只手上啄米，在她的茶碟里沐浴，也从里面喝水。侍女们说，喝人家沐浴过的水很不文雅。但是，“九月”公主说，那是艺术家的气质。小鸟用过早餐之后，便又开始唱歌了，歌声十分美妙，侍女们很是惊讶，因为她们从来都没有听过如此美妙的歌声。“九月”公主感到很自豪，很快乐。

“现在我想让你见见我的八个姐姐。”公主说。

她伸出右手的食指，当作一个栖息处，小鸟飞了下来，坐落在手指上。然后，后面跟随着她的侍女们，她

① glide [glaid] *v.* 游动

② saucer ['sɔːsə] *n.* 茶碟

she went through the palace and called on each of the Princesses in turn, starting with January, for she was mindful of **etiquette**①, and going all the way down to August. And for each of the Princesses the little bird sang a different song. But the parrots could only say God save the King and Pretty Polly. At last she showed the little bird to the King and Queen. They were surprised and delighted.

"I knew I was right to send you to bed without any supper," said the Queen.

"This bird sings much better than the parrots," said the King.

"I should have thought you got quite tired of hearing people say God save the King," said the Queen. "I can't think why those girls wanted to teach their parrots to say it too."

"The sentiment is admirable," said the King, "and I never mind how often I hear it. But I do get tired of hearing those parrots say Pretty Polly."

"They say it in seven different languages," said the Princesses.

"I daresay they do," said the King, "but it reminds me too much of my **Councillors**②. They say the same thing in seven different ways and it never means anything in any way they say it."

The Princesses, their characters as I have already said being naturally embittered, were vexed at this, and the parrots looked very **glum**③ indeed. But the Princess September ran through all the rooms of the palace, singing like a **lark**④, while the little bird flew round and round her, singing like a nightingale, which indeed it was.

Things went on like this for several days and then the eight Princesses put their heads together. They went to September and sat down in a circle round her, hiding their feet as is proper for Siamese princesses to do.

"My poor September," they said. "We are sorry for the death of your beautiful parrot. It must be dreadful for you not to have a pet bird as we have. So we have all put our pocket-money together and we are going to buy you a lovely green and yellow parrot."

走遍了王宫，从“一月”开始，挨个地拜访了每一位公主，因为她很在乎礼仪规范，一直拜访下去，直到“八月”。面对每一位公主，小鸟都会唱一支不同的歌。但是，鹦鹉只会说“上帝拯救国王”和“漂亮的鹦哥”。最后，她带着小鸟拜见了国王和王后。他们感到很惊讶，很开心。

“我知道，不让你吃晚饭便打发你去睡觉，我的这种做法是正确的。”王后说。

“这只鸟唱歌比鹦鹉强多了。”国王说。

“我本应想到你听人们说‘上帝拯救国王’都听得疲倦了，”王后说，“但我无法想象，为何公主们也要叫鹦鹉们说这话。”

“这种情怀很值得赞赏啊，”国王说，“我绝不在意会时常听到这句话。但是，我确实厌倦了听那些鹦鹉说‘漂亮的鹦哥’。”

“鹦鹉用七种不同的语言说这句话。”公主们说。

“我相信确实如此，”国王说，“但是，这在很大程度上让我想到了我的那些顾问们。他们用七种不同的方式说同一件事情，而他们那样说时，从来不表达任何方面的任何意思。”

我已经说过了，公主们的性格已经很自然地打上了愤懑的烙印。她们听了这话后很恼火，而鹦鹉们看起来确实闷闷不乐。但是，“九月”公主跑遍了王宫里所有的房间，像云雀一样唱着歌儿，那只小鸟一直飞着在她的头顶盘旋，像一只夜莺一样唱歌，事实上，它就是一只夜莺。

这种情形持续了几天时间，然后，那八位公主凑到了一块儿商议。她们跑到“九月”公主那儿去，形成一个圆圈围着她坐下来，把她们的脚掩盖起来了，因为对于暹罗国的人来说，这样做才是得体的。

“可怜的‘九月’啊，”她们说，“你那只美丽的鹦鹉死了，我们感到很难过。你不能像我们一样养一只宠物鸟，这对于你来说，一定是一件很可怕的事情。因此，我们把零用钱凑到了一块儿，准备给你买一只黄绿相间的鹦鹉。”

① etiquette ['etiket] *n.* 礼节

② councillor ['kaunsələ] *n.* 顾问

③ glum [glʌm] *a.* 忧郁的

④ lark [lɑːk] *n.* 云雀

"Thank you for nothing," said September. (This was not very civil of her, but Siamese princesses are sometimes a little short with one another.) "I have a pet bird which sings the most charming songs to me and I don't know what on earth I should do with a green and yellow parrot."

January **sniffed**①, then February sniffed, then March sniffed: in fact all the Princesses sniffed, but in their proper order of **precedence**②. When they had finished September asked them:

"Why do you sniff? Have you all got colds in the head?"

"Well, my dear," they said, "it's absurd to talk of your bird when the little fellow flies in and out just as he likes." They looked round the room and raised their eyebrows so high that their foreheads entirely disappeared.

"You'll get dreadful wrinkles," said September.

"Do you mind our asking where your bird is now?" they said.

"He's gone to pay a visit to his father-in-law," said the Princess September.

"And what makes you think he'll come back?" asked the Princesses.

"He always does come back," said September.

"Well, my dear," said the eight Princesses, "if you'll take our advice you won't run any risks like that. If he comes back, and mind you, if he does you'll be lucky, pop him into the cage and keep him there. That's the only way you can be sure of him."

"But I like to have him fly about the room," said the Princess September.

"Safety first," said her sisters **ominously**③.

They got up and walked out of the room, shaking their heads, and they left September very uneasy. It seemed to her that her little bird was away a long time and she could not think what he was doing. Something might have happened to him. What with **hawks**④ and men with **snares**⑤ you never knew what trouble he might get into. Besides, he might forget her, or he might take a fancy to somebody

"得了，不麻烦你们啦。"'九月'公主说。（她这样说话不是很礼貌，但是，暹罗国的公主们有时候相互之间态度有点粗鲁。）"我已经有一只宠物鸟了，它能为我唱出美妙的歌儿。我还真是不知道，面对一只黄绿相间的鹦鹉时，自己到底该怎么办呢。"

"一月"公主擤了一下鼻子，"二月"公主接着擤了一下鼻子，"三月"公主接着也擤了一下鼻子：事实上，所有公主都擤了一下鼻子，不过都是按照她们长幼的先后顺序来的。等到她们全都擤完鼻子时，"九月"公主问她们：

"你们擤鼻子干什么啊？你们全都受风寒了吗？"

"得了吧，亲爱的，"她们说，"说到你的那只小鸟，真是荒唐透顶啊，小东西跟随你随心所欲地飞来飞去。"她们环顾了一番房间，高高地抬起了眉头，连她们的额头都完全不见了。

"你们这样会生出可怕的皱纹的。""九月"公主说。

"你在意我们问一声，你的那只小鸟现在在哪儿吗？"她们说。

"它去拜访它的岳父去了，""九月"公主回答说。

"那你凭什么认为它会飞回来呢？"众公主问了一声。

"它一直都会飞回来的，""九月"公主说。

"得了吧，亲爱的，"八位公主说，"你若是听从我们的劝告，你就不会冒这样的风险了。它若是飞回来了，听好啦，它若是飞回来了，算你运气，那就把它关进鸟笼里，让它一直待在那儿。你能够确保拥有它，这是唯一的办法。"

"但是，我喜欢它在房间里飞来飞去。""九月"公主说。

"安全第一啊。"她的姐姐们说，语气中透出不详的意味。

她们起身走出了房间，摇了摇头，她们离开后，"九月"公主变得很不安。她意识到，自己的小鸟飞走已经很长时间了。她想象不出小鸟会在干些什么。它也许遇到什么麻烦了。比如老鹰啊，设下陷阱捕鸟的人啊，你根本就不知道小鸟可能遇到什么麻烦。此外，它有可能

① sniff [snif] *v.* 抽鼻子
② precedence ['presidəns] *n.* 先后次序
③ ominously ['ɔminəsli] *ad.* 不吉利地
④ hawk [hɔ:k] *n.* 鹰
⑤ snare [snεə] *n.* 陷阱

else; that would be dreadful; oh, she wished he were safely back again, and in the golden cage that stood there empty and ready. For when the Maids of Honour had buried the dead parrot they had left the cage in its old place.

Suddenly September heard a **tweet-tweet**① just behind her ear and she saw the little bird sitting on her shoulder. He had come in so quietly and **alighted**② so softly that she had not heard him.

"I wondered what on earth had become of you," said the Princess.

"I thought you'd wonder that," said the little bird. "The fact is I very nearly didn't come back tonight at all. My father-in-law was giving a party and they all wanted me to stay, but I thought you'd be anxious."

Under the circumstances this was a very unfortunate remark for the little bird to make.

September felt her heart go **thump**③, thump against her chest, and she made up her mind to take no more risks. She put up her hand and took hold of the bird. This he was quite used to, she liked feeling his heart go **pit-a-pat**④, so fast, in the hollow of her hand, and I think he liked the soft warmth of her little hand. So the bird suspected nothing and he was so surprised when she carried him over to the cage, popped him in, and shut the door on him that for a moment he could think of nothing to say. But in a moment or two he hopped up on the ivory perch and said:

"What is the joke?"

"There's no joke," said September, "but some of mamma's cats are prowling about tonight, and I think you're much safer in there."

"I can't think why the Queen wants to have all those cats," said the little bird, rather crossly.

"Well, you see, they're very special cats," said the Princess, "they have blue eyes and a **kink**⑤ in their tails, and they're a speciality of the royal family, if you understand what I mean."

"Perfectly," said the little bird, "but why did you put me in this cage without saying anything about it? I don't think it's the sort of place I like."

忘掉她了，或者喜欢上别的什么人了。太可怕了。噢，她希望小鸟能够安全飞回来，飞进那只空着的金鸟笼里面。因为侍女们把那只死亡的鹦鹉掩埋了之后，她们便把鸟笼搁在先前的位置上。

突然，“九月”公主听见自己耳朵后面传来小鸟啾啾的声音。她看见那只小鸟落坐在她的一只肩膀上。小鸟悄无声息地飞进来，又轻柔地落下，她都没有听见。

“我不知道你到底遇到什么情况了。”公主说。

“我猜到你会好奇，”小鸟说，“实际上，我今晚差一点就不回来了。我岳父举办了一场晚会，他们大家全都要我留下，但是，我想到，你会很着急。”

在这种情况下，小鸟说出了这句很不吉利的话。

“九月”感觉自己的心脏嘭嘭地撞击着自己的胸腔。她决定不再冒什么风险了。她抬起了一只手，抓住了小鸟。面对这个举动，小鸟已经很习惯了。她喜欢小鸟落在自己的手掌上，它的心扑通扑通跳得很快的感觉。我觉得，小鸟喜欢她的小手那种柔软而又温暖的感觉。所以，小鸟毫无防备，但等到她把它关进笼子时，它感到很惊讶。她把小鸟关了起来，一时间，它不知道该说什么。但是，又过了一会儿，小鸟跳上了象牙栖木，并且说：

“这开的是什么玩笑啊？”

“不是开玩笑，”“九月”公主说，“但是，今晚，母后的那些猫当中有一些会四处徘徊，我觉得你待在里面会安全很多。”

“我真不知道，王后为何想要养那些猫啊。”小鸟非常生气地说。

“是啊，你看吧，那些猫可不一般，”公主说，“它们长着蓝色的眼睛，尾巴上有个扭结。它们是皇宫里特有的，不知你是否听懂了我的话。”

“完全听懂了，”小鸟说，“但是，你为何不解释一下就把我关进这里呢？这儿可不是我喜欢待的地方啊。”

① tweet [twi:t] *n.* 啾啾声
② alight [ə'lait] *v.* 飞落
③ thump [θʌmp] *v.* 砰然地响
④ pit-a-pat [ˌpitə'pæt] *a.* 卜卜的
⑤ kink [kiŋk] *n.* 扭结

"I shouldn't have slept a wink all night if I hadn't known you were safe."

"Well, just for this once I don't mind," said the little bird, "so long as you let me out in the morning."

He ate a very good supper and then began to sing. But in the middle of his song he stopped.

"I don't know what is the matter with me," he said, "but I don't feel like singing tonight."

"Very well," said September, "go to sleep instead."

So he put his head under his wing and in a minute was fast asleep. September went to sleep too. But when the dawn broke she was awakened by the little bird calling her at the top of his voice.

"Wake up, wake up," he said. "Open the door of this cage and let me out. I want to have a good fly while the dew is still on the ground."

"You're much better off where you are," said September. "You have a beautiful golden cage. It was made by the best workman in my papa's kingdom, and my papa was so pleased with it that he cut off his head so that he should never make another."

"Let me out, let me out," said the little bird.

"You'll have three meals a day served by my Maids of Honour; you'll have nothing to worry you from morning till night, and you can sing to your heart's content."

"Let me out, let me out," said the little bird. And he tried to slip through the bars of the cage, but of course he couldn't, and he beat against the door but of course he couldn't open it. Then the eight Princesses came in and looked at him. They told September she was very wise to take their advice. They said he would soon get used to the cage and in a few days would quite forget that he had ever been free. The little bird said nothing at all while they were there, but as soon as they were gone he began to cry again: "Let me out, let me out."

"Don't be such an old silly," said September. "I've only put you in the cage because I'm so fond of you. I know what's good for you much better than you

“若是没有确认你的安全，我恐怕一宿都无法合眼啊。”

“啊，仅仅这一回，那我倒是不在乎，”小鸟说，“只是你到了早晨把我放出去就行。”

小鸟美美地吃了一顿晚餐，然后开始唱歌。但是，歌唱到一半，它便停下来了。

“我不知道我这是怎么了，”小鸟说，“但今晚就是不想唱了。”

“很好，”“九月”公主说，“那就睡觉吧。”

于是，小鸟把头藏到了翅膀下面，不一会儿过后，便睡着了。“九月”公主也睡觉去了。但是，黎明时分，小鸟把嗓子扯到最高呼喊她，她惊醒了。

“醒一醒，醒一醒，”小鸟说，“打开鸟笼门，放我出去。趁着大地上布满露珠时，我想要痛快地飞翔一番。”

“你待在里面会感觉舒服得多，”“九月”公主说，“你有一只美丽的金鸟笼。这是父王的王国里技术最精湛的工匠制作的。我父王高兴极了，于是砍掉了他的脑袋，这样一来，他就不可能再制作另外一只鸟笼了。”

“放我出去，放我出去。”小鸟说。

“我的侍女们每天会为你送上三餐，从早到晚，你不会有任何你揪心的事情。你可以尽情地唱歌。”

“放我出去，放我出去。”小鸟说。它试图想要从鸟笼的隔栏之间钻出来，但当然无法做到。它击打着鸟笼的门，但当然无法打开。后来，那八位公主来了，看着小鸟。她们告诉“九月”公主说，她听从了她们的劝告，很明智。她们说，小鸟很快就会习惯鸟笼里的生活。过不了多少天，小鸟就会忘却自己曾经拥有过的自由生活。公主们在场时，小鸟什么话也没有说。但是，公主们刚一离去，小鸟便开始叫了起来：“放我出去，放我出去。”

“别这么傻，”“九月”公主说，“我之所以把你放到笼子里，是因为我喜欢你啊。什么对你有好处，我比

do yourself. Sing me a little song and I'll give you a piece of brown sugar."

But the little bird stood in the corner of his cage, looking out at the blue sky, and never sang a note. He never sang all day.

"What's the good of sulking?" said September. "Why don't you sing and forget your troubles?"

"How can I sing?" answered the bird. "I want to see the trees and the lake and the green rice growing in the fields."

"If that's all you want I'll take you for a walk," said September.

She picked up the cage and went out and she walked down to the lake round which grew the willow-trees, and she stood at the edge of the rice fields that stretched as far as the eye could see.

"I'll take you out every day," she said. "I love you and I only want to make you happy."

"It's not the same thing," said the little bird. "The rice fields and the lake and the willow-trees look quite different when you see them through the bars of a cage."

So she brought him home again and gave him his supper. But he wouldn't eat a thing. The Princess was a little anxious at this, and asked her sisters what they thought about it.

"You must be firm," they said.

"But if he won't eat, he'll die," she answered.

"That would be very ungrateful of him," they said. "He must know that you're only thinking of his own good. If he's **obstinate**① and dies it'll serve him right and you'll be well rid of him."

September didn't see how that was going to do her very much good, but they were eight to one and all older than she, so she said nothing.

"Perhaps he'll have got used to his cage by tomorrow," she said.

And next day when she awoke she cried out good-morning in a cheerful voice. She got no answer. She jumped out of bed and ran to the cage. She gave a startled cry, for there the little bird lay, at the bottom, on his side, with his eyes closed, and he looked as if he were dead. She opened the door and putting her

你自己更加清楚呢。给我唱一小曲，给你一块红糖吃。”

但是，小鸟站立在鸟笼的一角，遥望着外面的蓝天，决不唱一个音符。小鸟整天都不再唱歌了。

“生气不说话有什么好处啊？”“九月”公主说，“为何不唱歌来排遣掉你的烦恼呢？”

“我怎么唱啊？”小鸟回答说，“我想要看到树木、湖泊、田野里生长着的绿色禾苗。”

“如果这就是你想要的，我可以带着你去散步呀。”“九月”公主说。

她提起鸟笼出门了，走到下面柳树环绕的湖边，伫立在一眼望不到边的稻田边上。

“我每天都会带着你出来，”她说，“我爱你，就想让你开心。”

“这不是一回事啊，”小鸟说，“你若是透过鸟笼的隔栏看，稻田、湖泊和柳树看起来不是一样的。”

于是，她又带着小鸟回家了，给它吃糖。但是，小鸟不吃东西。对此，公主有点担忧，询问她的姐姐们，问她们如何看这件事情。

“你必须态度坚决啊。”她们说。

“但是，小鸟若是不吃东西会死的。”她回答说。

“这说明小鸟很忘恩负义，”她们说，“它必须知道，你是一心为它好。它若是执拗任性死了，那是它活该，你摆脱了它是件好事。”

“九月”公主看不出，这样做如何会给她自己带来好处。但是，她们是八个对一个，而且都比她年长，于是，她也就没有说什么了。

“说不定小鸟明天就能习惯待在笼子里了。”她说。

翌日，公主醒来时，兴致勃勃地大喊着“早上好”，但没有听到回音。她跳下床，跑向鸟笼。她惊恐地哭了起来，因为小鸟侧着身子躺着，双目紧闭，看起来好像已经死了。她打开了鸟笼的门，伸手把小鸟提出来。她

① obstinate ['ɔbstinit] *a.* 顽固的

hand in lifted him out. She gave a sob of relief, for she felt that his little heart was beating still.

"Wake up, wake up, little bird," she said.

She began to cry and her tears fell on the little bird. He opened his eyes and felt that the bars of the cage were no longer round him.

"I cannot sing unless I'm free and if I cannot sing, I die," he said.

The Princess gave a great sob.

"Then take your freedom," she said, "I shut you in a golden cage because I loved you and wanted to have you all to myself. But I never knew it would kill you. Go. Fly away among the trees that are round the lake and fly over the green rice fields. I love you enough to let you be happy in your own way."

She threw open the window and gently placed the little bird on the **sill**①. He shook himself a little.

"Come and go as you will, little bird," she said. "I will never put you in a cage any more."

"I will come because I love you, little Princess," said the bird. "And I will sing you the loveliest songs I know. I shall go far away, but I shall always come back, and I shall never forget you." He gave himself another shake. "Good gracious me, how still I am," he said.

Then he opened his wings and flew right away into the blue. But the little Princess burst into tears, for it is very difficult to put the happiness of someone you love before your own, and with her little bird far out of sight she felt on a sudden very lonely. When her sisters knew what had happened they mocked her and said that the little bird would never return. But he did at last. And he sat on September's shoulder and ate out of her hand and sang her the beautiful songs he had learned while he was flying up and down the fair places of the world. September kept her window open day and night so that the little bird might come into her room whenever he felt inclined, and this was very good for her; so she grew extremely beautiful. And when she was old enough she married the King of Cambodia and was carried all the way to the city in which

抽泣着松了口气，因为她感觉到，小鸟的心脏还在跳动。

“醒一醒，醒一醒，小鸟。”她喊着。

她开始哭了起来，泪水滴到了小鸟身上。小鸟睁开了眼睛，感觉到自己的周围没有了鸟笼的隔栏。

“除非获得了自由，否则我无法唱歌；而我若是不能唱歌，我会死的。”小鸟说。

公主大声抽泣起来。

“那就享受自由吧，”公主说，“我之所以把你关进金鸟笼，那是因为我爱你，想要把你据为己有。但是，我怎么也不知道，这样反而会要了你的命。走吧，到湖畔的树丛中飞翔去吧，飞过绿色的稻田吧。我很爱你，要让你按照自己的方式享受快乐。”

① sill [sil] *n.* 窗台

公主推开窗户，动作轻柔地把小鸟放在窗棂上。小鸟稍稍抖了抖身子。

“好吧，或来或走都遵循你自己的意愿吧，小鸟，”她说，“我决不会再把你关进鸟笼里啦。”

“我会回来的，因为我爱你，小公主，”小鸟说。“我会把自己熟悉的最美妙动听的歌唱给你听的。我要飞到很远的地方去，但是，我永远都会回来，永远不会忘记你的。”小鸟再次抖了抖身子。“天哪，我多么平静啊。”小鸟说。

紧接着，小鸟展开了翅膀，直接飞向了蓝天。但是，小公主突然哭了起来，因为把你所爱的人的幸福快乐放在自我幸福之上，是很难做到的。随着小鸟消失在视线中，她突然感到很孤独。她的姐姐们知道了事情的原委之后，都嘲笑她，并且说，小鸟不可能返回了。但是，小鸟最后回来了。它坐落在“九月”公主的肩膀上，从她的手上啄食。小鸟在世界上美丽地方飞上飞下时，学会了美妙的歌曲。它把那些歌曲唱给公主听。无论白天黑夜，“九月”公主都让自己卧室的窗户敞开着，以便小鸟随时都可以飞进来，而这样做对她有好处。因此，她长得格外美丽。她成年之后便嫁给了柬埔寨的国王，坐在大象背上一路走向他居住的城

he lived on a white elephant. But her sisters never slept with their windows open, so they grew extremely ugly as well as disagreeable, and when the time came to marry them off they were given away to the King's Councillors with a pound of tea and a Siamese cat.

市。但是，她的姐姐们睡觉时从不打开卧室窗户，所以，她们长得既不可爱，又其丑无比。等到她们到了要嫁人时，她们被打发嫁给了国王的顾问们，带去一磅茶叶和一只暹罗猫。

The Letter

Outside on the quay the sun beat fiercely. A stream of motors, lorries and buses, private cars and hirelings, sped up and down the crowded **thoroughfare**①, and every **chauffeur**② blew his horn; **rickshaws**③ threaded their nimble path amid the throng, and the panting coolies found breath to yell at one another; coolies, carrying heavy bales, **sidled**④ along with their quick jog-trot and shouted to the passer-by to make way; **itinerant**⑤ vendors proclaimed their wares. Singapore is the meeting-place of a hundred peoples; and men of all colours, black Tamils, yellow Chinks, brown Malays. Armenians, Jews and Bengalis, called to one another in **raucous**⑥ tones. But inside the office of Messrs Ripley, Joyce and Naylor it was pleasantly cool; it was dark after the dusty **glitter**⑦ of the street and agreeably quiet after its unceasing **din**⑧. Mr. Joyce sat in his private room, at the table, with an electric fan turned full on him. He was leaning back, his elbows on the arms of the chair, with the tips of the outstretched fingers of one hand resting neatly against the tips of the outstretched fingers of the other. His gaze rested on the battered volumes of the Law Reports which stood on a long shelf in front of him. On the top of a cupboard were square boxes of **japanned**⑨ tin, on which were painted the names of various clients.

信

① thoroughfare ['θʌrəfεə] *n.* 大街
② chauffeur ['ʃəufə] *n.* 汽车司机
③ rickshaw ['rikʃɔː] *n.* 人力车
④ sidle [saidl] *v.* 侧身而行
⑤ itinerant [i'tinərənt] *a.* 流动的
⑥ raucous ['rɔːkəs] *a.* 沙哑的
⑦ glitter ['glitə] *n.* 闪光
⑧ din [din] *n.* 喧闹声
⑨ japanned [dʒə'pænd] *a.* 漆过的

烈日烤晒着外面的码头。汽车、卡车、公共汽车、私家车和出租车川流不息，快速驶过熙来攘往的主街道。每一位司机都会摁响喇叭。人力车行动敏捷，穿行在人群中。苦力们气喘吁吁，相互之间喊着号子，以便调整呼吸。苦力们扛着沉重的大包，迈着碎步，侧身前行，冲着来往行人大喊着让道。流动商贩大声吆喝着，叫卖自己的小商品。新加坡是个万国民众的聚首之地。各种肤色的人都有：有黑皮肤的泰米尔人[1]，黄皮肤的支那人[2]，棕皮肤的马来人。还有亚美尼亚人，犹太人和孟加拉人。他们相互之间扯着嗓子吆喝着。但是，里普利–乔伊斯–内勒律师事务所内，感觉清凉舒心。虽说外面的街道上尘土飞扬，阳光耀眼，但这儿却光线昏暗。虽说街道上声音嘈杂，没完没了，但这儿却舒适宁静。乔伊斯先生坐在自己个人办公室的桌子边，一台电风扇正对着自己吹。他后仰着身子，胳膊肘搁在椅子两边的扶手上，两手张开，指尖相互顶着。他目不转睛盯着立在自己前面书架上一本本磨损了的《案例汇编》。一只小厨的上方放着几个涂了黑漆的方形铁皮盒子，盒子上面写着诉讼委托人的姓名。

1　泰米尔人（Tamil）是一个居住在印度南部和斯里兰卡等地的民族，在新加坡是仅次于华族、马来族的第三大民族。

2　支那人（Chink）是人们对中国人的贬称。

There was a knock at the door.

"Come in."

A Chinese clerk, very neat in his white ducks, opened it.

"Mr. Crosbie is here, sir."

He spoke beautiful English, accenting each word with precision, and Mr. Joyce had often wondered at the extent of his vocabulary. Ong Chi Seng was a Cantonese, and he had studied law at Gray's Inn. He was spending a year or two with Messrs Riply, Joyce and Naylor in order to prepare himself for practice on his own account. He was industrious, obliging, and of **exemplary**① character.

"Show him in," said Mr. Joyce.

He rose to shake hands with his visitor and asked him to sit down. The light fell on him as he did so. The face of Mr. Joyce remained in shadow. He was by nature a silent man, and now he looked at Robert Crosbie for quite a minute without speaking. Crosbie was a big fellow, well Over six feet high, with broad shoulders, and muscular. He was a rubber-planter, hard with the constant exercise of walking over the estate, and with the tennis which was his relaxation when the day's work was over. He was deeply sun-burned. His hairy hands, his feet in clumsy boots, were enormous, and Mr. Joyce found himself thinking that a blow of that great fist would easily kill the fragile Tamil. But there was no fierceness in his blue eyes, they were confiding and gentle; and his face, with its big, undistinguished features, was open, frank and honest. But at this moment it bore a look of deep distress. It was drawn and **haggard**②.

"You look as though you hadn't had much sleep the last night or two," said Mr. Joyce.

"I haven't."

Mr. Joyce noticed now the old felt hat, with its broad double brim, which Crosbie had placed on the table; and then his eyes travelled to the khaki shorts he wore, showing his red hairy **thighs**③, the tennis shirt open at the neck, without a

有人敲门。

"进来。"

一位华人职员打开了门。他穿着整洁的白色帆布裤子。

"克罗斯比先生来了，先生。"

他说着一口流利的英语，每个词的发音都很精准。面对他巨大的词汇量，乔伊斯先生常常惊叹不已。王志成是广东人，曾在格雷律师学院[1]研修法律。他眼下正花一两年时间在里普利－乔伊斯－内勒律师事务所见习，日后自己独立开业。他勤奋努力，恭谦内敛，品性模范。

"请他进来吧。"乔伊斯先生说。

乔伊斯先生站起身同客人握手，请他坐下。他站起身时，太阳的光线照到了他身上，但面部还处在阴处。他是个生性沉默寡言的人，此时打量了罗伯特·克罗斯比好一会儿，没有开口说话。克罗斯比是个高大个儿，身高超过六英尺[2]，肩膀宽阔，肌肉发达。他是位橡胶种植园主，因常常在园区内行走得到锻炼，一天的工作结束之后还要打网球进行放松，因此身体很结实。他的皮肤被太阳晒得黝黑，双手毛茸茸的，脚上套着笨重的靴子，显得奇大无比。乔伊斯心里寻思着，这样的一个大拳头打出去准会要了一个身子骨虚弱的泰米尔人的性命。但是，他那双蓝色眼睛中并没有透出凶悍的光芒，而是充满了信任和谦和。面部五官虽然粗大、平常，但显得开朗、坦率和真诚。不过，此时此刻，脸上挂着深深的忧愁，显得阴郁而憔悴。

"你看起来这两个晚上没有睡好觉啊。"乔伊斯先生说。

"是没有睡好。"

乔伊斯先生此时注意到了那顶旧毡帽，属于宽边双檐的那种。克罗斯比刚才把帽子放在了桌子上面。他的目光随后移到了对方的卡其布短裤，短裤下面露出了毛茸茸的红色大腿，上身穿着网球衫，领口敞开着，没有

① exemplary [ig'zempləri] *a.* 模范的

② haggard ['hægəd] *a.* 憔悴的

③ thigh [θai] *n.* 大腿

1　格雷律师学院（Gray's Inn）是伦敦四个培养律师的机构之一，成立于 1569 年。另外三个是林肯律师学院（1422 年）、中殿律师学院（1501 年）和内殿律师学院（1505 年），但四个律师学院互不隶属。

2　一英尺相当于 0.3048 米。

tie, and the dirty khaki jacket with the ends of the sleeves turned up. He looked as though he had just come in from a long tramp among the rubber trees. Mr. Joyce gave a slight frown.

"You must pull yourself together, you know. You must keep your head."

"Oh, I'm all right."

"Have you seen your wife today?"

"No, I'm to see her this afternoon. You know, it is a damned shame that they should have arrested her."

"I think they had to do that," Mr. Joyce answered in his level, soft tone.

"I should have thought they'd have let her out **on bail**①."

"It's a very serious charge."

"It is damnable. She did what any decent woman would do in her place. Only, nine women out of ten wouldn't have the **pluck**②. Leslie's the best woman in the world. She wouldn't hurt a fly. Why, hang it all, man, I've been married to her for twelve years, do you think I don't know her? God, if I'd got hold of the man I'd have **wrung**③ his neck, I'd have killed him without a moment's hesitation. So would you."

"My dear fellow, everybody's on your side. No one had a good word to say for Hammond. We're going to get her off. I don't suppose either the **assessors**④ or the judge will go into court without having already made up their minds to bring in a **verdict**⑤ of not guilty."

"The whole thing's a **farce**⑥," said Crosbie violently. "She ought never to have been arrested in the first place, and then it's terrible, after all the poor girl's gone through, to subject her to the ordeal of a trial. There's not a soul I've met since I've been in Singapore, man or woman, who hasn't told me that Leslie was absolutely justified. I think it's awful to keep her in prison all these weeks."

"The law is the law. After all, she confesses that she killed the man. It is terrible, and I'm dreadfully sorry for both you and for her."

"I don't matter a hang," interrupted Crosbie.

配领带，然后是那件脏兮兮的卡其布外套，袖子是向上卷起的。他看起来就像是刚刚在橡胶林中长途跋涉后出来。乔伊斯先生微微皱了皱眉头。

“你得打起精神来啊，这你是知道的。必须要保持头脑清醒。”

“噢，我挺好的。”

“你今天看到了你夫人吗？”

“没有呢，我打算今天下午去看她。你知道的，他们竟然逮捕了她，真他妈丢人啊。”

“我觉得他们不得不那么做。”乔伊斯先生回答说，声音平和，轻柔。

“我本来以为，他们会允许把她保释出来的。”

“案情很重大啊。”

“见他妈的鬼去吧。她做了任何处在她的位置的体面女人所做的事情，只是十个女人里有九个没有那个胆量罢了。莱斯利是世界上最最善良的女人，连一只苍蝇都不忍心伤害。哎呀，真是倒霉啊，老兄。我同她结婚十二年了，你觉得我会不了解她吗？上帝啊，我若是逮着那个家伙，非拧断他脖子不可。我会毫不迟疑地要了他的命。换了是你也会啊。”

“亲爱的伙计啊，所有人都站在你这一边呢。谁也不会替哈蒙德说半句好话的。我们会把她救出来的。我估计，无论是陪审团还是法官，不对她宣告无罪是不会离开法庭的。”

“整件事情就是一场闹剧，”克罗斯比说，性情暴躁，“首先，她本来就不应该被捕。其次是，可怜的女人经历了种种磨难，还要接受审判，这真是可怕啊。自从我来到新加坡之后，但凡我遇到的人，无论男女，都说莱斯利那样做是绝对正当的。她竟然被关押在监牢里达几个星期之久，我觉得这太可怕啊。”

“法律就是法律，毕竟她承认杀死了那个人。这件事情真可怕，我很替你和她感到难受。”

“我倒是没什么。”克罗斯比接话说。

① on bail 保释

② pluck [plʌk] *n.* 勇气

③ wring [riŋ] *v.* 拧

④ assessor [ə'sesə] *n.* 陪审

⑤ verdict ['vəːdikt] *n.* 裁决

⑥ farce [fɑːs] *n.* 闹剧

"But the fact remains that murder has been committed, and in a civilized community a trial is inevitable."

"Is it murder to **exterminate**① **noxious**② **vermin**③? She shot him as she would have shot a mad dog."

Mr. Joyce leaned back again in his chair and once more placed the tips of his ten fingers together. The little construction he formed looked like the **skeleton**④ of a roof. He was silent for a moment.

"I should be wanting in my duty as your legal adviser," he said at last, in an even voice, looking at his client with his cool, brown eyes, "if I did not tell you that there is one point which causes me just a little anxiety. If your wife had only shot Hammond once, the whole thing would be absolutely plain sailing. Unfortunately she fired six times."

"Her explanation is perfectly simple. In the circumstances anyone would have done the same."

"I daresay," said Mr. Joyce, "and of course I think the explanation is very reasonable. But it's no good closing our eyes to the facts. It's always a good plan to put yourself in another man's place, and I can't deny that if I were prosecuting for the Crown that is the point on which I should centre my inquiry."

"My dear fellow, that's perfectly idiotic."

Mr. Joyce shot a sharp glance at Robert Crosbie. The shadow of a smile hovered over his shapely lips. Crosbie was a good fellow, but he could hardly be described as intelligent.

"I daresay it's of no importance," answered the lawyer, "I just thought it was a point worth mentioning. You haven't got very long to wait now, and when it's all over I recommend you to go off somewhere with your wife on a trip, and forget all about it. Even though we are almost dead certain to get an acquittal, a trial of that sort is anxious work, and you'll both want a rest."

For the first time Crosbie smiled, and his smile strangely changed his face. You forgot the **uncouthness**⑤ and saw only the goodness of his soul.

"I think I shall want it more than Leslie. She's borne up wonderfully. By

“但是，事实依然是，她犯了谋杀罪。这在文明社会中，审判是不可避免的。”

“除掉一个十恶不赦的恶棍也算是谋杀吗？她对着他开枪，如同会对着一条疯狗开枪一样。”

乔伊斯先生再次仰靠在椅子上，再次把两只手的指尖相互顶着，好像搭起了一个很小的屋顶框架。他沉默了片刻。

“只是在一个问题上令我有点担心，”他终于开口说，语气很平和，棕褐色的眼睛冷静地看着自己的委托人，“作为你的法律顾问，若是不如实相告，那就没有尽到责任。你夫人若是只朝着哈蒙德开了一枪，整桩案件处理起来就会顺利多了。不幸的是，她连开了六枪。”

“她的解释再简单不过了。面对那种情形，谁都会那样做的。”

“或许如此吧，”乔伊斯先生说，“当然，我觉得，她的解释是很合情合理的。但是，我们不能不无视事实啊。理想的做法是，站在第三者的立场上来考虑问题。我不能否认，我若是代表王国政府来提起公诉的话，我会特别针对这一点来提出质询的。”

“亲爱的伙计啊，这才是十足白痴的做法呢。”

乔伊斯先生用犀利的目光瞥了罗伯特·克罗斯比一眼。他棱角分明的嘴唇上略过一丝淡淡的微笑。克罗斯比是个好人，但脑子不开窍。

“我寻思着，这一点或许不重要，”律师回答说，“我只是觉得，这事有必要提出来。你现在不用等待很长时间了，等到一切都结束了之后，我建议，你领着夫人出去，到什么地方旅游去，忘掉这一切。尽管我们断定她会无罪释放，但审判的过程是令人揪心的，你们二位都需要好好休息一下。”

克罗斯比第一次露出了微笑，他的脸庞也随之发生奇特的变化。您忘却了他那副凶悍的样子，看到的只有美好的心灵。

“我觉得，我比莱斯利更加需要休息。她神奇地挺过

① exterminate [ik'stə:mineit] v. 铲除
② noxious ['nɔkʃəs] a. 可憎的
③ vermin ['və:min] n. 坏蛋
④ skeleton ['skelitən] n. 框架
⑤ uncouthness [ˌʌn'ku:θnis] n. 粗鲁

God, there's a **plucky**[1] little woman for you."

"Yes, I've been very much struck by her self-control," said the lawyer. "I should never have guessed that she was capable of such determination."

His duties as her counsel had made it necessary for him to have a good many interviews with Mrs. Crosbie since her arrest. Though things had been made as easy as could be for her, the fact remained that she was in **gaol**[2], awaiting her trial for murder, and it would not have been surprising if her nerves had failed her. She appeared to bear her ordeal with composure. She read a great deal, took such exercise as was possible, and by favour of the authorities worked at the pillow lace which had always formed the entertainment of her long hours of leisure. When Mr. Joyce saw her, she was neatly dressed in cool, fresh, simple frocks, her hair was carefully arranged, and her nails were **manicured**[3]. Her manner was collected. She was able even to **jest upon**[4] the little inconveniences of her position. There was something casual about the way in which she spoke of the tragedy, which suggested to Mr. Joyce that only her good breeding prevented her from finding something a trifle **ludicrous**[5] in a situation which was eminently serious. It surprised him, for he had never thought that she had a sense of humour.

He had known her off and on for a good many years. When she paid visits to Singapore she generally came to dine with his wife and himself, and once or twice she had passed a week-end with them at their bungalow by the sea. His wife had spent a fortnight with her on the estate, and had met Geoffrey Hammond several times. The two couples had been on friendly, if not on intimate, terms, and it was on this account that Robert Crosbie had rushed over to Singapore immediately after the catastrophe and begged Mr. Joyce to take charge personally of his unhappy wife's defence.

The story she told him the first time he saw her, she had never varied in the smallest detail. She told it as coolly then, a few hours after the tragedy, as she told it now. She told it connectedly, in a level, even voice, and her only sign of confusion was when a slight colour came into her cheeks as she described

① plucky ['plʌki] *a.* 有勇气的

② gaol [dʒeil] *n.* 监狱

③ manicure ['mænikjuə] *v.* 修剪

④ jest upon 嘲弄

⑤ ludicrous ['lju:dikrəs] *a.* 荒谬可笑的

来了。天哪，你接受委托的可是个勇敢的小女人呀。”

“是啊，她做到镇定自若，这给我留下了深刻的印象呢，”律师说，“我无论如何都想不到，她竟然能够做出那样的决断。”

作为克罗斯比夫人的辩护律师，自从她被捕以来，乔伊斯先生必须要多次同她会面。尽管已经想方设法，让她尽可能感觉到轻松，但她毕竟关押在牢房，等待她的是因为谋杀罪接受审判，面对如此情形，她若是精神崩溃，那也不足为奇。面对严峻的考验，她表现得很镇定。她大量阅读，尽可能做些运动。同时，征得监管人许可后，她做些刺绣枕头的活儿，这一直是她消磨漫长闲暇时间的一项娱乐活动。每当乔伊斯先生同她会面时，她会着装整洁，身穿凉爽、清新、朴素的外套，头发经过精心梳理，指甲也精心修剪过。她举止落落大方，甚至还会针对自己所处的不利处境调侃上几句。她在谈到那桩悲剧时，显得有点漫不经心。这让乔伊斯先生不禁感觉到，她只有凭着自己良好的修养才没有发现严重的事态中有些许荒唐可笑的因素。令他感到惊讶的是，他根本没有想到，她很有幽默感。

很多年来，乔伊斯先生同她断断续续有交往。她但凡来新加坡，一般都会同他们夫妇一块儿吃饭。有一两次，她还和他们一块儿在他们的海滨别墅共度周末。他夫人曾经在她的种植园里度过了两个星期时间，并且几次见到过杰弗里·哈蒙德。他们两对夫妇之间的关系虽然说不上是至交，但还是称得上是好友。正因为如此，灾祸发生之后，罗伯特·克罗斯比便立刻跑到新加坡，请求乔伊斯先生亲自担任他不幸的夫人的辩护律师。

乔伊斯先生第一次同她会面时，她便对他叙述了事情的经过。她对此没有做过任何更改。悲剧发生几个小时之后，她便把事情的经过告诉了他，态度很冷静，现在也还是如此。她叙述时，内容连贯，语气平和。她只

one or two of its incidents. She was the last woman to whom one would have expected such a thing to happen. She was in the early thirties, a fragile creature, neither short nor tall, and graceful rather than pretty. Her wrists and ankles were very delicate, but she was extremely thin, and you could see the bones of her hands through the white skin, and the veins were large and blue. Her face was colourless, slightly **sallow**①, and her lips were pale. You did not notice the colour of her eyes. She had a great deal of light brown hair, and it had a slight natural wave; it was the sort of hair that with a little touching-up would have been very pretty, but you could not imagine that Mrs. Crosbie would think of resorting to any such device. She was a quiet, pleasant, unassuming woman. Her manner was engaging, and if she was not very popular it was because she suffered from a certain shyness. This was comprehensible enough, for the planter's life is lonely, and in her own house, with people she knew, she was in her quiet way charming. Mrs. Joyce, after her fortnight's stay, had told her husband that Leslie was a very agreeable hostess. There was more in her, she said, than people thought; and when you came to know her you were surprised how much she had read and how entertaining she could be.

She was the last woman in the world to commit murder.

Mr. Joyce dismissed Robert Crosbie which such reassuring words as he could find and, once more alone in his office, turned over the pages of the brief. But it was a mechanical action, for all its details were familiar to him. The case was the sensation of the day, and it was discussed in all the clubs, at all the dinner tables, up and down the Peninsula, from Singapore to Penang. The facts that Mrs. Crosbie gave were simple. Her husband had gone to Singapore on business, and she was alone for the night. She dined by herself, late, at a quarter to nine, and after dinner sat in the sitting-room working at her lace. It opened on the veranda. There was no one in the bungalow, for the servants had retired to their own quarters at the back of the compound. She was surprised to hear a step on the gravel path in the garden, a booted step, which suggested a white man rather than a native, for she had not heard a motor drive up, and she could

有在叙述到其中的一两个细节时，脸上泛起了红晕，显得有点迷茫。谁都不会想到，这样的事情竟然会发生她这样的一个女人身上。她年龄三十出头一点，很柔弱的一个人，身材适中，与其说是容貌俊秀，不如说是气质高雅。她手腕和脚踝都显得很纤细，她十分瘦削，透过双手白皙的皮肤可以看到骨头，青筋毕露。她脸上毫无血色，还微微有点泛黄，嘴唇苍白。眼睛的颜色不明显。她长着一头浓密的浅棕褐色头发，头发略呈自然卷，属于略加修饰便会很漂亮的那种。不过，您很难想像，克罗斯比夫人会借助于诸如此类的修饰手段。她文静娴雅，受人喜爱，从不做作。她举止态度很优雅，若是说她不那么引人注目，那是因为她略显羞怯。这一点很能够理解，因为种植园主的生活很寂寞。她在自己家里同熟悉的人相处时，显得文静娴雅，魅力四射。乔伊斯夫人在种植园待了两个星期之后告诉自己丈夫，莱斯利是个和蔼友善的女主人。她说了，莱斯利的内涵比人们想象的要丰富。您一旦对她熟悉了，就会很惊讶地发现，她博览群书，风度迷人。

① sallow ['sæləu] *a.* 灰黄色的

她是世界上最不可能会犯谋杀罪的女人。

乔伊斯先生尽可能多地说了宽心的话之后，让罗伯特·克罗斯比离开了。他随后独自一人待在办公室里翻阅卷宗。不过，这只是个机械的动作罢了，因为他对案件的细节全都了如指掌。本案轰动一时，从新加坡到槟榔岛，半岛上下，所有俱乐部，所有餐桌旁，人们都热议着。克罗斯比夫人提供的事实很简单。她丈夫先前到新加坡办事情去了，她晚上独自一人待在家里，独自一人用餐，时间很晚了，九点差一刻，用过晚餐之后，坐在起居室里做刺绣活儿。起居室的门对着露台敞开着。孟加拉平房里没有任何人，因为仆人们回到他们自己在院落后面的住处去了。她听到了花园里铺了石子的小路上传来了脚步声，感到很惊讶。那是穿着靴子的脚步声，说明来者是白人，而非土著居民，因为她没有听见汽车发动机的声音。她无法想

not imagine who could be coming to see her at that time of night. Someone ascended the few stairs that led up to the bungalow, walked across the veranda, and appeared at the door of the room in which she sat. At the first moment she did not recognize the visitor. She sat with a shaded lamp, and he stood with his back to the darkness.

"May I come in?" he said.

She did not even recognize the voice.

"Who is it?" she asked.

She worked with spectacles, and she took them off as she spoke.

"Geoff Hammond."

"Of course. Come in and have a drink."

She rose and shook hands with him cordially. She was a little surprised to see him, for though he was a neighbour neither she nor Robert had been lately on very intimate terms with him, and she had not seen him for some weeks. He was the manager of a rubber estate nearly eight miles from theirs, and she wondered why he had chosen this late hour to come and see them.

"Robert's away," she said. "He had to go to Singapore for the night."

Perhaps he thought his visit called for some explanation, for he said:

"I'm sorry. I felt rather lonely tonight, so I thought I'd just come along and see how you were getting on."

"How on earth did you come? I never heard a car."

"I left it down the road. I thought you might both be in bed and asleep."

This was natural enough. The planter gets up at dawn in order to take the roll-call of the workers, and soon after dinner he is glad to go to bed. Hammond's car was in point of fact found next day a quarter of a mile from the bungalow.

Since Robert was away there was no whisky and soda in the room. Leslie did not call the boy, who was probably asleep, but fetched it herself. Her guest mixed himself a drink and filled his pipe.

象，这么晚了，还会有谁登门。有人登上了通向孟加拉平房的台阶，穿过了露台，出现在她所在的房间门口。一开始，她没有认出来者何人，因为她坐在一盏带灯罩的灯旁边，而他则站立在那儿，背对着暗的一面。

“我可以进来吗？”来者问了一声。

她连是谁的声音都没有听出来。

“是谁呀？”她问了一声。

她做刺绣时戴着眼镜，但说话时摘下了眼镜。

“杰夫·哈蒙德[1]。”

“当然可以呀。进来喝一杯吧。”

她站起身，热情地同他握手。她见到他时心里觉得有点惊讶，因为尽管他算是邻居，但无论是她还是罗伯特近来都和他没有什么密切交往，况且她有好几个星期没有见到过他。他经营着橡胶种植园，离他们的种植园将近八英里。令她感到诧异的是，他怎么会这么晚上他们家来。

“罗伯特不在家呢，”她说，“他晚上得在新加坡过夜。”

他或许觉得，自己登门来需要有个解释，于是说：

“很对不起。我今晚觉得很寂寞，所以便过来了，看看你们情况如何。”

“您究竟是怎么过来的？我没有听见汽车的声音啊。”

“我把车停在大路上呢。我寻思着，你们二位都可能已经上床睡觉了。”

这样说显得很自然。种植园主通常黎明即起，查看工人出勤的情况，因此，用过晚餐不久，便就乐于上床睡觉了。翌日，人们确实在距离孟加拉平房半英里处发现了哈蒙德的汽车。

由于罗伯特不在家里，起居室里便没有准备威士忌和苏打水。男仆可能已经睡了，莱斯利没有叫他，而是亲自去拿。客人给自己调制了一杯，然后装上烟斗。

1　杰夫是乔治的昵称。

Geoff Hammond had a host of friends in the colony. He was at this time in the late thirties, but he had come out as a **lad**[1]. He had been one of the first to volunteer on the outbreak of war, and had done very well. A wound in the knee caused him to be **invalided**[2] out of the army after two years, but he returned to the Federated Malay States with a DSO and an MC. He was one of the best billiard-players in the colony. He had been a beautiful dancer and a fine tennis-player, but though able no longer to dance, and his tennis, with a stiff knee, was not so good as it had been, he had the gift of popularity and was universally liked. He was a tall, good-looking fellow, with attractive blue eyes and a fine head of black, curling hair. Old stagers said his only fault was that he was too fond of the girls, and after the catastrophe they shook their heads and vowed that they had always known this would get him into trouble.

He began now to talk to Leslie about the local affairs, the forthcoming races in Singapore, the price of rubber, and his chances of killing a tiger which had been lately seen in the neighbourhood. She was anxious to finish by a certain date the piece of lace on which she was working, for she wanted to send it home for her mother's birthday, and so put on her spectacles again, and drew towards her chair the little table on which stood the pillow.

"I wish you wouldn't wear those great horn-spectacles," he said. "I don't know why a pretty woman should do her best to look plain."

She was a trifle taken aback at this remark. He had never used that tone with her before. She thought the best thing was to **make light of**[3] it.

"I have no pretensions to being a **raving**[4] beauty, you know, and if you ask

① lad [læd] n. 小伙子

② invalid ['invəli:d] v.（因伤痛）令……退役

杰夫·哈蒙德在这个殖民地有众多朋友。他年龄此时四十挨边了，但他出来时还是个小伙子。战争[1]爆发后，他是第一批志愿上战场的人，而且在战斗中表现得很勇敢。两年后，膝盖部受伤了，只得离开军队。但是，他佩戴着“杰出服务勋章”和“军功十字勋章”返回到了马来联邦[2]。他是这个殖民地最优秀的台球手之一。他曾经是个完美的舞者，出色的网球手。不过现在不能跳舞了，由于膝盖僵硬，打网球的水平也不如从前了。他很善于交际，而且也广受人们喜爱。他身材高大，仪表堂堂，一双吸引人的眼睛，一头乌黑卷曲的秀发。经验老道的人说，他唯一的缺点就是过分沉溺女色。灾难发生之后，他们摇着头诅咒发誓说，他们早就知道，这一点会让他惹上麻烦的。

他此时开始和莱斯利谈本地的一些事情，比如即将在新加坡举行的赛马，橡胶的价格，还有人们最近在附近看到了一只老虎，他差一点猎杀到了。莱斯利手头正在刺绣的东西需要在一定日期完成，感到心急火燎的，因为她打算寄回家去，作为母亲的生日礼物。于是重新戴上眼镜，并且把放着枕头套的小桌子往自己坐着的椅子边拖近了一点。

“你若是不戴这种巨大的牛角边框眼睛该有多好啊，”他说，“我就不明白了，一个漂漂亮亮的女人，偏要设法让自己看起来显得其貌不扬。”

她听到这句评价之后感到有点震惊。他过去可是从来都没有用这种腔调对她说话来着。她觉得，最理想的做法就是不予理睬。

“我可是从来都没有装模作样冒充什么绝色美人，

③ make light of 轻视

④ raving ['reiviŋ] a. 迷人的

1　此处指第一次时间大战。

2　马来联邦（Federated Malay States，当时华人称之为四州府），是英国在马来半岛的殖民政体之一，由半岛上四个接受英国保护的马来王朝所组成，包括雪兰莪、森美兰、霹雳和彭亨，于1895年成立，首府吉隆坡。四州自《邦咯条约》开始，逐步为英国控制，外交和防务由英国负责。内政方面，除涉及马来习俗和伊斯兰教的事务外，都须听从英国派出参政司的的意见。这种情况一直维持到1946年。

me point blank, I'm bound to tell you that I don't care two pins if you think me plain or not."

"I don't think you're plain. I think you're awfully pretty."

"Sweet of you," she answered, ironically. "But in that case I can only think you half-witted."

He chuckled. But he rose from his chair and sat down in another by her side.

"You're not going to have the face to deny that you have the prettiest hands in the world," he said.

He made a gesture as though to take one of them. She gave him a little tap.

"Don't be an idiot. Sit down where you were before and talk sensibly, or else I shall send you home."

He did not move.

"Don't you know that I'm awfully in love with you?" he said.

She remained quite cool.

"I don't. I don't believe it for a minute, and even if it were true I don't want you to say it."

She was the more surprised at what he was saying, since during the seven years she had known him he had never paid her any particular attention. When he came back from the war they had seen a good deal of one another, and once when he was ill Robert had gone over and brought him back to their bungalow in his car. He had stayed with them then for a fortnight. But their interests were dissimilar, and the acquaintance had never ripened into friendship. For the last two or three years they had seen little of him. Now and then he came over to play tennis, now and then they met him at some planter's who was giving a party, but it often happened that they did not set eyes on him for a month at a time.

Now he took another whisky and soda. Leslie wondered if he had been drinking before. There was something odd about him, and it made her a trifle uneasy. She watched him help himself with disapproval.

"I wouldn't drink any more if I were you," she said, good-humouredly still.

He emptied his glass and put it down.

这您是知道的。您若是直白地问我，我一定会对您直言相告，您是否觉得我其貌不扬，我并不在乎。”

“我觉得你并非其貌不扬，而是绝色美女。”

“您真会甜言蜜语，”她回答说，话里带着刺儿，“但是，若真是这样，我只能认为您缺乏眼光。”

他咯咯地笑了起来。但是，他从坐着的椅子上站立起来，在她旁边的另外一把椅子上坐下。

“你不至于否认，你的这双手可是世界上最美丽的手啊。”他说。

他做了个动作，好像是要握住她的一只手。她则轻轻地拍了他一下。

“别干傻事，坐回您先前坐的地方，有话好好说，否则我就要求您离开。”

他一动不动。

“你难道真不知道我深深地爱着你吗？”他说。

她仍然保持冷静的态度。

“我不知道，我也绝不相信，即便此话当真，我也不想您说出来。”

听到他说的话后，她更加感到惊讶了，因为他们认识七年来，他从来没有对她表现出过关注。他从战场上回来的那阵子，他们倒是经常见面。有一回，他生病了，罗伯特到他那边去，用车他把接到了他们的孟加拉平房。他和他们在一起待了两个星期时间。但是，他们的志趣各不相同，所以，这种相识的关系始终都没有发展为友情。最近两三年，他们很少见到他。他偶尔会过来打打网球，他们偶尔会在某个种植园主举行的聚会上遇见他。但是，一个月不见他，那是常有的事。

他这时又喝了一杯威士忌加苏打水。莱斯利怀疑他来之前就喝过酒了，因为他的行为举止有点怪异，她感到略微有点不安。她注视着他自顾自喝酒的样子。

“我若是您，我就不会再喝了。”她说，语气仍然显得心平气和。

"Do you think I'm talking to you like this because I'm drunk?" he asked abruptly.

"That is the most obvious explanation, isn't it?"

"Well, it's a lie. I've loved you ever since I first knew you. I've held my tongue as long as I could, and now it's got to come out. I love you, I love you, I love you."

She rose and carefully put aside the pillow.

"Good-night," she said.

"I'm not going now."

At last she began to lose her temper.

"But, you poor fool, don't you know that I've never loved anyone but Robert, and even if I didn't love Robert you're the last man I should care for?"

"What do I care? Robert's away."

"If you don't go away this minute I shall call the boys, and have you thrown out."

"They're out of earshot."

She was very angry now. She made a movement as though to go on to the veranda from which the house-boy would certainly hear her, but he seized her arm.

"Let me go," she cried furiously.

"Not much. I've got you now."

She opened her mouth and called "Boy, boy", but with a quick gesture he put his hand over it. Then before she knew what he was about he had taken her in his arms and was kissing her passionately. She struggled, turning her lips away from his burning mouth.

"No, no, no," she cried. "Leave me alone. I won't."

She grew confused about what happened then. All that had been said before she remembered accurately, but now his words assailed her ears through a mist of horror and fear. He seemed to plead for her love. He broke into violent **protestations**① of passion. And all the time he held her in his **tempestuous**② embrace. She was helpless, for he was a strong, powerful man, and her arms

他喝干了杯中酒，放下了杯子。

“你觉得我这么说话是因为我喝醉了酒吗？”他突然问了一声。

“这再明显不过了，不是吗？”

“啊，谎话。我刚认识你时就爱上你啦。只是一直忍着没有说出来罢了，现在把话说了出来。我爱你，我爱你，我爱你。”

她站起身，小心翼翼地放下枕头套。

“晚安。”她说。

“我现在不走。”

最后，她终于脾气上来了。

“啊，你这个可怜的蠢货，你难道不知道，我除了罗伯特没有爱过任何人吗？我即便不爱罗伯特，我也绝对不会爱上你的。”

“我会在乎吗？罗伯特又不在家。”

“你若是不立刻离开，我就要喊仆人了，把你扔出去。”

“他们听不见的。”

她气愤不已，正要朝着露台走去，因为在那儿叫喊，仆人们是可以听见的，但他一把抓住了她的一条胳膊。

“放开我。”她大声说，怒不可遏。

“没用的，我已经抓住你啦。”

她张开嘴，喊着“来人啦，来人啦”，但他急忙用一只手捂住了她的嘴。紧接着，她还没有来得及弄明白他的企图，他便把她抱在了怀里，疯狂地吻她。她挣扎着，拼命避开他灼热的嘴唇。

“不，不，不，”她大声说着，“放开我，我不。”

关于随后发生的事情，她思绪有些混乱。先前说过的话，她记得一清二楚，但此时，她诚惶诚恐，心思恍惚，只觉得他在自己耳边说着什么。他好像是在向她求爱，心情激动地向她倾诉自己的感情。这期间，他激情澎湃，紧紧地把她搂在怀里。她无能为力，因为他强壮有力，她的双臂被他牢牢固定在自己身子的两侧，她挣扎也没有用。她感觉自己越来越虚弱，担心会晕过去。

① protestation [ˈprəuteˈsteiʃən] *n.* 郑重声明

② tempestuous [temˈpestjuəs] *a.* 激烈的

were **pinnioned**① to her sides; her struggles were unavailing, and she felt herself grow weaker; she was afraid she would faint, and his hot breath on her face made her feel desperately sick. He kissed her mouth, her eyes, her cheeks, her hair. The pressure of his arms was killing her. He lifted her off her feet. She tried to kick him, but he only held her more closely. He was carrying her now. He wasn't speaking any more, but she knew that his face was pale and his eyes hot with desire. He was taking her into the bedroom. He was no longer a civilized man, but a savage. And as he ran he stumbled against a table which was in the way. His stiff knee made him a little awkward on his feet, and with the burden of the woman in his arms he fell. In a moment she had snatched herself away from him. She ran round the sofa. He was up in a flash, and flung himself towards her. There was a **revolver**② on the desk. She was not a nervous woman, but Robert was to be away for the night, and she had meant to take it into her room when she went to bed. That was why it happened to be there. She was frantic with terror now. She did not know what she was doing. She heard a report. She saw Hammond stagger. He gave a cry. He said something, she didn't know what. He **lurched**③ out of the room on to the veranda. She was in a frenzy now, she was beside herself, she followed him out, yes, that was it, she must have followed him out, though she remembered nothing of it, she followed firing automatically, shot after shot, till the six chambers were empty. Hammond fell down on the floor of the veranda. He **crumpled**④ up into a bloody **heap**⑤.

When the boys, startled by the reports, rushed up, they found her standing over Hammond with the revolver still in her hand, and Hammond lifeless. She looked at them for a moment without speaking. They stood in a frightened, huddled bunch. She let the revolver fall from her hand, and without a word turned and went into the sitting-room. They watched her go into her bedroom and turn the key in the lock. They dared not touch the dead body, but looked at it with terrified eyes, talking excitedly to one another in undertones. Then the head-boy collected himself; he had been with them for many years, he was Chinese and a level-headed fellow. Robert had gone into Singapore on his motorcycle, and the car stood in the garage. He told the seik to get it out; they must go at once to the

① pinion ['pinjən] v. 束缚

② revolver [ri'vɔlvə] n. 左轮手枪

③ lurch [ləːtʃ] v. 颠簸着行进

④ crumple ['krʌmpl] v. 倒下

⑤ heap [hiːp] n.（一）堆

而他呼出的热气冲到了她的脸上，让她感到说不出的恶心。他吻她的嘴唇，她的眼睛，她的脸颊，她的头发。他双臂的压力都快要她的命了。他抱起她，两脚都离地了。她试图用脚踢他，但他把她搂得更紧了。他此时把她抱起来了，没有再吭声说什么，但莱斯利看得出，他脸色苍白，眼睛里燃烧着欲火。他抱着她正要进入卧室。他已经不再是个文明人了，而是个野蛮人。匆忙向前当中，他撞着挡在途中的一张桌子上。他的膝盖本来僵硬，所以走路不是很灵便，加上怀里抱着个女人，结果倒下了。莱斯利瞬间挣脱了他，跑着绕过了沙发。他一骨碌爬了起来，朝着她扑了过去。桌上放着一支左轮手枪。她不是个提心吊胆的女人，但是，罗伯特夜间不在家，她本来打算睡觉时把枪拿进卧室的。这就是枪碰巧放在桌子上的原因。她此刻惊恐万状，情绪激动，不知道自己在干什么。她听见了一声枪响，看见哈蒙德打了趔趄。他大叫了一声，说了句什么话，但她没有听清楚。他踉踉跄跄地走到了露台上。她此时情绪处于狂乱状态，失去了控制，跟随着他到了室外，是啊，情况就是这样的，她一定跟随着他到了室外，不过，她对这个情况一点都记不起来了。她不由自主地连续开枪，直到枪膛里的六发子弹全部打光。哈蒙德倒在露台的地上，蜷缩成一团，血肉模糊。

枪声惊动了仆人们。他们冲了上来，发现她站立在哈蒙德的身边，手上仍然握着枪。哈蒙德则已经毫无声息了。她打量了他们片刻，没有开口说话。他们站立着，诚惶诚恐，挤作一团。枪从她手上掉落了，她没有吭声，转身走向卧室。仆人们注视着她走进自己的卧室，扭动锁孔里的钥匙把门反锁上。他们不敢碰死者的尸体，只是看着，目光恐惧，相互之间情绪激动地低声议论着。紧接着，领头的仆人镇定了下来，他跟随他们一家人许多年了，是个华人，头脑冷静。罗伯特是骑着摩托车去新加坡的，所以汽车留在车库里。他吩咐司机把车开出来。他们必须立刻去找区域警务助理，向他报告这里发

Assistant District Officer and tell him what had happened. He picked up the revolver and put it in his pocket. The ADO, a man called Withers, lived on the outskirts of the nearest town, which was about thirty-five miles away. It took them an hour and a half to reach him. Everyone was asleep, and they had to rouse the boys. Presently Withers came out and they told him their **errand**①. The head-boy showed him the revolver in proof of what he said. The ADO went into his room to dress, sent for his car, and in a little while was following them back along the deserted road. The dawn was just breaking as he reached the Crosbies' bungalow. He ran up the steps of the veranda, and stopped short as he saw Hammond's body lying where he fell. He touched the face. It was quite cold.

"Where's mem?" he asked the house-boy.

The Chinese pointed to the bedroom. Withers went to the door and knocked. There was no answer. He knocked again.

"Mrs. Crosbie," he called.

"Who is it?"

"Withers."

There was another pause. Then the door was unlocked and slowly opened. Leslie stood before him. She had not been to bed, and wore the tea-gown in which she had dined. She stood and looked silently at the ADO.

"Your house-boy fetched me," he said. "Hammond. What have you done?"

"He tried to rape me, and I shot him."

"My God. I say, you'd better come out here. You must tell me exactly what happened."

"Not now. I can't. You must give me time. Send for my husband."

Withers was a young man, and he did not know exactly what to do in an emergency which was so out of the run of his duties. Leslie refused to say anything till at last Robert arrived. Then she told the two men the story, from which since then, though she had repeated it over and over again, she had never

① errand ['erənd] *n.* 差事；使命；差使

生的情况。他捡起手枪，放进自己的衣服口袋里。区域警务助理名叫威瑟斯，住在离此地最近一座城镇的镇郊，距离有三十五英里。他们开车一个半小时之后才到达了他的住处。那儿的每一个人都已经睡觉了，他们只好唤醒仆人。不一会儿，威瑟斯出来了，他们把来意告诉给了他。领头的仆人拿出手枪给他看，以便证明自己说的话。区域警务助理进入卧室更衣，吩咐人把车开出来。一会儿过后，他便跟随着他们返回，行进在没有行人的公路上。他抵达克罗斯比的孟加拉平房时，天刚蒙蒙亮。他一路跑着上了通向露台的台阶，看到哈蒙德的尸体躺在原地时，突然停住了。他触摸了一下死者的脸庞，已经冰凉了。

"夫人呢？"他对着仆人问了一声。

华人仆人指了指卧室。威瑟斯走到门口，敲了敲门。没有反应，他再敲。

"克罗斯比夫人。"他喊了一声。

"谁呀？"

"威瑟斯。"

又是一阵停顿。然后，门锁开了，房门慢慢打开。莱斯利站立在他面前。她并没有上床睡觉，因为她身上仍然穿着那身吃晚饭时穿的茶会礼服。她站立着，一声不吭，打量着区域警务助理。

"您家的仆人叫我过来，"他说，"关于哈蒙德。您都干什么啦？"

"他企图强奸我，于是我朝他开枪了。"

"天哪，我说啊，您最好出来。您一定要把情况原原本本地告诉我。"

"现在不成，我无法做到。您得给我时间才是，请派人去把我丈夫找回来。"

威瑟斯人很年轻，面对这样一种超出了自己职责范围的紧急情况，他并不确切地知道该如何是好。莱斯利拒绝陈述任何情况，直到最后见到了罗伯特，她才向两个人陈述了事情的原委。从那之后，尽管她一次次重复，

in the slightest degree diverged.

The point to which Mr. Joyce **recurred**① was the shooting. As a lawyer he was bothered that Leslie had fired not once, but six times, and the examination of the dead man showed that four of the shots had been fired close to the body. One might almost have thought that when the man fell she stood over him and emptied the contents of the revolver into him. She confessed that her memory, so accurate for all that had preceded, failed her here. Her mind was blank. It pointed to an uncontrollable fury; but uncontrollable fury was the last thing you would have expected from this quiet and **demure**② woman. Mr. Joyce had known her a good many years, and had always thought her an unemotional person; during the weeks that had passed since the tragedy her composure had been amazing.

Mr. Joyce shrugged his shoulders.

"The fact is, I suppose," he reflected, "that you can never tell what hidden possibilities of savagery there are in the most respectable of women."

There was a knock at the door.

"Come in."

The Chinese clerk entered and closed the door behind him. He closed it gently, with deliberation, but decidedly, and advanced to the table at which Mr. Joyce was sitting.

"May I trouble you, sir, for a few words' private conversation?" he said.

The elaborate accuracy with which the clerk expressed himself always faintly amused Mr. Joyce, and now he smiled.

"It's no trouble, Chi Seng," he replied.

"The matter on which I desire to speak to you, sir, is delicate and confidential."

"Fire away."

Mr. Joyce met his clerk's shrewd eyes. As usual Ong Chi Seng was dressed in the height of local fashion. He wore very shiny patent leather shoes and gay silk socks. In his black tie was a pearl and ruby pin, and on the fourth finger of

① recur [ri'kəː] v. 重新提起

② demure [di'mjuə] a. 端庄的

但每一次都没有任何更改。

乔伊斯先生反复思索了开枪这个问题。作为辩护律师，他感到伤脑筋的是，莱斯利不只是开了一枪，而是开了六枪。查验死者的尸体后发现，其中有四枪是在距离死者很近处开的。人们几乎可以认定，死者倒地后，她就站立在他身边，把手枪内的子弹全部射向了他。她承认，尽管自己对那之前发生的情况记得很清楚，但关于开枪这一段，却完全记不得了。她脑袋一片空白，这说明她当时已经是怒不可遏了。但是，若是说这样一位文静娴雅、举止端庄的女性会怒不可遏，人们是始料未及的。乔伊斯先生认识她也有许多年了，一直都觉得，她不是个感情用事的人。悲剧发生后的几个星期当中，她表现得镇定自若，这也着实令人感到惊叹。

乔伊斯先生耸了耸肩膀。

"我觉得吧，事实上，"他心里寻思着，"你永远都不可能清楚，即便是再端庄体面的女人身上，可能隐藏着什么样的野蛮性。"

有人敲门。

"进来。"

那位华人职员进来了，带上了门。他关门时动作轻柔，谨小慎微，但又坚决果断，然后走向乔伊斯先生的办公桌边。

"先生，我能否打搅您一下，私下里同您说句话？"他问了一声。

这位职员每次表达自己的意思时总会字斟句酌，而乔伊斯先生则总会觉得有趣。他此时就露出了笑容。

"说不上是打搅啊，志成。"他回答说。

"我想要对您说的事情，先生，很微妙也很机密。"

"直说吧。"

乔伊斯先生捕捉到自己这位职员狡黠的目光。和平常一样，王志成身穿本地最时髦的服装。脚上是铮亮的漆皮鞋和鲜艳的丝袜。黑色的领带上别着镶嵌了珍珠和红宝石的饰针。左手的无名指上戴着一颗钻戒。洁白的

his left hand a diamond ring. From the pocket of his neat white coat protruded a gold fountain pen and a gold pencil. He wore a gold wrist-watch, and on the bridge of his nose invisible pince-nez. He gave a little cough.

"The matter has to do with the case R. v. Crosbie, sir."

"Yes?"

"A circumstance has come to my knowledge, sir, which seems to me to put a different complexion on it."

"What circumstance?"

"It has come to my knowledge, sir, that there is a letter in existence from the defendant to the unfortunate victim of the tragedy."

"I shouldn't be at all surprised. In the course of the last seven years I have no doubt that Mrs. Crosbie often had occasion to write to Mr. Hammond."

Mr. Joyce had a high opinion of his clerk's intelligence and his words were designed to conceal his thoughts.

"That is very probable, sir. Mrs. Crosbie must have communicated with the deceased frequently, to invite him to dine with her for example, or to propose a tennis game. That was my first thought when the matter was brought to my notice. This letter, however, was written on the day of the late Mr. Hammond's death."

Mr. Joyce did not flicker an eyelash. He continued to look at Ong Chi Seng with the smile of faint amusement with which he generally talked to him.

"Who has told you this?"

"The circumstances were brought to my knowledge, sir, by a friend of mine."

Mr. Joyce knew better than to insist.

"You will no doubt recall, sir, that Mrs. Crosbie has stated that until the fatal night she had had no communication with the deceased for several weeks."

"Have you got the letter?"

"No, sir."

"What are its contents?"

"My friend gave me a copy. Would you like to **peruse**① it, sir?"

上衣口袋里露出一支镀金自来水笔和一支镀金铅笔。手腕上戴着一块镀金手表，鼻梁上架着一副隐形夹鼻眼镜。他先轻声地咳嗽了一声。

“这件事情一定牵涉到罗伯特·克洛斯比夫人的案件，先生。”

“嗯？”

“我了解到一个情况，先生。我觉得这个情况会让本案呈现出不同面貌。”

“是什么情况呢？”

“先生，我知道的情况是，有那么一封信，这封信是被告人写给本案受害者的。”

“我并不觉得有什么奇怪的。最近七年中，我毫不怀疑，格罗斯比夫人会经常写信给哈蒙德先生。”

乔伊斯先生平常高度赞赏自己这位职员的聪明睿智，但他说这样的话实在有意掩盖自己的想法。

“这是非常有可能的，先生，克洛斯比夫人一定经常同死者联系，比如邀请他来同自己一块儿吃饭，或者建议打网球。我刚刚知道这个情况时，最初就是这么想的。不过，那封信是已故哈蒙德先生死亡那天写的。”

乔伊斯先生没有眨一下眼睛，而是持续不断地看着王志成，脸带微笑，和平常一样饶有兴趣听着对方说话。

“这个情况是谁告诉你的？”

“我是从我的一位朋友那儿听说这个情况的，先生。”

乔伊斯先生心里清楚，最好不要再追问了。

“您一定还记得，先生，克洛斯比夫人表达过，悲剧发生之前几个星期，她都没有同死者联系过。”

“你拿到了那封信吗？”

“没有啊，先生。”

“信里面写了什么？”

“我朋友给了我一份抄写件。您想看一看吗，先生？”

① peruse [pə'ru:z] v. 阅读

"I should."

Ong Chi Seng took from an inside pocket a bulky wallet. It was filled with papers, Singapore dollar notes and cigarette cards. From the confusion he presently extracted a half sheet of thin notepaper and placed it before Mr. Joyce. The letter read as follows:

> *"R. will be away for the night. I absolutely must see you. I shall expect you at eleven. I am desperate, and if you don't come I won't answer for the consequences. Don't drive up. — L."*

It was written in the flowing hand which the Chinese were taught at the foreign schools. The writing, so lacking in character, was oddly **incongruous**① with the ominous words.

"What makes you think that this note was written by Mrs. Crosbie?"

"I have every confidence in the **veracity**② of my informant, sir," replied Ong Chi Seng. "And the matter can very easily be put to the proof. Mrs. Crosbie will, no doubt, be able to tell you at once whether she wrote such a letter or not."

Since the beginning of the conversation Mr. Joyce had not taken his eyes off the respectable countenance of his clerk. He wondered now if he **discerned**③ in it a faint expression of mockery.

"It is inconceivable that Mrs. Crosbie should have written such a letter," said Mr. Joyce.

"If that is your opinion, sir, the matter is of course ended. My friend spoke to me on the subject only because he thought, as I was in your office, you might like to know of the existence of this letter before a communication was made to the Deputy Public Prosecutor."

"Who has the original?" asked Mr. Joyce sharply.

Ong Chi Seng made no sign that he perceived in this question and its manner a change of attitude.

"You will remember, sir, no doubt, that after the death of Mr. Hammond it was discovered that he had had relations with a Chinese woman. The letter is at

"看看吧。"

王志成从内侧的衣服口袋里掏出一个鼓鼓囊囊的皮夹子，里面塞满了纸条、新加坡钞票和烟卷卡。不一会儿，他便从这一对乱糟糟的东西当中取出了半张薄薄的字条，然后放在乔伊斯先生面前。信的内容如下：

罗今晚不在家。我一定要见到你，十一点钟见面。我豁出去了，你若不来，后果我不负责。别把汽车开上来。

莱

信的抄件是用外国学校里教华人书写的那种连体书法写的。这种字写得缺乏个性，与信中那些充满不祥意义的词语很不协调，显得很怪异。

"你凭什么认定这封信就是克洛斯比夫人写的呢？"

"我完全信得过给我提供信息的人，先生，"王志成回答说，"这件事情很容易便可得到证实。毫无疑问，克洛斯比夫人是否写过这样一封信，她立刻便能够告诉您。"

自从谈话伊始，乔伊斯先生的目光从未离开过他的这位职员谦逊体面的面容。他此刻心里想着，自己是否从中觉察出了一丝揶揄的表情。

"要说克洛斯比夫人写了这样一封信，这简直不可想象啊。"乔伊斯先生说。

"您若是这么看的话，先生，此事当然就到此为止了。我朋友之所以把这个情况告诉我，那是因为他考虑到我在您的事务所里做事，您或许希望知道有这么一封信存在，然后再去同副检察长交流情况。"

"信的原件在谁手上？"乔伊斯先生问，语气咄咄逼人。

王志成并没有表露出，自己从对方的这个问题和提问的语气中觉察出了态度上的变化。

"毫无疑问，您一定记得，先生，哈蒙德先生死亡后，人们发现，他曾与一位华人妇女同居过。那封信眼

① incongruous [in'kɔŋgruəs] *a.* 不相称的

② veracity [və'ræsəti] *n.* 诚实

③ discern [di'səːn] *v.* 觉察出

present in her possession."

That was one of the things which had turned public opinion most vehemently against Hammond. It came to be known that for several months he had had a Chinese woman living in his house.

For a moment neither of them spoke. Indeed everything had been said and each understood the other perfectly.

"I'm obliged to you, Chi Seng. I will give the matter my consideration."

"Very good, sir. Do you wish me to make a communication to that effect to my friend?"

"I daresay it would be as well if you kept in touch with him," Mr. Joyce answered with gravity.

"Yes, sir."

The clerk noiselessly left the room, shutting the door again with deliberation, and left Mr. Joyce to his reflections. He stared at the copy, in its neat, impersonal writing, of Leslie's letter. Vague suspicions troubled him. They were so disconcerting that he made an effort to put them out of his mind. There must be a simple explanation of the letter, and Leslie without doubt could give it at once, but, by heaven, an explanation was needed. He rose from his chair, put the letter in his pocket, and took his topi. When he went out Ong Chi Seng was busily writing at his desk.

"I'm going out for a few minutes, Chi Seng," he said.

"Mr. George Reed is coming by appointment at twelve o'clock, sir. Where shall I say you've gone?"

Mr. Joyce gave him a thin smile.

"You can say that you haven't the least idea."

But he knew perfectly well that Ong Chi Seng was aware that he was going to the gaol. Though the crime had been committed in Belanda and the trial was to take place at Belanda Bharu, since there was in the gaol no convenience for the **detention**① of a white woman Mrs. Crosbie had been brought to Singapore.

When she was led into the room in which he waited she held out her thin,

下就在她的手上呢。”

公众舆论之所以强烈谴责哈蒙德，这件事情是其原因之一。人们知道，他先前让那个华人妇女在自己家里住了好几个月。

他们两个人沉默了片刻。事实上，要说的话都已经说了，而双方都完全心知肚明。

“非常感谢你，志成。我会仔细斟酌这件事情的。”

“太好啦，先生，您是否希望我把这个意思向我朋友转述呢？”

“我觉得，你可以同他保持联系。”乔伊斯先生回答说，态度郑重其事。

“那行，先生。”

职员轻手轻脚地退出了房间，小心谨慎地再把房门关上，留下乔伊斯先生独自思考。莱斯利信的抄件书写工整，但缺乏个性。他盯着信的抄件看，心里不禁有了种种模糊的疑惑，颇费思忖。他感到很不舒服，极力想要驱散心中的疑惑。信的事情必须要有一个明确的解释。莱斯利无疑可以立刻给出解释。但是，天哪，解释是必须的。他从坐着的椅子上站起身，把信放进衣服口袋，拿起自己那顶遮阳帽。乔伊斯先生走到室外时，王志成正在自己的办公室忙碌地写着什么。

“我要出去一会儿，志成。”他说。

“根据事先的约定，乔治·里德先生十二点钟要来，先生。我该说您去哪儿了呢？”

乔伊斯先生对着他淡淡地微笑着。

“你就说不知道。”

不过，乔伊斯先生明确知道，王志成其实很清楚，他这是要去监狱看看。虽说命案发生在贝兰达，案件的审理也会在贝兰达巴鲁进行，但由于那儿的监舍条件不适合于关押白人妇女，所以，克罗斯比夫人被押送到了新加坡。

克洛斯比夫人被带到乔伊斯先生等待的房间后，便

① detention [di'tenʃən] *n.* 拘留

distinguished hand, and gave him a pleasant smile. She was as ever neatly and simply dressed, and her abundant, pale hair was arranged with care.

"I wasn't expecting to see you this morning," she said, graciously.

She might have been in her own house, and Mr. Joyce almost expected to hear her call the boy and tell him to bring the visitor a **gin pahit**①.

"How are you?" he asked.

"I'm in the best of health, thank you." A flicker of amusement flashed across her eyes. "This is a wonderful place for a rest cure."

The attendant withdrew and they were left alone.

"Do sit down," said Leslie.

He took a chair. He did not quite know how to begin. She was so cool that it seemed almost impossible to say to her the thing he had come to say. Though she was not pretty there was something agreeable in her appearance. She had elegance, but it was the elegance of good breeding in which there was nothing of the artifice of society. You had only to look at her to know what sort of people she had and what kind of surroundings she had lived in. Her fragility gave her a singular refinement. It was impossible to associate her with the vaguest idea of **grossness**②.

"I'm looking forward to seeing Robert this afternoon," she said, in her good-humoured, easy voice. (It was a pleasure to hear her speak, her voice and her accent were so distinctive of her class.) "Poor dear, it's been a great trial to his nerves. I'm thankful it'll all be over in a few days."

"It's only five days now."

"I know. Each morning when I awake I say to myself 'one less'." She smiled then. "Just as I used to do at school and the holidays were coming."

"By the way, am I right in thinking that you had no communication whatever with Hammond for several weeks before the catastrophe?"

"I'm quite positive of that. The last time we met was at a tennis-party at the MacFarrens. I don't think I said more than two words to him. They have two

伸出了自己一只纤细优雅的手，朝着他莞尔一笑。她还和平常一样衣着整洁朴素，一头浓密淡色的秀发经过精心的梳理。

“没想到上午就见到您了。”她说，态度优雅随和。

她如同在自己家里一样，乔伊斯先生几乎都指望着她会召唤男仆给客人上杜松子酒了。

“你身体好吧？”他问候了一声。

“可好啦，谢谢你。”她的眼睛里掠过一丝快乐的神情。“这儿是修养生息的绝佳所在啊。”

监狱的看守离开了房间，就剩下他们两个人了。

“快请坐吧。”莱斯利说。

他坐在一把椅子上。他不是很清楚该从何开始说起。她的表情神态显得格外冷静，他本来到这儿来要对她说的话，现在觉得几乎无法启口了。尽管她算不得很漂亮，但她的音容相貌确有令人感到开心愉悦的地方。她风度优雅，但那种优雅源自良好的教养，绝无社交场上的那种矫揉造作之态。您只需要看一看，便知道她同什么样的人交往，生活在什么样的环境中。她体质虚弱，但却反而显得独具风韵。人们丝毫都不可能把她同粗鲁俗气联系起来。

“我等着今天下午见罗伯特呢，”她说，语气平静轻松。（听她说话真是一种享受，语气和腔调具有她所属的那个阶层的特质。）“可怜的人啊，这件事情让他备受折磨。令我充满了感激之情的是，这事再过几天就要了结了。”

“从现在算起只有五天了。”

“我知道。我每天早晨一醒来便会对自己说，‘又少了一天了’。”她笑着说，“完全就像我过去上学时盼着放假的情形一样。”

“对了，悲剧发生之前的几个星期里，你和哈蒙德没有任何联系，我这样认为不错吧？”

“这一点我很肯定。我们上一次见面是在麦克法伦家举行的网球聚会上。我认为，自己当时同他说的话最

① gin pahit 一种见于东南亚的苦味杜松子酒（“pahit”源自马来语，意为“苦的”）

② grossness ['grəusnis] *n.* 粗野

courts, you know, and we didn't happen to be in the same sets."

"And you hadn't written to him?"

"Oh, no."

"Are you quite sure of that?"

"Oh, quite," she answered, with a little smile. "There was nothing I should write to him for except to ask him to dine or to play tennis, and I hadn't done either for months."

"At one time you'd been on fairly intimate terms with him. How did it happen that you had stopped asking him to anything?"

Mrs. Crosbie shrugged her thin shoulders.

"One gets tired of people. We hadn't anything very much in common. Of course, when he was ill Robert and I did everything we could for him, but the last year or two he'd been quite well, and he was very popular. He had a good many calls on his time, and there didn't seem to be any need to **shower**① invitations upon him."

"Are you quite certain that was all?"

Mrs. Crosbie hesitated for a moment.

"Well, I may just as well tell you. It had come to our ears that he was living with a Chinese woman, and Robert said he wouldn't have him in the house. I had seen her myself."

Mr. Joyce was sitting in a straight-backed armchair, resting his chin on his hand, and his eyes were fixed on Leslie. Was it his fancy that, as she made this remark, her black **pupils**② were filled on a sudden, for the fraction of a second, with a dull red light? The effect was startling. Mr. Joyce shifted in his chair. He placed the tips of his ten fingers together. He spoke very slowly, choosing his words.

"I think I should tell you that there is in existence a letter in your handwriting to Geoff Hammond."

He watched her closely. She made no movement, nor did her face change colour, but she took a noticeable time to reply.

多没有超过两句。麦克法伦家有两个网球场，这你是知道的。我们碰巧不在一个组。

“而你没有给他写过信吗？”

“噢，没有。”

“这一点你肯定吗？”

“噢，很肯定，”她回答说，露出了一丝微笑。“我写信给他也就是邀请他来吃饭或者打网球，实际上，我已经有好几个月没有因为这两件事情给他写信了。”

“你们一度同他关系挺密切的，后来怎么又停止邀请他来开展活动啦？”

克洛斯比夫人耸了耸瘦削的肩膀。

“人会厌烦同别人交往的。我们之间没多少共同点。当然，他若是生病了，我和罗伯特会尽我们的一切努力去帮助他，但是，过去一两年当中，他身体挺好的，而且人缘很广，平时应酬活动很多。所以，我们似乎没有必要经常向他发出邀请了。”

“你对此很肯定吗？”

克洛斯比夫人迟疑了片刻。

“好吧，我也不妨告诉你。别人的话也传到我们的耳朵来了，说他同一位华人妇女同居。罗伯特说过，他不会再让他上门了。我本人也见过那个女人。”

乔伊斯先生坐在一把直背扶手椅上，一只手托着下巴颏，眼睛盯着莱斯利看。她说上面这番话时，乌黑的瞳孔里突然闪现了一道暗红色的光，转瞬即逝。乔伊斯感到十分惊讶。乔伊斯先生坐在椅子上变换了一下姿势，两手的指尖相互顶着。他说话了，语速缓慢，字斟句酌。

“我觉得，我应该告诉你，有一封写给杰夫·哈蒙德的信，是你的笔迹。”

乔伊斯先生紧盯着她看。她一动不动，面不改色，只是停顿了好一阵子才回话。

① shower ['ʃauə] *v.* 大量给予

② pupil ['pjupəl] *n.* 瞳孔

"In the past I've often sent him little notes to ask him to something or other, or to get me something when I knew he was going to Singapore."

"This letter asks him to come and see you because Robert was going to Singapore."

"That's impossible. I never did anything of the kind."

"You'd better read it for yourself."

He took it out of his pocket and handed it to her. She gave it a glance and with a smile of scorn handed it back to him.

"That's not my handwriting."

"I know, it's said to be an exact copy of the original."

She read the words now, and as she read a horrible change came over her. Her colourless face grew dreadful to look at. It turned green. The flesh seemed on a sudden to fall away and her skin was tightly stretched over the bones. Her lips **receded**①, showing her teeth, so that she had the appearance of **making a grimace**②. She stared at Mr. Joyce with eyes that started from their sockets. He was looking now at a **gibbering**③ death's head.

"What does it mean?" she whispered.

Her mouth was so dry that she could utter no more than a hoarse sound. It was no longer a human voice.

"That is for you to say," he answered.

"I didn't write it. I swear I didn't write it."

"Be very careful what you say. If the original is in your handwriting it would be useless to deny it."

"It would be a **forgery**④."

"It would be difficult to prove that. It would be easy to prove that it was genuine."

A shiver passed through her lean body. But great beads of sweat stood on her forehead. She took a handkerchief from her bag and wiped the palms of her hands. She glanced at the letter again and gave Mr. Joyce a sidelong look.

“过去，我倒是常常会给他去个便条，为了这样那样的事情，或者知道他去新加坡时，请他给我捎点东西。”

“刚才提到的那封信是要他过来看你，因为罗伯特要去新加坡。”

“这不可能。我从没有干过这一类的事情。”

“你还是自己看看信吧。”

他从衣服口袋里掏出信，递给了她。她瞥了一眼信，轻蔑地微笑了一下，把信还回给了他。

“这不是我的笔迹。”

“我知道，但据说是一份和原件一模一样的抄写件。”

她这时看着信上面的文字内容，看着看着，便有了一种可怕的变化。毫无血色的脸庞看上去更加吓人，铁青着，脸上的肌肉仿佛顿时消失了，只剩下皮囊紧紧地裹着骨头。嘴唇向后收缩，露出了牙齿。做鬼脸时就是这样一副模样。眼睛在眼眶里暴突着，盯着乔伊斯先生看。乔伊斯先生觉得自己看到的是一具骷髅，正在胡言乱语地说着什么呢。

① recede [ri'siːd] *v.* 向后倾斜

② make a grimace 做鬼脸

③ gibbering ['dʒibəriŋ] *a.* 语无伦次的

“这是什么意思啊？”克洛斯比夫人低声说。

她口干舌燥，只能发出嘶哑的声音，但根本就不像是人在说话。

“什么意思得由你来说呢。”他回答说。

“信不是我写的。我发誓，信不是我写的。”

“说话可要谨慎啊。信的原件若是你的笔迹，否认是没有用的。”

“信一定是伪造的。”

④ forgery ['fɔːdʒəri] *n.* 伪造品

“是否伪造，证明起来很困难啊。但证明信是真实的却很容易。”

她瘦削的身子颤抖了起来。但豆大的汗珠子却从额头上冒了出来。她从包里面拿出了一块手帕，擦了擦了手心。她再次瞥了一眼信，然后斜睨了一眼乔伊斯先生。

“上面没有标明日期。我即便写过这样一封信，而且忘记了标明日期，那也可能是几年前写的。你若是给我时间，我定会设法回忆起这个事情来的。”

"It's not dated. If I had written it and forgotten all about it, it might have been written years ago. If you'll give me time, I'll try and remember the circumstances."

"I noticed there was no date. If this letter were in the hands of the prosecution they would cross-examine the boys. They would soon find out whether someone took a letter to Hammond on the day of his death."

Mrs. Crosbie clasped her hands violently and **swayed**① in her chair so that he thought she would faint.

"I swear to you that I didn't write that letter."

Mr. Joyce was silent for a little while. He took his eyes from her **distraught**② face, and looked down on the floor. He was reflecting.

"In these circumstances we need not go into the matter further," he said slowly, at last breaking the silence. "If the possessor of this letter sees fit to place it in the hands of the prosecution you will be prepared."

His words suggested that he had nothing more to say to her, but he made no movement of departure. He waited. To himself he seemed to wait a very long time. He did not look at Leslie, but he was conscious that she sat very still. She made no sound. At last it was he who spoke.

"If you have nothing more to say to me I think I'll be getting back to my office."

"What would anyone who read the letter be inclined to think that it meant?" she asked then.

"He'd know that you had told a deliberate lie," answered Mr. Joyce sharply.

"When?"

"You have stated definitely that you had had no communication with Hammond for at least three months."

"The whole thing has been a terrible shock to me. The events of that dreadful night have been a nightmare. It's not very strange if one detail has escaped my memory."

"It would be unfortunate when your memory, has reproduced so exactly every particular of your interview with Hammond, that you should have

① sway [swei] v. 摆动

② distraught [dis'trɔːt] a. 焦虑不安的

“我注意到上面确实没有标明日期。此信若是到了检方的手上，他们定会对府上的仆人进行反诘问[1]的。他们很快就会发现，是否有人在哈蒙德死亡的当天给过他信。”

克洛斯比夫人两只手猛然紧紧握在一块儿，身子在椅子上摇晃着。乔伊斯先生感觉她要晕过去了。

“我向你发誓，我没有写过这样一封信。”

乔伊斯先生沉默了片刻，目光从她那变了形的脸上移开，看着地面。他沉思了起来。

“既然如此，我们没有必要再谈这件事情了，”他最后打破了沉默，语气缓慢地说，“持有此信的人若是认准了要把信交给检方，你得有所准备才是。”

乔伊斯先生话里面的意思是，他没有更多话要对她说了。但是，他并没有起身告辞。他等待着。他自己倒是觉得已经等了很长时间。他没有看莱斯利一眼，但清楚地意识到，她坐着一动不动，没有吭声。最后还是他开口说话的。

“你若是没有什么更多的情况要对我说的，我想我这就回自己的事务所去了。”

“有人若是看过这封信，那会觉得此信是什么意思呢？”她紧接着问了一声。

“人家会觉得，你蓄意说谎来着。”乔伊斯先生回答说，语气严厉。

“什么时候？”

“你明确地说过了，你先前至少有三个月没有同哈蒙德联系过。”

“整个这件事情对我带来了沉重的打击。那个恐怖的夜晚发生的一桩桩一件件简直就是一场噩梦。我若是忘却了一个细节，那也没有什么好奇怪的。”

“关于你和哈蒙德会面的详情，你都记得一清二楚。但你竟然忘记了他是应你的紧急要求前去见你的这

1　反诘问（cross-examine）是法律用语，指诉讼当事人的一方向对方证人就其所提供的的证词进行盘问以便发现矛盾，推翻其证词。

forgotten so important a point as that he came to see you in the bungalow on the night of his death at your express desire."

"I hadn't forgotten. After what happened I was afraid to mention it. I thought you'd none of you believe my story if I admitted that he'd come at my invitation. I daresay it was stupid of me; but I lost my head, and after I'd said once that I'd had no communication with Hammond I was obliged to stick to it."

By now Leslie had recovered her admirable composure, and she met Mr. Joyce's appraising glance with **candour**①. Her gentleness was very **disarming**②.

"You will be required to explain, then, why you asked Hammond to come and see you when Robert was away for the night."

She turned her eyes full on the lawyer. He had been mistaken in thinking them insignificant, they were rather fine eyes, and unless he was mistaken they were bright now with tears. Her voice has a little break in it.

"It was a surprise I was preparing for Robert. His birthday is next month. I knew he wanted a new gun and you know I'm dreadfully stupid about sporting things. I wanted to talk to Geoff about it. I thought I'd get him to order it for me."

"Perhaps the terms of the letter are not very clear to your recollection. Will you have another look at it?"

"No, I don't want to," she said quickly.

"Does it seem to you the sort of letter a woman would write to a somewhat distant acquaintance because she wanted to consult him about buying a gun?"

"I daresay it's rather extravagant and emotional. I do express myself like that, you know. I'm quite prepared to admit it's very silly." She smiled. "And after all, Geoff Hammond wasn't quite a distant acquaintance. When he was ill I'd nursed him like a mother. I asked him to come when Robert was away, because Robert wouldn't have him in the house."

Mr. Joyce was tired of sitting so long in the same position. He rose and

个十分重要的情节，这样说很不合适吧。”

“我没有忘记，但是，发生了那样的惨剧之后，我就不敢提起这一点了。我若是承认，他是应我的邀请过来的，我觉得你们谁都不会相信我说的话。可以说，我这样做很愚蠢，但是，我昏了头，既然我都已经说过了，自己之前很长时间没有同哈蒙德联系过，那我就只能一口咬定了。”

到了这个时候，莱斯利完全恢复了自己镇定自若的神态，能够坦然面对乔伊斯先生审视的目光。她温柔娴雅的神态很能别人释怀。

“这样一来，检方就会要求你做出解释，你为何偏偏在罗伯特不在家的那个夜晚邀请他到家里来。”

她的目光完全聚焦在了律师身上。他先前觉得她的眼睛微不足道，这实在是看错了。她的眼睛很迷人，他若是没有弄错的话，眼下那双眼睛里正闪烁着晶莹的泪水。她说话的声音有点哽咽。

“我本来是准备给罗伯特一个惊喜的，下个月就是他的生日了。我知道，他想要一支新枪。但是，你可知道，关于狩猎方面的事情，我真是一窍不通。我想要把这个事情告诉杰夫来着。我想到了，自己可以请他替我订购一支。”

“你或许不大记得信中是怎么写的了吧。你要不要再看一看信呢？”

“不，我不想看了。”她急忙说。

“你觉得，一个女人想要向一位并不是很熟悉的朋友请教关于购买枪支的事情，她会写出这样一封信来吗？”

“可以说，这样做确实有点过分，感情用事。你知道，我确实会这样表现自己。我也承认，这样做很傻。”她微笑着说，“但毕竟说起来，杰夫·哈蒙德也并不是关系很疏远的关系。他过去生病时，我像母亲一样照顾他来着。我之所以在罗伯特不在家时请他到家里来，那是因为，罗伯特不让他到家里来。”

乔伊斯先生感到疲倦了，因为他保持同一个姿势坐

① candour ['kændə] *n.* 真诚

② disarming [dis'ɑːmiŋ] *a.* 释人疑虑的

walked once or twice up and down the room, choosing the words he proposed to say; then he leaned over the back of the chair in which he had been sitting. He spoke slowly in a tone of deep gravity.

"Mrs. Crosbie, I want to talk to you very, very seriously. This case was comparatively plain sailing. There was only one point which seemed to me to require explanation: as far as I could judge, you had fired no less than four shots into Hammond when he was lying on the ground. It was hard to accept the possibility that a delicate, frightened, and habitually self-controlled woman, of gentle nature and refined instincts, should have surrendered to an absolutely uncontrolled frenzy. But of course it was admissible. Although Geoffrey Hammond was much liked and on the whole thought highly of, I was prepared to prove that he was the sort of man who might be guilty of the crime which in justification of your act you accused him of. The fact, which was discovered after his death, that he had been living with a Chinese woman gave us something very definite to go upon. That robbed him of any sympathy which might have been felt for him. We made up our minds to make use of the **odium**① which such a connection cast upon him in the minds of all respectable people. I told your husband this morning that I was certain of an acquittal, and I wasn't just telling him that to give him heart. I do not believe the assessors would have left the court."

They looked into one another's eyes. Mrs. Crosbie was strangely still. She was like a little bird paralysed by the fascination of a snake. He went on in the same quiet tones.

"But this letter has thrown an entirely different complexion on the case. I am your legal adviser, I shall represent you in court. I take your story as you tell it me, and I shall conduct your defence according to its terms. It may be that I believe your statements, and it may be that I doubt them. The duty of counsel is to persuade the court that the evidence placed before it is not such as to justify it in bringing in a verdict of guilty, and any private opinion he may have of the guilt or innocence of his client is entirely beside the point."

He was astonished to see in Leslie's eyes the flicker of a smile. **Piqued**②, he

了很长时间。他站起身，在房间里走了一两个来回，斟酌着自己打算要说的话。然后，他倚靠在自己刚才一直坐着的那个椅子的靠背上。他说话时语速缓慢，语气深沉而又严肃。

“克罗斯比夫人，我想要非常非常严肃地同你说。相对而言，本案的进展很顺利。我觉得，其中只有一点需要做出解释：根据我的判断，哈蒙德倒在地上之后，你对准他至少开了四抢。一个女人若是纤细瘦弱，战战兢兢，惯常有控制力，加上性情娴雅，素有教养，说她会完全失去控制，疯狂桀骜，这未免令人难以相信。但这当然也可以为人所接受。尽管杰夫·哈蒙德广受人们喜爱，人们对他的总体评价也很高，但我还是打算要证明，你替自己的行为辩护时指控他所犯有的那种罪行。他死亡之后，人们发现，他和一位华人妇女同居。我们完全可以依据这个事实对他提出指控。这样可以消除人们对他的同情。我们已经打定了主意，一定要充分利用这种关系在体面人士的心目中对他形成的厌恶感。我今天上午已经对你丈夫说过了，我有把握让你无罪释放。我告诉他这个情况不仅仅是为了给他增强信心。我相信，陪审团不判定你无罪是不会离开法庭的。”

他们相互对视着。令人感到奇怪的是，克洛斯比夫人一动不动，如同一只被蛇迷住了的小鸟，动弹不得。他继续用同样平静的语气说说下去。

“但是，这封信让本案呈现出了一种完全不同的面貌。我既然是你的法律顾问，那就应该在法庭上代表你说话。我会接受你向我陈述的经过，并根据其内容替你辩护。我可能相信你的陈述，也可能怀疑你的陈述。辩护律师有义务让法庭相信，庭上展示的证据不足以做出有罪判决。至于他私下里认为自己的当事人有罪还是无辜，那完全是另外一回事。”

乔伊斯先生看到莱斯利的眼中掠过一丝微笑，很是惊讶。他感觉到自己的自尊心受到了伤害，于是继续往下说时语气显得有点冷漠。

① odium ['əudiəm] *n.* 强烈的厌恶

② piqued [pi:kt] *a.* 激怒的

went on somewhat dryly.

"You're not going to deny that Hammond came to your house at your urgent, and I may even say, hysterical invitation?"

Mrs. Crosbie, hesitating for an instant, seemed to consider.

"They can prove that the letter was taken to his bungalow by one of the house-boys. He rode over on his bicycle."

"You mustn't expect other people to be stupider than you. The letter will put them on the track of suspicions which have entered nobody's head. I will not tell you what I personally thought when I saw the copy. I do not wish you to tell me anything but what is needed to save your neck."

Mrs. Crosbie gave a shrill cry. She sprang to her feet, white with terror.

"You don't think they'd hang me?"

"If they came to the conclusion that you hadn't killed Hammond in self-defence, it would be the duty of the assessors to bring in a verdict of guilty. The charge is murder. It would be the duty of the judge to sentence you to death."

"But what can they prove?" she gasped.

"I don't know what they can prove. You know. I don't want to know. But if their suspicions are aroused, if they begin to make inquiries, if the natives are questioned—what is it that can be discovered?"

She crumpled up suddenly. She fell on the floor before he could catch her. She had fainted. He looked round the room for water, but there was none there, and he did not want to be disturbed. He stretched her out on the floor, and kneeling beside her waited for her to recover. When she opened her eyes he was disconcerted by the **ghastly**① fear that he saw in them.

"Keep quite still," he said. "You'll be better in a moment."

"You won't let them hang me," she whispered.

She began to cry, hysterically, while in undertones he sought to quieten her.

"For goodness' sake pull yourself together," he said.

"Give me a minute."

“应你的紧急邀请，甚至可以说是应你歇斯底里的邀请，哈蒙特这才上你家来的。你对此不至于否认吧？”

克罗斯比夫人迟疑了片刻，好像是在思索。

“检方能够证明，信是由府上的某个仆人送到哈蒙德的孟加拉平房去的。他骑了自行车过去。”

“你可一定不要以为别人都不如你聪明。尽管人们至今还没有怀疑过，但是，有了这封信之后，他们一定会起疑心的。我不打算告诉你，自己刚一看到这封信的抄件时，心里面有何感受。别的不用说，我只想要你告诉我能够让你免受绞刑的情况。”

克洛斯比夫人尖叫了一声，一跃而起，吓得脸色煞白。

“你觉得他们不至于绞死我吧？”

“陪审团若是得出结论，你枪杀哈蒙德并非出于自卫，那他们便有责任对你做出有罪裁定。罪名就是谋杀。既然如此，那法官就有责任判定你死刑。”

“但是，他们能证明什么呢？”她气喘吁吁说。

“我不知道他们能证明什么。要知道，我也不想知道。但是，他们若是起了疑心了，若是开始调查了，若是询问那些土著居民了——那有可能会发现什么情况呢？”

克罗斯比夫人突然瘫成一团。乔伊斯先生还没有来得及伸手扶她一把，她便晕倒在了地上。他环顾了一番房间，想要看看是否有水，但没有看到。他又不想受到外人的惊扰，于是让她平躺在地上，双膝跪在她身边，等着她苏醒过来。当她睁开眼睛时，他看见她的眼中充满了可怕的恐惧，一时间不知道该怎么办。

“躺着别动，”他说，“过一会儿就好啦。”

“你不会让他们绞死我的。”她低声说着。

她控制不了自己的情绪，开始哭了起来。而他则低声细语地想要让她平静下来。

“看在上帝的份上，请你镇定。”他说。

“稍稍等一会儿吧。”

① ghastly ['gɑːstli] *a.* 可怕的

Her courage was amazing. He could see the effort she made to regain her self-control, and soon she was once more calm.

"Let me get up now."

He gave her his hand and helped her to her feet. Taking her arm, he led her to the chair. She sat down wearily.

"Don't talk to me for a minute or two," she said.

"Very well."

When at last she spoke it was to say something which he did not expect. She gave a little sigh.

"I'm afraid I've made rather a mess of things," she said.

He did not answer, and once more there was a silence.

"Isn't it possible to get hold of the letter?" she said at last.

"I do not think anything would have been said to me about it, if the person in whose possession it is was not prepared to sell it."

"Who's got it?"

"The Chinese woman who was living in Hammond's house."

Aspot of colour flickered for an instant on Leslie's cheekbones.

"Does she want an awful lot for it?"

"I imagine that she has a very shrewd idea of its value. I doubt if it would be possible to get hold of it except for a very large sum."

"Are you going to let me be hanged?"

"Do you think it's so simple as all that to secure possession of an unwelcome piece of evidence? It's no different from suborning a witness. You have no right to make any such suggestion to me."

"Then what is going to happen to me?"

"Justice must take its course."

She grew very pale. A little shudder passed through her body.

"I put myself in your hands. Of course I have no right to ask you to do anything that isn't proper."

Mr. Joyce had not bargained for the little break in her voice which her

她的勇气令人惊叹。他能够看得出，她竭尽全力让自己恢复镇定，而且很快便就平静下来了。

“扶我起来吧。”

他向她伸出了自己的一只手，扶着她站立起来。他抓住她的一条胳膊，把她搀扶到椅子边。她有气无力地坐了下来。

“等一两分钟，先不要对我说话。”她说。

“很好。”

她最后开口说话时，便说出了一些出乎他的预料的情况。她微微地叹息了一声。

“我恐怕已经把事情弄得很糟糕了。”她说。

他没有接她的茬儿，又是一阵沉默。

“就没有办法把那封信搞到手了吗？”她最后说。

“我觉得，手上掌握着那封信的人若是没有要出卖信件的意思，那也不会有人来告诉我这个情况了。”

“信会在谁的手上呢？”

“住在哈蒙德家里的那位华人妇女。”

莱斯利脸部的颧骨上泛起一块红晕。

“她的要价会很高吗？”

“我觉得吧，那个女人头脑精明，知道此信很有价值。我寻思着，除非出大价，否则不可能得到那封信。”

“你会眼睁睁看着我被绞死吗？”

“你觉得把一件对我们很不利的证据搞到手是那么简单的事情吗？这与买通证人没有任何区别啊。你没有权利向我提出这样的建议。”

“那到头来我会是一个什么样的结果呢？”

“正义必定要得到伸张。”

她脸色煞白。身子微微地颤抖着。

“我把自己全交给你了，当然没有权利要求你做什么不合适的事情。”

乔伊斯先生不曾预料到，她说话声音中会出现些许

habitual self-restraint made quite intolerably moving. She looked at him with humble eyes, and he thought that if he rejected their appeal they would haunt him for the rest of his life. After all, nothing could bring poor Hammond back to life again. He wondered what really was the explanation of that letter. It was not fair to conclude from it that she had killed Hammond without provocation. He had lived in the East a long time and his sense of professional honour was not perhaps so acute as it had been twenty years before. He stared at the floor. He made up his mind to do something which he knew was unjustifiable, but it stuck in his throat and he felt dully resentful towards Leslie. It embarrassed him a little to speak.

"I don't know exactly what your husband's circumstances are?"

Flushing a rosy red, she shot a swift glance at him.

"He has a good many tin shares and a small share in two or three rubber estates. I suppose he could raise money."

"He would have to be told what it was for."

She was silent for a moment. She seemed to think.

"He's in love with me still. He would make any sacrifice to save me. Is there any need for him to see the letter?"

Mr. Joyce frowned a little, and, quick to notice, she went on.

"Robert is an old friend of yours. I'm not asking you to do anything for me, I'm asking you to save a rather simple, kind man who never did you any harm from all the pain that's possible."

Mr. Joyce did not reply. He rose to go and Mrs. Crosbie, with the grace that was natural to her, held out her hand. She was shaken by the scene, and her look was haggard, but she made a brave attempt to speed him with courtesy.

"It's so good of you to take all this trouble for me. I can't begin to tell you how grateful I am."

Mr. Joyce returned to his office. He sat in his own room, quite still, attempting to do no work, and pondered. His imagination brought him many

哽咽，她惯常的自我克制令这种哽咽很感人，让人受不了。她看着他，眼睛里流露出谦卑的神情。他感觉到，自己若是拒绝了那种乞求的目光，自己的下半辈子都恐怕摆脱不掉那种目光。毕竟说起来，不可能有任何力量能够让已故的哈蒙德死而复生。他想要知道，那封信的真相如何。如果凭借那封信得出结论，说她在没有受到任何挑衅的情况下便杀害了哈蒙德，这未免有失公正。乔伊斯先生在东方生活了很长时间，他的职业荣誉感可能也不像二十年前那样强烈了。他盯着地板看，心里打定了主意，准备做一件自己明明知道不公正的事情。不过，他觉得自己的喉咙哽咽住了，因此内心里感到对莱斯利有一种隐隐的憎恨。他开口说话时，感到有点尴尬。

“我不太清楚你丈夫那边的情况怎么样啊？”

她脸上涨得通红，很快瞥了他一眼。

“他持有大量的锡矿股份，两三座橡胶种植园中也有少量股份。我估计，他有办法筹到钱。”

“得告诉他钱款的用途啊。”

她沉默了片刻，好像是在思索。

“他仍然是爱我的。为了拯救我，他会愿意做出任何牺牲的。有必要让他看到那封信吗？”

乔伊斯稍稍皱了皱眉头。她很快便注意到了，于是接着说。

“罗伯特是你的老朋友。我这不是在求你帮我的忙，而是在求你帮一位淳朴、善良而且从未冒犯过你的人的忙，使其免受可能面临的痛苦。”

乔伊斯先生没有回答。他站起身离开。克罗斯比夫人举止自然，态度优雅，伸出了一只手。她对眼前的情景感到格外震惊，而且面容憔悴，但她仍然强打起精神，礼貌周到地同他告别。

“你真好，为了我的事情不辞辛劳。我对你的感激之情无法用言语表达。”

乔伊斯先生返回到了自己的律师事务所。他在自己的办公室里坐下，平静地坐着，不想干任何事情，只是

strange ideas. He shuddered a little. At last there was the discreet knock on the door which he was expecting. Ong Chi Seng came in.

"I was just going out to have my **tiffin**①, sir," he said.

"All right."

"I didn't know if there was anything you wanted before I went, sir."

"I don't think so. Did you make another appointment for Mr. Reed?"

"Yes, sir. He will come at three o'clock."

"Good."

Ong Chi Seng turned away, walked to the door, and put his long slim fingers on the handle. Then, as though on an afterthought, he turned back.

"Is there anything you wish me to say to my friend, sir?"

Although Ong Chi Seng spoke English so admirably he had still a difficulty with the letter R, and he pronounced it "fliend".

"What friend?"

"About the letter Mrs. Crosbie wrote to Hammond deceased, sir."

"Oh! I'd forgotten about that. I mentioned it to Mrs. Crosbie and she denies having written anything of the sort. It's evidently a forgery."

Mr. Joyce took the copy from his pocket and handed it to Ong Chi Seng. Ong Chi Seng ignored the gesture.

"In that case, sir, I suppose there would be no objection if my friend delivered the letter to the Deputy Public Prosecutor."

"None. But I don't quite see what good that would do your friend."

"My friend, sir, thought it was his duty in the interests of justice."

"I am the last man in the world to interfere with anyone who wishes to do his duty, Chi Seng."

The eyes of the lawyer and of the Chinese clerk met. Not the shadow of a smile hovered on the lips of either, but they understood each other perfectly.

"I quite understand, sir," said Ong Chi Seng, "but from my study of the case, R. v. Crosbie I am of the opinion that the production of such a letter would be

① tiffin ['tifin] *n.* 午餐

沉思着。他想象着，头脑中掠过许许多多怪异的念头。他微微地颤抖着。最后，终于响起来预料中的谨慎敲门声。王志成走了进来。

“我正要出去用午餐，先生。”他说。

“好吧。”

“不知道我离开之前，您是否还有什么吩咐的，先生。”

“没什么事。你另外约了里德先生吗？”

“约了，先生。他下午三点钟会过来。”

“很好。”

王志成转身离开，走到了门口，细长的手指放在门把手上。紧接着，他好像突然又想起了什么，转身返回。

“您有什么话想要我转告我朋友的吗，先生？”

尽管王志成英语说得很流利，但他发“R”音还是有困难，把“friend”发成了“fliend”。

“什么朋友？”

“同克罗斯比夫人写给已故哈蒙德的那封信有关的朋友，先生。”

“噢！我把这事都给忘了。我在克罗斯比夫人面前提到了这事，但她否认写过诸如此类的东西。那很显然是一封伪造的信啊。”

乔伊斯先生从自己的衣服口袋里掏出那封信的抄件，交还给王志成。王志成没有理会对方的动作。

“情况若是如此，我觉得，我朋友若是把信交给副检察长，那就不会有什么问题了。”

“毫无问题。但是，我看此事对你的那位朋友也不会带来什么好处的。”

“先生，我朋友认为，他有义务伸张正义。”

“有人若是想要履行好自己的义务，我是绝不可能会去干涉人家的，志成啊。”

律师和华人职员两个人的目光相遇了。双方的嘴边都没有呈现一丝笑容，但是，两个人都心照不宣。

“我非常清楚，先生，”王志成说，“但是，根据我对克罗斯比夫人案件的研究，我觉得，假如出示了这样

damaging to our client."

"I have always had a very high opinion of your legal acumen, Chi Seng."

"It has occurred to me, sir, that if I could persuade my friend to **induce**① the Chinese woman who has the letter to deliver it into our hands it would save a great deal of trouble."

Mr. Joyce idly drew faces on his blotting-paper.

"I suppose your friend is a business man. In what circumstances do you think he would be induced to part with the letter?"

"He has not got the letter. The Chinese woman has the letter. He is only a relation of the Chinese woman. She is an ignorant woman; she did not know the value of that letter till my **fliend**② told her."

"What value did he put on it?"

"Ten thousand dollars, sir."

"Good God! Where on earth do you suppose Mrs. Crosbie can get ten thousand dollars! I tell you the letter's a forgery."

He looked up at Ong Chi Seng as he spoke. The clerk was unmoved by the outburst. He stood at the side of the desk, civil, cool, and observant.

"Mr. Crosbie owns an eighth share of the Betong Rubber Estate and a sixth share of the Selantan River Rubber Estate. I have a friend who will lend him the money on the security of his property."

"You have a large circle of acquaintances, Chi Seng."

"Yes sir."

"Well, you can tell them all to go to hell. I would never advise Mr. Crosbie to give a penny more than five thousand for a letter that can be very easily explained."

"The Chinese woman does not want to sell the letter, sir. My fliend took a long time to persuade her. It is useless to offer her less than the sum mentioned."

Mr. Joyce looked at Ong Chi Seng for at least three minutes. The clerk bore the searching **scrutiny**① without embarrassment. He stood in a respectful

的一封信，那对我们的当事人是很不利的。”

“我可是一向都看好你在法律事务上的判断力啊，志成。”

“我有个想法，先生，那位华人妇女手上掌握着那封信，我若是能够说服我朋友敦促她把信交到我们手上，那可就省事多啦。”

乔伊斯先生漫不经心地在自己的吸墨纸上勾勒出各种脸谱。

“我估计，你那位朋友是个生意人。你觉得什么样的条件才能促使他交出信呢？”

“信不在他手上。那位华人妇女掌握着信呢。他只是那个华人妇女的亲戚而已。那女人不懂什么，我朋友告诉她之前，她根本就不知道那封信的价值。”

“他开的是什么价呢？”

“一万元，先生。”

“天哪！你觉得，克罗斯比夫人究竟从哪儿去弄到一万元啊！我告诉你，那封信是伪造的。”

乔伊斯先生一边说话一边抬头看了看王志成。这个职员面对对方激动的情绪时不动声色，而是站立在办公桌的另一边，彬彬有礼，态度冷静，观形察色。

“克罗斯比先生持有勿洞橡胶园八分之一的股份和南角河橡胶园六分之一的股份。用他的那些财产做抵押，我的一位朋友可以把钱借给他。”

“你认识的人还真是很多啊，志成。”

“是的，先生。”

“好啦，你可以告诉他们，让他们见鬼去。一封可以很容易解释清楚的信，最多值五千元。我决不会劝克罗斯比先生多出一个子儿。”

“那位华人妇女不想出售那封信啊，先生。我朋友费了很大功夫才说服了她。少于刚才说的那个数额，事情办不成的。”

乔伊斯先生打量着王志成至少有三分钟。职员坦然面对着这种审视的坚定目光，毫不感到窘迫。他站立着，

① induce [in'dju:s] *v.* 说服

② fliend 即 friend, 作者有意展现当地人口音，故如此拼写

③ scrutiny ['skru:tini] *n.* 详细审查

attitude with downcast eyes. Mr. Joyce knew his man. Clever fellow, Chi Seng, he thought, I wonder how much he's going to get out of it.

"Ten thousand dollars is a very large sum."

"Mr. Crosbie will certainly pay it rather than see his wife hanged, sir."

Again Mr. Joyce paused. What more did Chi Seng know than he had said? He must be pretty sure of his ground if he was obviously so unwilling to bargain. That sum had been fixed because whoever it was that was managing the affair knew it was the largest amount that Robert Crosbie could raise.

"Where is the Chinese woman now?" asked Mr. Joyce.

"She is staying at the house of my friend, sir."

"Will she come here?"

"I think it more better if you go to her, sir. I can take you to the house tonight and she will give you the letter. She is a very ignorant woman, sir, and she does not understand cheques."

"I wasn't thinking of giving her a cheque. I will bring banknotes with me."

"It would only be waste of valuable time to bring less than ten thousand dollars, sir."

"I quite understand."

"I will go and tell my friend after I have had my tiffin, sir."

"Very good. You'd better meet me outside the club at ten o'clock tonight."

"With pleasure, sir," said Ong Chi Seng.

He gave Mr. Joyce a little bow and left the room. Mr. Joyce went out to have luncheon, too. He went to the club and here, as he had expected, he saw Robert Crosbie. He was sitting at a crowded table, and as he passed him, looking for a place, Mr. Joyce touched him on the shoulder.

"I'd like a word or two with you before you go," he said.

"Right you are. Let me know when you're ready."

Mr. Joyce had made up his mind how to tackle him. He played a rubber of bridge after luncheon in order to allow time for the club to empty itself. He did

眼睛朝下看，一副毕恭毕敬的姿态。乔伊斯先生了解自己的手下。聪明的家伙，志成啊，他心里想着，我真是不知道他自己能够从中捞取多少好处。

“一万元可是个大数额啊。”

“克罗斯比先生肯定宁可支付这个数额，也不愿意眼睁睁看着自己的夫人被绞死的，先生。”

乔伊斯先生再次陷入了沉思。除了所说的情况之外，志成还知道些什么？既然他明显不愿意讨价还价，说明他一定心里很有数了。之所以确定这么个数额，那是因为，不管从中运作的人是谁，他一定知道，这个数额是罗伯特·克罗斯比能够筹集到的最多钱款。

“那位华人妇女现在在哪儿呢？”乔伊斯先生问了一声。

“她眼下待在我朋友的家里，先生。”

“她会来这儿吗？”

“我觉得，最好还是您去找她，先生。我今晚可以领着您去那个人家里。她会把信给您。她是个什么都不懂的女人啊，先生。她连支票是怎么回事都不懂。”

“我本来就没有考虑给她支票。我会带现金去的。”

“您若是带去的钱少于一万元，那只会浪费宝贵的时间，先生。”

“我心里有数。”

“我用过午餐后就去告诉我的朋友，先生。”

“很好。你最好今晚十点钟在俱乐部外面和我会面。”

“没有问题，先生。”王志成说。

他对着乔伊斯先生微微鞠了一躬，离开了办公室。乔伊斯先生也出去用午餐了。他去了俱乐部。正如他预料的那样，他在那儿看到了罗伯特·克罗斯比。后者坐在一张挤满了人的桌子边，乔伊斯先生寻找位子经过他身边时，触碰了一下他的肩膀。

“你离开前我有几句话对你说。”乔伊斯先生说。

“好吧，你吃完后招呼我一声就行。”

该如何同罗伯特·克罗斯比谈，乔伊斯先生已经有了主意了。他用过午餐后打了一局桥牌消磨时间，目的

not want on this particular matter to see Crosbie in his office. Presently Crosbie came into the card-room and looked on till the game was finished. The other players went on with their various affairs, and the two were left alone.

"A rather unfortunate thing has happened, old man," said Mr. Joyce, in a tone which he sought to render as casual as possible. "It appears that your wife sent a letter to Hammond asking him to come to the bungalow on the night he was killed."

"But that's impossible," cried Crosbie. "She's always stated that she had had no communication with Hammond. I know from my own knowledge that she hadn't set eyes on him for a couple of months."

"The fact remains that the letter exists. It's in the possession of the Chinese woman Hammond was living with. Your wife meant to give you a present on your birthday, and she wanted Hammond to help her get it. In the emotional excitement that she suffered from after the tragedy, she forgot all about it, and having once denied having any communication with Hammond she was afraid to say that she had made a mistake. It was, of course, very unfortunate, but I daresay it was not unnatural."

Crosbie did not speak. His large, red face bore an expression of complete bewilderment, and Mr. Joyce was at once relieved and exasperated by his lack of comprehension. He was a stupid man, and Mr. Joyce had no patience with stupidity. But his distress since the catastrophe had touched a soft spot in the lawyer's heart; and Mrs. Crosbie had struck the right note when she asked him to help her, not for her sake, but for her husband's.

"I need not tell you that it would be very awkward if this letter found its way into the hands of the prosecution. Your wife has lied, and she would be asked to explain the lie. It alters things a little if Hammond did not intrude, an unwanted guest, but came to your house by invitation. It would be easy to arouse in the assessors a certain indecision of mind."

Mr. Joyce hesitated. He was face to face now with his decision. If it had

是等俱乐部里面的人都离开。他不想因为这样一件很特别的事情让别人看见克罗斯比在他的事务所里出现。不一会儿，克罗斯比进入了桥牌室，在一旁当看客，一直等到桥牌打完了。另外几位一同玩桥牌的人都忙自己的事情去了，房间里就剩下他们二位。

“出了一个挺不幸的情况啊，老朋友，”乔伊斯先生说，说话的语气尽可能显得随意。“看起来，哈蒙德遇害的那天夜里，你夫人给他去了个信，邀请他到你们府上的孟加拉平房去。”

“但这事不可能呀，”克罗斯比大声说，“她一直都说，她先前根本没有和哈蒙德联系过。就我所知，她已经有几个月没有见过他啦。”

“事实上，那封信是存在的。信眼下在与哈蒙德同居的那个华人妇女手上。你夫人打算给你一件生日礼物。她想要哈蒙德替她办理。悲剧发生之后，她情绪过于激动，竟然把这件事情忘得一干二净了。由于先前否认了同哈蒙德有过联系，所以，她担心前面说错了话。这件事情当然很不幸，但是，我觉得，也不是什么违背常理的事情。”

克罗斯比没有吭声。他宽大的红脸庞上挂着一副完全困惑茫然的表情。乔伊斯先生看见他一副懵懂迟钝的样子，立刻感到既宽慰又愤慨。他是脑袋不开窍的人，乔伊斯先生面对愚笨迟钝的行为没有耐性。但是，悲剧发生之后，律师看见他一副痛苦悲伤的姿态，心也软了，深表同情。克罗斯比夫人请求律师帮她的忙时，说到她不是为了她自己，而是为了她丈夫。此话更是触动了他的心弦。

“用不着我告诉你，此信若是落到了检察官的手上，那事情会有多么被动。你夫人说了谎话，而她会被要求解释为何说谎。哈蒙德如若不是个不速之客，而是你夫人邀请人家来的，那情况就稍微有点不同了。陪审团成员在做出裁定时就很容易动摇心思。”

乔伊斯先生犹豫迟疑着，现在正是面临着要做出决

been a time for humour, he could have smiled at the reflection that he was taking so grave a step, and that the man for whom he was taking it had not the smallest conception of its gravity. If he gave the matter a thought, he probably imagined that what Mr. Joyce was doing was what any lawyer did in the ordinary run of business.

"My dear Robert, you are not only my client, but my friend. I think we must get hold of that letter. It'll cost a good deal of money. Except for that I should have preferred to say nothing to you about it."

"How much?"

"Ten thousand dollars."

"That's a devil of a lot. With the slump and one thing and another it'll take just about all I've got."

"Can you get it at once?"

"I suppose so. Old Charlie Meadows will let me have it on my tin shares and on those two estates I'm interested in."

"Then will you?"

"Is it absolutely necessary?"

"If you want your wife to be acquitted."

Crosbie grew very red. His mouth sagged strangely.

"But..." he could not find words, his face now was purple. "But I don't understand. She can explain. You don't mean to say they'd find her guilty? They couldn't hang her for putting a noxious vermin out of the way."

"Of course they wouldn't hang her. They might only find her guilty of manslaughter. She'd probably get off with two or three years."

Crosbie started to his feet and his red face was distraught with horror.

"Three years."

Then something seemed to dawn in that slow intelligence of his. His mind was darkness across which shot suddenly a flash of lightning, and though the succeeding darkness was as profound, there remained the memory of something

断的时刻。他想到眼下自己正要替另外一个人决定采取一个至关重要的措施，而那个人却丝毫未领会事情的重要性。如若这是幽默的时候，他准备笑出来的。克罗斯比若是再仔细想一想，说不定他会认为，乔伊斯先生所做的事情同一位律师代理普通案件时所做的一样呢。

“亲爱的罗伯特，你不仅是我的代理人，而且还是我的朋友啊。我认为，我们必须要把那封信弄到手。那样做需要花费一大笔钱呢。要不是因为这个原因，关于这件事情，我宁可什么都不同你说。”

“要多少钱？”

“一万元。”

“这笔数额大得惊人。现在生意不景气，加上这样那样的开支，这差不多要耗尽我的全部家当啦。”

“你能否立刻筹措到这笔钱？”

“我估计能够吧。我若是把锡矿的股份和另外那两家地产的权益用来做抵押，老查理·梅多斯会把钱借给我的。”

“那你准备这样做吗？”

“是否绝对需要这样做呢？”

“你若是想要你夫人无罪释放的话。”

克罗斯比脸涨得通红，嘴向下耷拉着，显得很怪异。

“但是……”他找不到合适词来表达，脸部现在成了紫色，“但是，我不理解。她可以做出解释的。你该不会是说他们认为她确实有罪吧？他们不会因为她除掉了一个流氓恶棍而绞死她吧。”

“他们当然不会绞死她。他们只能判她犯了杀人罪。她可能要坐过两三年牢。”

克罗斯比怔了一下站立起来，涨红了的脸庞因恐惧而变了形。

“三年。”

这时候，克罗斯比迟钝的脑袋似乎有点开窍了。他漆黑一团的内心现在突然闪过了一道亮光。尽管接下来黑暗还是那么深沉，但那儿却是有了对某种看不见的东西的记

not seen but perhaps just descried. Mr. Joyce saw that Crosbie's big red hands, coarse and hard with all the odd jobs he had set them to, trembled.

"What was the present she wanted to make me?"

"She says she wanted to give you a new gun."

Once more that great red face flushed a deeper red.

"When have you got to have the money ready?"

There was something odd in his voice now. It sounded as though he spoke with invisible hands clutching at his throat.

"At ten o'clock tonight. I thought you could bring it to my office at about six."

"Is the woman coming to you?"

"No, I'm going to her."

"I'll bring the money. I'll come with you."

Mr. Joyce looked at him sharply.

"Do you think there's any need for you to do that? I think it would be better if you left me to deal with this matter by myself."

"It's my money, isn't it? I'm going to come."

Mr. Joyce shrugged his shoulders. They rose and shook hands. Mr. Joyce looked at him curiously.

At ten o'clock they met in the empty club.

"Everything all right?" asked Mr. Joyce.

"Yes. I've got the money in my pocket."

"Let's go then."

They walked down the steps. Mr. Joyce's car was waiting for them in the square, silent at that hour, and as they came to it Ong Chi Seng stepped out of the shadow of a house. He took his seat beside the driver and gave him a direction. They drove past the Hotel de l'Europe and turned up by the Sailors' Home to get into Victoria Street. Here the Chinese shops were still open, idlers lounged about, and in the road-way rickshaws and motor-cars and gharries gave a busy air to the scene. Suddenly their car stopped and Chi Seng turned round.

"I think it more better if we walk here, sir," he said.

忆烙印。乔伊斯先生看到，克罗斯比那双通红的大手颤抖着，那双手因为干过各种各样的活儿变得粗糙坚实。

“她想要送我个什么礼物来着？”

“她说，她打算送你一支新枪。”

克罗斯比宽大的脸庞涨得更红了。

“你需要什么时候把钱筹措好呢？”

现在，克罗斯比说话时显得有点怪异，听起来好像有一双无形的手扼住了喉咙似的。

“今晚十点钟吧。我认为，你可以在六点钟左右把钱带到我的事务所去。”

“那个女人会去见你吗？”

“不会，我去见她。”

“我带上钱，和你一块儿去。”

乔伊斯先生看了他一眼，目光犀利。

“你觉得你这样做有这个必要吗？我认为，你若是把这件事情交由我一个人来办，结果会更加理想一些。”

“但那是我的钱，对吧？我要去。”

乔伊斯先生耸了耸肩膀。他们站起身，握手告别。乔伊斯先生看着对方，充满了好奇的目光。

晚上十点钟，他们在空无一人的俱乐部见面了。

“全都准备好了吗？”乔伊斯先生问了一声。

“准备好了，钱在我的衣服口袋里面呢。”

“那我们就走吧。”

他们走下了台阶。乔伊斯先生的汽车在广场上等着他们。这时候，广场上一片寂静。他们走到汽车旁边时，王志成从一幢房屋的阴影处走了出来。他在汽车的副驾驶位置上坐了下来，给司机指路。汽车从欧洲饭店旁边驶过，然后在“水手之家”旁边拐弯，驶入维多利亚大街。街道上的华人店铺仍然还在营业，无所事事的人还在闲逛着。街道中间，人力车、汽车和出租马车来来往往，一幅热闹景象。他们的车突然停了下来，王志成转过头来。

“我觉得，我们从这儿走过去比较好些，先生。”他说。

They got out and he went on. They followed a step or two behind. Then he asked them to stop.

"You wait here, sir. I go in and speak to my fliend."

He went into a shop, open to the street, where three or four Chinese were standing behind the counter. It was one of those strange shops where nothing was on view, and you wondered what it was they sold there. They saw him address a stout man in a duck suit with a large gold chain across his breast, and the man shot a quick glance out into the night. He gave Chi Seng a key and Chi Seng came out. He beckoned to the two men waiting and slid into a doorway at the side of the shop. They followed him and found themselves at the foot of a flight of stairs.

"If you wait a minute I will light a match," he said, always resourceful. "You come upstairs, please."

He held a Japanese match in front of them, but it scarcely dispelled the darkness and they groped their way up behind him. On the first floor he unlocked a door and going in lit a gas-jet.

"Come in, please," he said.

It was a small square room, with one window, and the only furniture consisted of two low Chinese beds covered with matting. In one corner was a large chest, with an elaborate lock, and on this stood a shabby tray with an opium pipe on it and a lamp. There was in the room the faint, acrid scent of the drug. They sat down and Ong Chi Seng offered them cigarettes. In a moment the door was opened by the fat Chinaman whom they had seen behind the counter. He bade them good-evening in very good English, and sat down by the side of his fellow-countryman.

"The Chinese woman is just coming," said Chi Seng.

A boy from the shop brought in a tray with a teapot and cups and the Chinaman offered them a cup of tea. Crosbie refused. The Chinese talked to one another in undertones, but Crosbie and Mr. Joyce were silent. At last there was the sound of a voice outside; someone was calling in a low tone;

他们下了车，王志成走在前面，他们在后面相差一两步跟着。他随即叫他们停下来。

“您在此等着，先生。我进去同我朋友说一声。”

他走进了一家店铺，是朝街面开着的，柜台后面站立着三四个华人。有些店铺很奇怪，看不到陈列了什么，人们不知道他们经营什么商品的。这家店铺就属于那种。他们看见王志成对着一位身体结实的男子说话。那人身穿帆布衣服，胸前挂着一条很粗的金链子，朝着外面的夜色快速瞥了一眼。他给了志成一把钥匙，志成便走出来了。他想着两个等待的人示意，进入了店铺旁边的一道侧门。他们跟随在后面，到达了一段楼梯脚下。

“稍等，我划根火柴，”他说着，总是一副有办法的样子，“请上楼吧。”

他点亮了一根日本火柴在前面引路，但是，火柴的亮光无法驱散黑暗。他们在他身后摸索着上楼。上到了二楼后，他打开了一扇房门，进入后点亮了一盏煤气灯。

“请进来。”他喊了一声。

这是个方方正正的小房间，只有一扇窗户，里面就只摆放了两张铺着垫子的中国式矮床。房间的一角摆放着一只大箱子，用一把精巧的锁锁着。箱子上面有一只破旧的托盘，托盘上摆着一管吸食鸦片的烟枪和烟灯。房间里弥漫着一股淡淡的苦涩烟草味儿。他们坐了下来，王志成递给他们烟卷。不一会儿，房门打开了，进来一位胖墩墩的华人，就是他们刚才看见站在柜台后面的那位。他用十分纯正的英语同打招呼，问晚安，然后在他的华人同胞身边坐下来。

“那位华人妇女马上就来了。”志成说。

店铺里跑腿的端着一只托盘进来了，上面放着茶壶和茶杯。胖胖的华人给他们每人倒了一杯茶。克罗斯比谢绝了。几个华人相互间低声交谈着，但是，克罗斯比和乔伊斯先生默不作声。最后，室外传来有人说话的声音。有人小声叫门。胖华人走向门边。他打开了门，说了几句话，然后领着个女人进入房间。乔伊斯先生看着

and the Chinaman went to the door. He opened it, spoke a few words, and **ushered**① a woman in. Mr. Joyce looked at her. He had heard much about her since Hammond's death, but he had never seen her. She was a stoutish person, not very young, with a broad, phlegmatic face, she was powdered and rouged and her eyebrows were a thin black line, but she gave you the impression of a woman of character. She wore a pale blue jacket and a white skirt, her costume was not quite European nor quite Chinese, but on her feet were little Chinese silk slippers. She wore heavy gold chains round her neck, gold bangles on her wrists, gold ear-rings and elaborate gold pins in her black hair. She walked in slowly, with the air of a woman sure of herself, but with a certain heaviness of tread, and sat down on the bed beside Ong Chi Seng. He said something to her and nodding she gave an incurious glance at the two white men.

"Has she got the letter?" asked Mr. Joyce.

"Yes, sir."

Crosbie said nothing, but produced a roll of five-hundred-dollar notes. He counted out twenty and handed them to Chi Seng.

"Will you see if that is correct?"

The clerk counted them and gave them to the fat Chinaman.

"Quite correct, sir."

The Chinaman counted them once more and put them in his pocket. He spoke again to the woman and she drew from her bosom a letter. She gave it to Chi Seng who cast his eyes over it.

"This is the right document, sir," he said, and was about to give it to Mr. Joyce when Crosbie took it from him.

"Let me look at it," he said.

Mr. Joyce watched him read and then held out his hand for it.

"You'd better let me have it."

Crosbie folded it up deliberately and put it in his pocket.

"No, I'm going to keep it myself. It's cost me enough money."

Mr. Joyce made no **rejoinder**②. The three Chinese watched the little passage,

她。自从哈蒙德死亡之后，关于她的事情，乔伊斯先生听到的可多了，但从未谋过面。女人的体态显得有点胖，不太年轻，宽大的脸庞毫无表情。她脸上涂过脂粉，五官粗糙，两道眉毛描得又细又黑。但人们看到她后会觉得，这是个有个性的女人。她身穿淡蓝色的上衣，白色的裙子，穿着打扮既不属于欧式的，也不属于中式的，不过脚上倒是趿拉着一双很小的中国式丝绸拖鞋。她脖子上挂着沉甸甸的金项链，手腕上戴着金手镯，耳朵上吊着金坠子，乌黑的头发上别着精致的金簪子。她缓步进入房间，一副很自信的姿态，只是步态略显沉重。她在床上坐下，紧挨着王志成。他对她说了句什么。她点了点头，漫不经心地朝着两个白人瞥了一眼。

“她把信带过来了吗？”乔伊斯先生问了一声。

“带过来了，先生。”

卡罗斯比没有吭声，但掏出了一卷五百元的钞票。他数出了二十张，交给了志成。

“看看是不是这个数好吗？”

职员把钱数了一遍，随即交给了胖华人。

“没错，先生。”

那位又数了一遍，把钱放进了自己的衣服口袋里。他又对着那个女人说话，女人从胸前掏出一封信。她把信交给了志成，志成看了看信。

“正是那封信呢，先生。”他说，正要把信给乔伊斯先生，但克罗斯比却一把从他手上夺过了信。

“让我看一看吧。”克罗斯比说。

乔伊斯先生看着他把信读完，然后伸手要信。

“你最好还是让我拿着信。”

克罗斯比小心翼翼地把信折起来，然后放入自己的衣服口袋里。

“不，信还是由我自己保管着，我可是花费了够多钱啊。”

乔伊斯先生没有反驳。三位华人观看着这一段小小的插曲，但脸上毫无表情，心里对此是怎么想的，或者

① usher [ˈʌʃə] *v.* 带领

② rejoinder [riˈdʒɔində] *n.* 反驳

but what they thought about it, or whether they thought, it was impossible to tell from their impassive countenances. Mr. Joyce rose to his feet.

"Do you want me any more tonight, sir?" said Ong Chi Seng.

"No." He knew that the clerk wished to stay behind in order to get his agreed share of the money, and he turned to Crosbie. "Are you ready?"

Crosbie did not answer, but stood up. The Chinaman went to the door and opened it for them. Chi Seng found a bit of candle and lit it in order to light them down, and the two Chinese accompanied them to the street. They left the woman sitting quietly on the bed smoking a cigarette. When they reached the street the Chinese left them and went once more upstairs.

"What are you going to do with that letter?" asked Mr. Joyce.

"Keep it."

They walked to where the car was waiting for them and here Mr. Joyce offered his friend a lift. Crosbie shook his head.

"I'm going to walk." He hesitated a little and shuffled his feet. "I went to Singapore on the night of Hammond's death partly to buy a new gun that a man I knew wanted to dispose of. Good-night."

He disappeared quickly into the darkness.

Mr. Joyce was quite right about the trial. The assessors went into court fully determined to acquit Mrs. Crosbie. She gave evidence on her own behalf. She told her story simply and with straightforwardness. The DPP was a kindly man and it was plain that he took no great pleasure in his task. He asked the necessary questions in a deprecating manner. His speech for the prosecution might really have been a speech for the defence, and the assessors took less than five minutes to consider their popular verdict. It was impossible to prevent the great outburst of applause with which it was received by the crowd that packed the court house. The judge congratulated Mrs. Crosbie and she was a free woman.

No one had expressed a more violent disapprobation of Hammond's behaviour than Mrs. Joyce; she was a woman loyal to her friends and she

是否有想法，无从知晓。乔伊斯先生站起身。

“您今晚还有什么事情需要我做的吗，先生？”王志成问了一声。

“没有了。”乔伊斯先生知道，他的职员想要留在后面，以便分到他们事先商定好了的钱数，于是转身对着克罗斯比，“可以走了吧？”

克罗斯比没有接话，但站立起来了。胖子华人走向门边，替他们打开了门。志成找到了一小段蜡烛，点亮了，照着他们下楼，两位华人一直陪伴他们到了街上。他们让那个妇女留在房间里，安安静静地坐在床上，抽着烟卷。他们一行人到达街上后，两位华人同他们告辞，再次返回到了楼上。

“你打算拿这封信做什么啊？”乔伊斯先生问了一声。

“保留着。”

他们走到了汽车等待他们的地方。乔伊斯先生提出要捎自己的朋友一程，克罗斯比摇了摇头。

“我打算走一走。”他犹豫迟疑了片刻，但缓慢地挪动着脚步。“哈蒙德死亡的那天晚上，我之所以去了新加坡，部分原因就是为了去买一支新枪，因为我的一位熟人想要脱手卖掉。晚安吧。”

克罗斯比很快便消失在了黑暗中。

关于审判的事情，果然不出乔伊斯先生所料。陪审团走进法庭时，信心满满，一致决定要无罪释放克罗斯比夫人。她为自己提供了证词，叙述了事情的经过，简明扼要，直截了当。副检察长是个善良之辈。很显然，他履行自己的使命时并不是很开心。他提出了几个必要的问题，态度显得不以为然。他代表公诉方的陈词实际上可以当成对被告的辩护词。陪审团商议不到五分钟便做出了令人称快的裁决。法庭内挤满了人，宣判过后，人群中爆发出了雷鸣般的掌声，经久不息，无法阻止。法官向克罗斯比夫人表示祝贺，她已重获自由。

人们对哈蒙德的行径表达了强烈的谴责，但态度强烈者莫过于乔伊斯夫人。她对自己的朋友们诚挚忠诚，

had insisted on the Crosbies' staying with her after the trial, for she in common with everyone else had no doubt of the result, till they could make arrangements to go away. It was out of the question for poor, dear, brave Leslie to return to the bungalow at which the horrible catastrophe had taken place. The trial was over by half-past twelve and when they reached the Joyces' house a grand luncheon was awaiting them. Cocktails were ready, Mrs. Joyce's million-dollar cocktail was celebrated through all the Malay States, and Mrs. Joyce drank Leslie's health. She was a talkative, vivacious woman, and now she was in the highest spirits. It was fortunate, for the rest of them were silent. She did not wonder, her husband never had much to say, and the other two were naturally exhausted from the long strain to which they had been subjected. During luncheon she carried on a bright and spirited monologue. Then coffee was served.

"Now, children," she said in her gay, bustling fashion, "you must have a rest and after tea I shall take you both for a drive to the sea."

Mr. Joyce, who lunched at home only by exception, had of course to go back to his office.

"I'm afraid I can't do that, Mrs. Joyce," said Crosbie. "I've got to get back to the estate at once."

"Not today?" she cried.

"Yes, now. I've neglected it for too long and I have urgent business. But I shall be very grateful if you will keep Leslie until we have decided what to do."

Mrs. Joyce was about to expostulate, but her husband prevented her.

"If he must go, he must, and there's an end of it."

There was something in the lawyer's tone which made her look at him quickly. She held her tongue and there was a moment's silence. Then Crosbie spoke again.

"If you'll forgive me, I'll start at once so that I can get there before dark."

审判过后，坚持要克罗斯比夫妇住到她家里去，因为她和其他每一个人一样，对于审判的结果毫不怀疑，等到克罗斯比夫妇能够做出安排离开再说。绝对不能让可怜、可爱而又勇敢的莱斯利返回到那幢孟加拉平房去，那儿可是发生过那桩恐怖的灾难之地啊。审判十二点半钟结束，他们到达乔伊斯的宅邸时，那儿已经备好了丰盛的午餐，调好了鸡尾酒。乔伊斯夫人价值百万的鸡尾酒在整个马来联邦闻名遐迩。乔伊斯夫人为莱斯利的健康干杯。她是个能言善聊、性情活泼的女人，此时正情绪高涨。幸亏如此，因为其他人全都沉默不语。她倒是并不觉得很奇怪，因为自己丈夫本来就话不多。至于另外两个人，这么长时间以来一直精神紧张，备受煎熬，自然精疲力竭了。午餐期间，她一个人兴致勃勃，情绪高昂，一直独白着。然后，咖啡上来了。

“好啦，孩子们，”她说着，说话的态度兴高采烈，风风火火，“你们一定得好好休息一下，喝过茶后，我开车带你们到海边兜风去。”

乔伊斯先生本来很少在家用午餐，当然要回到事务所去。

“恐怕不行啊，乔伊斯夫人，”克罗斯比说，“我得立刻返回到种植园去。”

“今天不回去可以吗？”她大声说。

“要回去，就现在。我已经很长时间没有顾及到种植园里的事情了，有些紧要的事情要去处理。但是，你若是把莱斯利留下来待一阵子，等到我们决定该怎么办，我将不胜感激。”

乔伊斯夫人想要再次挽留他，但她丈夫制止了她。

“他若是一定要离开，他就一定会离开，就这样吧。”

律师说话的口气有弦外之音，她急忙看着他。她打住没有说下去，一时间，在场的人全都沉默不语。后来还是克罗斯比重新开口说话。

“你若是肯谅解我，我这就出发了，这样可以在天黑

He rose from the table. "Will you come and see me off, Leslie?"

"Of course."

They went out of the dining-room together.

"I think that's rather inconsiderate of him," said Mrs. Joyce. "He must know that Leslie wants to be with him just now."

"I'm sure he wouldn't go if it wasn't absolutely necessary."

"Well, I'll just see that Leslie's room is ready for her. She wants a complete rest, of course, and then amusement."

Mrs. Joyce left the room and Joyce sat down again. In a short time he heard Crosbie start the engine of his motorcycle and then noisily **scrunch**① over the **gravel**② of the garden path. He got up and went into the drawing-room. Mrs. Crosbie was standing in the middle of it, looking into space, and in her hand was an open letter. He recognized it. She gave him a glance as he came in and saw that she was deathly pale.

"He knows," she whispered.

Mr. Joyce went up to her and took the letter from her hand. He lit a match and set the paper afire. She watched it burn. When he could hold it no longer he dropped it on the tiled floor and they both looked at the paper curl and blacken. Then he trod it into ashes with his foot.

"What does he know?"

She gave him a long, long stare and into her eyes came a strange look. Was it contempt or despair? Mr. Joyce could not tell.

"He knows that Geoff was my lover."

Mr. Joyce made no movement and uttered no sound.

"He'd been my lover for years. He became my lover almost immediately after he came back from the war. We knew how careful we must be. When we became lovers I pretended I was tired of him, and he seldom came to the house when Robert was there. I used to drive out to a place we knew and he met me, two or three times a week, and when Robert went to Singapore he used to come to the bungalow late, when the boys had gone for the night.

前赶到那儿。”他从桌子边站起身。“送送我好吗，莱斯利？”

“当然可以。”

夫妻二人一同离开餐厅。

“我觉得他不太会体贴人，”乔伊斯夫人说，“他一定知道，此时此刻，莱斯利想要同他待在一块儿。”

“我可以肯定，他若不是迫不得已，绝不可能离开。”

“好吧，我去看看莱斯利的房间是否收拾好了。她当然需要彻底的休息，然后去娱乐一番。”

乔伊斯夫人离开了餐厅，乔伊斯重新坐了下来。不久，他听见克罗斯比发动了汽车的声音，然后是轮子碾过花园碎石路面时发出的吵闹的嘎吱声。乔伊斯先生站起身，进入客厅。克罗斯比夫人站立在客厅的正中央，怔怔地发呆，手上拿着一封展开的信。他认出了她手上的信。他进入客厅时，她瞥了他一眼。他看到，她脸色苍白。

① scrunch [skrʌntʃ] *v.* 碾

② gravel ['grævəl] *n.* 沙砾

“他知道了。”她轻声地说。

乔伊斯先生走向她身边，从她手上拿过信。他划了根火柴，点燃了信纸。她眼看着信纸付之一炬。等火快烧到手指时，他便把它扔到了砖头地上。两个人看着信纸卷缩变黑。他随后在上面踏上一脚，烧黑的信纸变成了灰烬。

“他知道什么了？”

她久久地盯着他看，眼睛里充满了奇异的目光。那是蔑视的目光呢，还是绝望的目光？乔伊斯先生无法辨认。

“他知道了，杰夫是我的情人。”

乔伊斯先生一动不动，一声未吭。

“多年来，他一直是我的情人。他差不多刚从战场上回来就立刻成了我的情人。我们知道，我们必须得谨小慎微。我们相好之后，我假装表现得厌恶他。罗伯特在家时，他也极少到家里来。我往往开车到我们熟悉的一处地方去，他在那儿同我会面，一个星期有个两三回。罗伯特若是去了新加坡，他便会在夜深人静时到孟加拉平房去，因为仆人全都已经就寝了。我们一直都相互会面来着，没有任何

We saw one another constantly, all the time, and not a soul had the smallest suspicion of it. And then lately, a year ago, he began to change. I didn't know what was the matter. I couldn't believe that he didn't care for me any more. He always denied it. I was frantic. I **made him scenes**①. Sometimes I thought he hated me. Oh, if you knew what agonies I endured. I passed through hell. I knew he didn't want me any more and I wouldn't let him go. Misery! Misery! I loved him. I'd given him everything. He was all my life. And then I heard he was living with a Chinese woman. I couldn't believe it. I wouldn't believe it. At last I saw her, I saw her with my own eyes, walking in the village, with her gold bracelets and her necklaces, an old, fat, Chinese woman. She was older than I was. Horrible! They all knew in the kampong that she was his mistress. And when I passed her, she looked at me and I knew that she knew I was his mistress too. I sent for him. I told him I must see him. You've read the letter. I was mad to write it. I didn't know what I was doing. I didn't care. I hadn't seen him for ten days. It was a lifetime. And when last we'd parted he took me in his arms and kissed me, and told me not to worry. And he went straight from my arms to hers."

She had been speaking in a low voice, vehemently, and now she stopped and wrung her hands.

"That damned letter. We'd always been so careful. He always tore up any word I wrote to him the moment he'd read it. How was I to know he'd leave that one? He came, and I told him I knew about the Chinawoman. He denied it. He said it was only scandal. I was beside myself. I don't know what I said to him. Oh, I hated him then. I tore him limb from limb. I said everything I could to wound him. I insulted him. I could have spat in his face. And at last he turned on me. He told me he was sick and tired of me and never wanted to see me again. He said I bored him to death. And then he acknowledged that it was true about the Chinawoman. He said he'd known her for years, before the war, and she was the only woman who really meant anything to him, and the rest was just

① make scenes 大吵大闹

人起过一丁点儿疑心。但是，到了近期，一年前的样子，他开始有了变化。我不知道其中的原由。我不相信，他会不再在乎我了。他一直都否认来着。我情绪疯狂，在他面前大吵大闹。有时候，我都觉得他恨我。噢，你若是知道我内心忍受着多大的痛苦该有多好啊。我仿佛在地狱里面过日子。我知道，他不再想要我了，但我不能让他走。悲痛啊！悲痛啊！我爱他。为了爱，我可以给他一切。他是我整个生命。后来，我听说他与一位华人女人同居了。这事我简直不能相信。这事我简直不愿意相信。最后，我见到她了，我亲眼见到了她，戴着金手镯和金项链，在村庄上走着，一个又老又胖的华人女人。她年纪比我更大。简直可怕啊！村上的人全都知道，她是他的情妇。我从她身边经过时，她盯着我看。我知道，她知道我也是他的情人。我派人去找他，告诉他说，我一定要见他。你已经看过这封信了。我情绪疯狂才写了这封信的。我简直不知道自己在干什么。但我不在乎。我先前有十天没有见到他。那简直就像是一辈子啊。我们最后分别时，他把我搂在怀里，还吻了我，告诉我说不用担心。而他却从我的怀里直接投入到了她的怀抱。”

她说话的声音一直很低，但情绪激动。她此时停了下来，用力搓揉着双手。

“这封该死的信。我们一直都做得小心谨慎。但凡我写给他的信，他都是一看完便撕毁。我怎么会知道他竟然留下了这一封啊？他来了，我告诉他说，我知道那个华人女人的事情。他矢口否认。他说这是有人造谣生事。我情绪失控了，都不知道自己对他说了些什么话。噢，我这时恨他了。我对着他又撕又扯来着。我尽说些伤害他的话，侮辱他，还可能还朝着他脸上啐了一口唾沫。最后，他对我发火了。他说他讨厌我了，烦腻我了，永远都不想再见到我。他说我令他烦死了。随后，他承认，那个华人女人的事情是真的。他说他认识她有很多年了，那是在战争爆发之前，她是他真正在乎的女人，同其他女人在一块儿时都只是逢场作戏而已。他说我知道了这件

pastime. And he said he was glad I knew, and now at least I'd leave him alone. And then I don't know what happened, I was beside myself, I saw red. I seized the revolver and I fired. He gave a cry and I saw I'd hit him. He staggered and rushed for the veranda. I ran after him and fired again. He fell, and I stood over him and I fired and fired till the revolver went click, click, and I knew there were no more **cartridges**①."

At last she stopped, panting. Her face was no longer human, it was distorted with cruelty, and rage and pain. You would never have thought that this quiet, refined woman was capable of such fiendish passion. Mr. Joyce took a step backwards. He was absolutely aghast at the sight of her. It was not a face, it was a gibbering, hideous mask. Then they heard a voice calling from another room, a loud, friendly, cheerful voice. It was Mrs. Joyce.

"Come along, Leslie darling, your room's ready. You must be dropping with sleep."

Mrs. Crosbie's features gradually composed themselves. Those passions, so clearly delineated, were smoothed away as with your hand you would smooth a crumpled paper, and in a minute the face was cool and calm and unlined. She was a trifle pale, but her lips broke into a pleasant, **affable**② smile. She was once more the well-bred and even distinguished woman.

"I'm coming, Dorothy dear. I'm sorry to give you so much trouble."

事情，他很高兴，现在至少可以让他清静了。后来，我不知道发生了什么事情，我情绪失控了，怒火中烧。我抓起手枪，开了枪。他惨叫了一声，我知道，枪击中了他。他踉踉跄跄，冲向了露台。我追赶了上去，再次开枪。他倒下了，我站立在他身边，开了一枪又一枪，直到手枪发出咔哒咔哒的声响。我知道，弹夹里没有子弹了。”

她最后打住了没说了，气喘吁吁。她的那张脸没有人样了，因为残忍、愤怒和痛苦而变了形。您根本想象不到，这样一个文静娴雅的女人会显露出如此凶恶的表情。乔伊斯先生后退了一步。看到她这副模样，他着实感到害怕。那已经不再是一张人的面孔了，简直就是一副癫狂狰狞的面具了。他们随后听见了另一个房间里传来呼喊的声音，声音很响亮，很友善，很快乐。那是乔伊斯夫人的声音。

“过来吧，莱斯利，亲爱的，你的房间已经收拾好啦。你一定要躺下来睡一觉啊。”

克罗斯比夫人的五官慢慢地恢复了原样。先前清楚地刻写在脸上的激情已经平复了，犹如用手把一张弄皱了纸抚平一样。片刻之后，那张脸庞冷静，平和，没有皱纹。她还略微显得有点苍白，但嘴唇边已经绽放出了可心的笑容了。她依然是那位素有教养、至情至性的女人了。

“我这就来，多萝西，亲爱的。给你添了这么多麻烦，真是对不起啊。”

① cartridge ['kɑːtridʒ] *n.* 弹药筒

② affable ['æfəbl] *adj.* 和蔼的；友善的；平易近人的

The Outstation

The new assistant arrived in the afternoon. When the Resident, Mr. Warburton, was told that the prahu was in sight he put on his solar **topee**① and went down to the landing-stage. The guard, eight little Dyak soldiers, stood to attention as he passed. He noted with satisfaction that their bearing was **martial**②, their uniforms neat and clean, and their guns shining. They were a credit to him. From the landing-stage he watched the bend of the river round which in a moment the boat would sweep. He looked very smart in his spotless ducks and white shoes. He held under his arm a gold-headed Malacca **cane**③ which had been given him by the Sultan of Perak. He awaited the newcomer with mingled feelings. There was more work in the district than one man could properly do, and during his periodical tours of the country under his charge it had been inconvenient to leave the station in the hands of a native clerk, but he had been so long the only white man there that he could not face the arrival of another without misgiving. He was accustomed to loneliness. During the war he had not seen an English face for three years; and once when he was instructed to put up an **afforestation**④ officer he was seized with panic, so that when the stranger was due to arrive,

海外驻地

① topee ['təupi] *n.* 遮阳帽

② martial ['mɑːʃəl] *a.* 军队生活的

③ cane [kein] *n.* 竹杖

④ afforestation [əˌfɔːri'steiʃn] *n.* 造林，造林地区

新助理下午到达。手下人告诉驻地专员沃伯顿先生，已经看见马来帆船[1]了。这时候，他戴上了自己的遮阳软草帽，走到下面的浮码头。他一路走过去时，一队卫兵——八位小个子迪雅克[2]士兵——立正致意。他欣喜地看到，他们的仪容仪表符合军人的要求，穿在身上的制服整洁干净，配备的枪支擦得铮亮。他们让他脸上有光。他站立在浮码头上，注视着河的弯曲处，因为过一会儿，那艘船就会快速绕过那儿。他穿着洁白的帆布裤子，脚上穿着白色皮鞋，显得很时髦。他腋下夹着一根顶端镶了金的马六甲白藤手杖。手杖是霹雳州[3]的苏丹赠送给他的。他等待着那位新来者，心情很复杂。本地区的工作任务一个人难以应付。他对自己负责的区域进行定期巡视期间，不方便把这个驻地交由某个土著职员来管理。但是，长期以来，这儿就他一个白人，所以，当他要面对另外一位白人的到来时，不可能不心存疑虑。他已经习惯了孤单寂寞的生活。战争期间，他有三年时间没有见到过一张英国人的面孔。有一次，他奉命接待一位造林官时，竟然感到诚惶诚恐。因此，那位

1 马来帆船（prahu）指马来人使用大三角帆的船只。

2 迪雅克（Dyak）指加里曼丹或沙捞越的土著居民。

3 霹雳州（Perak）是马来西亚马来地区的一个地方。

having arranged everything for his reception, he wrote a note telling him he was obliged to go up-river, and fled; he remained away till he was informed by a messenger that his guest had left.

Now the prahu appeared in the broad reach. It was manned by prisoners, Dyaks under various sentences, and a couple of warders were waiting on the landing-stage to lake them back to jail. They were **sturdy**① fellows, used to the river, and they rowed with a powerful stroke. As the boat reached the side a man got out from under the attap **awning**② and stepped on shore. The guard presented arms.

"Here we are at last. By God, I'm as **cramped**③ as the devil. I've brought you your mail."

He spoke with **exuberant**④ **joviality**⑤. Mr. Warburton politely held out his hand.

"Mr. Cooper, I presume?"

"That's right. Were you expecting anyone else?"

The question had a facetious intent, but the Resident did not smile.

"My name is Warburton. I'll show you your quarters. They'll bring your kit along."

He preceded Cooper along the narrow pathway and they entered a compound in which stood a small bungalow.

"I've had it made as habitable as I could, but of course no one has lived in it for a good many years,"

It was built on piles. It consisted of a long living-room which opened on to a broad verandah, and behind, on each side of a passage, were two bedrooms.

"This'll do me all right," said Cooper.

"I daresay you want to have a bath and a change. I shall be very much pleased if you'll dine with me tonight. Will eight o'clock suit you?"

"Any old time will do for me."

The Resident gave a polite, but slightly disconcerted smile, and withdrew. He returned to the Fort where his own residence was. The impression which

陌生人将要如期到达时，由于事先安排好了全部接待工作，他留下了一张字条，告诉客人说，他迫不得已到河的上游地区去了，然后便撒腿跑了。他一直在外地待着，直到信使告诉他说，他的客人已经离开了。

现在，马来帆船出现在河道的开阔处。船由囚犯们操纵着，是雅克人，其刑期各不相同，两三位狱卒在浮码头上等待着将他们收监。他们是些身强力壮的人，熟悉这条河，划船时力量强大。当船靠近岸边时，有位男子从聂帕榈叶的遮阳棚下面走了出来，跨上了岸。卫兵举枪致意。

“我们终于到了，谢天谢地啊，我给挤得够呛。我已经把您的邮件给带过来了。”

他说话时，热情洋溢，兴致勃勃。沃伯顿先生彬彬有礼地伸出一只手。

“我估计您就是库珀先生吧？”

“不错，您还在等别的什么人吗？”

这个问题本来是想要幽默一下的，但驻扎专员并没有露出笑容。

“我姓沃伯顿。我领着您去您的住处。他们随即会把您的行李送过来。”

他领着库珀一路沿着狭窄的小路走。他们随后进入了一座庭院，里面是一幢小型的孟加拉平房。

“我已经吩咐人收拾过了，尽量弄得好一些，住进去舒适。不过，当然啦，里面有很多年没有住过人了。”

房子是建在一系列桩子上的。一间很长的起居室，前面是一个很宽敞的露台。后面过道两边各有一间卧室。

“我住到这儿挺好的。”库珀说。

“我看您需要洗个澡，换一换衣服。您今晚若是能够同我一块儿用晚餐，我会感到很高兴的。八点钟，怎么样？”

“我随便什么时间都可以。”

驻扎专员露出了礼貌但略显窘迫的微笑，然后离开了。他返回到了“要塞”——自己的住处。艾伦•库珀给

① sturdy ['stə:di] *a.* 强壮的

② awning ['ɔ:niŋ] *n.* 遮日篷

③ cramped [kræmpt] *a.* 狭窄的

④ exuberant [ig'zju:bərənt] *a.*(情感等)充溢的

⑤ joviality [ˌdʒəuvi'æləti] *n.* 高兴

Allen Cooper had given him was not very favourable, but he was a fair man, and he knew that it was unjust to form an opinion on so brief a glimpse. Cooper seemed to be about thirty. He was a tall, thin fellow, with a sallow face in which there was not a spot of colour. It was a face all in one tone. He had a large, hooked nose and blue eyes. When, entering the bungalow, he had taken off his topee and flung it to a waiting boy, Mr. Warburton noticed that his large skull, covered with short, brown hair, contrasted somewhat oddly with a weak, small chin. He was dressed in khaki shorts and a khaki shirt, but they were shabby and soiled; and his battered topee had not been cleaned for days. Mr. Warburton reflected that the young man had spent a week on a coasting steamer and had passed the last forty eight hours lying in the bottom of a prahu.

"We'll see what he looks like when he comes in to dinner."

He went into his room where his things were as neatly laid out as if he had an English **valet**①, undressed, and, walking down the stairs to the bath-house, **sluiced**② himself with cool water. The only concession he made to the climate was to wear a white dinner-jacket; but otherwise, in a boiled shirt and a high collar, silk socks and patent-leather shoes, he dressed as formally as though he were dining at his club in Pall Mall. A careful host, he went into the dining-room to see that the table was properly laid. It was gay with **orchids**③, and the silver shone brightly. The napkins were folded into elaborate shapes. Shaded candles in silver candle-sticks shed a soft light. Mr. Warburton smiled his approval and returned to the sitting-room to await his guest. Presently he appeared. Cooper was wearing the khaki shorts, the khaki shirt, and the ragged jacket in which he had landed. Mr. Warburton's smile of greeting froze on his face.

"Hullo, you're all dressed up," said Cooper. "I didn't know you were going to do that. I very nearly put on a **sarong**④."

"It doesn't matter at all. I daresay your boys were busy."

"You needn't have bothered to dress on my account, you know."

他留下的印象不那么理想，但是，他是个讲究公平的人。他心里很清楚，这么匆匆一瞥便形成看法有失公平。库珀看上去三十岁的样子，身材又高又瘦，脸色蜡黄，没有血色。那是一张很单调的脸。他长着一个很大的鹰钩鼻，一双蓝眼睛。他刚才走进孟加拉平房前便取下了自己的遮阳软草帽，扔给了一位男仆。当时，沃伯顿先生注意到，他长着个大脑袋，上面盖着短短的棕褐色头发，弱小单薄的下巴颏与之对照起来，多少显得有点怪异。他身穿卡其布短裤，卡其布衬衫，但衣服又破又脏。他那顶破旧的遮阳草帽也有日子没有洗涤过。沃伯顿先生想到，年轻人在沿岸航行的汽船上待了一个星期时间，先前的四十八个小时还躺在马来帆船的船底呢。

“等他过来用晚餐时，我们再看看他是什么模样。”

他走进自己的房间，他的东西全部都摆放得整齐有序，好像他身边有一位英国仆人似的。他脱下衣服，然后下楼走进浴室，用凉水冲了个澡。他穿了一件白色无尾礼服，这是他向气候所做的唯一妥协。除此之外，浆洗过的衬衫、高领、丝袜和漆皮鞋，一应俱全，穿得很正式，犹如在蓓尔美尔大街[1]自己所属的俱乐部里就餐一般。由于他是个细心周到的东道主，他进入餐室查看一番，看看餐桌是否摆设妥当了。餐桌上摆放着盛开的兰花，银制餐具铮亮闪光。餐巾折叠成了精巧多样的形状。银制烛台里用罩子罩住的蜡烛放射出柔和的光线。沃伯顿先生会意地露出了微笑，返回到了起居室，等待他的客人到来。不一会儿，客人到了。库珀穿着卡其布短裤，卡其布衬衫，还有他上岸时穿的那件破旧短外套。沃伯顿先生表达问候的微笑凝固在了脸上。

“啊呀，您都全副武装啊，”库珀说，“我都不知道您会穿着这么讲究。我差一点就围一条土著人的围裙呢。”

“没有关系。我肯定，伺候您的那些仆人挺忙的。”

“您没有必要为了我穿得这么郑重其事，您知道。”

“不是，我吃饭前一直都穿戴整齐的。”

① valet ['vælit] n. 贴身男仆
② sluice [slu:s] v. 浇灌
③ orchid ['ɔ:kid] n. 兰花
④ sarong [sə'rɔŋ] n. 围裙

1 蓓尔美尔大街（Pall Mall）是伦敦的一条街道，以俱乐部云集而著称。

"I didn't. I always dress for dinner."

"Even when you're alone?"

"Especially when I'm alone," replied Mr. Warburton, with a frigid stare.

He saw a twinkle of amusement in Cooper's eyes, and he flushed an angry red. Mr. Warburton was a hot-tempered man; you might have guessed that from his red face with its **pugnacious**① features and from his red hair now growing white; his blue eyes, cold as a rule and observing, could flash with sudden **wrath**②; but he was a man of the world and he hoped a just one. He must do his best to get on with this fellow.

"When I lived in London I moved in circles in which it would have been just as **eccentric**③ not to dress for dinner every night as not to have a bath every morning. When I came to Borneo I saw no reason to discontinue so good a habit. For three years during the war I never saw a white man. I never omitted to dress on a single occasion on which I was well enough to come in to dinner. You have not been very long in this country; believe me, there is no better way to maintain the proper pride which you should have in yourself. When a white man surrenders in the slightest degree to the influences that surround him he very soon loses his self-respect, and when he loses his self-respect you may be quite sure that the natives will soon cease to respect him."

"Well, if you expect me to put on a boiled shirt and a stiff collar in this heat I'm afraid you'll be disappointed."

"When you are dining in your own bungalow you will, of course, dress as you think fit, but when you do me the pleasure of dining with me, perhaps you will come to the conclusion that it is only polite to wear the costume usual in civilised society."

Two Malay boys, in sarongs and songkoks, with smart white coats and brass buttons, came in, one bearing gin pahits, and the other a tray on which were olives and **anchovies**④. Then they went in to dinner. Mr. Warburton flattered himself that he had the best cook, a Chinese, in Borneo, and he took great trouble to have as good food as in the difficult circumstances was possible. He

"即便独自一人吃也一样吗？"

"独自一人吃饭时尤其如此。"沃伯顿先生回答说，眼睛盯他着看，目光严厉。

沃伯顿先生看到库珀的目光中透出一丝戏谑，于是生气了，脸涨得通红。沃伯顿先生是个脾气暴躁的人，您可以从他音容相貌看出这一点，他脸色通红，五官凶悍，红色的头发现在正在慢慢变得灰白。一双蓝色的眼睛，平常显得冷漠而又警觉，但可能会突然冒出怒气。但是，他是个见过世面的人，同时也希望行事公平。他一定会竭尽全力同眼前这个人友好相处的。

"我在伦敦时有一些属于自己的人脉圈子，每天晚上用餐前，若是不穿戴整齐，那会显得很怪异的，如同每天早晨不洗澡一样。来了婆罗洲之后，我觉得，没有任何理由不继续保持这个良好的习惯。战争期间的三年当中，我没有看见过一个白人。但凡用餐时，我没有一次不是穿戴整齐的，这个程序一次都没有省略过。您到这个国家的时间还不是很长。相信我好啦，您若是要保持自己应有的尊严，这样做是再好不过的办法。白人面对自己周围环境的影响，若是有丁点儿屈服，那他们很快就会失去自尊的。这样一来，您便可以肯定，土著人很快就不会再尊重他们啦。"

"啊，这么大热天，您若是指望着我会穿浆洗过的衬衫和硬邦邦的领子，恐怕您会失望的。"

"当然啦，您若是在自己的孟加拉平房里用餐，那您可以穿得随心所欲一些，但是，您若是看得起我，让我有幸同您一块儿用餐，可能您就会认同，只有按照文明社会的着装，那才是文明礼貌的表现呢。"

两个马来男仆进来了。他们围着围裙，戴着椭圆形无边帽，上身穿着洁白的外套，外套外面是黄铜色的纽扣。他们一个拿来了杜松子酒，另一个端了个盛着橄榄和凤尾鱼的托盘。随后，沃伯顿先生和库珀进入餐室用餐。沃伯顿先生自我炫耀着说，他有位华人厨子，是婆罗洲最好的。他想方设法，配备了困难条件下最好的餐

① pugnacious [pʌg'neiʃəs] *a.* 爱吵架的

② wrath [rɔθ] *n.* 愤怒

③ eccentric [ik'sentrik] *a.* 古怪的

④ anchovy ['æntʃəvi] *n.* 凤尾鱼

exercised much ingenuity in making the best of his materials.

"Would you care to look at the menu?" he said, handing it to Cooper.

It was written in French and the dishes had resounding names. They were waited on by the two boys. In opposite corners of the room two more waved immense fans, and so gave movement to the sultry air. The fare was **sumptuous**① and the champagne excellent.

"Do you do yourself like this every day?" said Cooper.

Mr. Warburton gave the menu a careless glance. "I have not noticed that the dinner is any different from usual," he said. "I eat very little myself but I make a point of having a proper dinner served to me every night. It keeps the cook in practice and it's good discipline for the boys."

The conversation proceeded with effort. Mr. Warburton was elaborately courteous, and it may be that he found a slightly malicious amusement in the embarrassment which he thereby occasioned in his companion. Cooper had not been more than a few months in Sembulu, and Mr. Warburton's inquiries about friends of his in Kuala Solor were soon exhausted.

"By the way," he said presently, "did you meet a lad called Hennerley? He's come out recently, I believe."

"Oh, yes, he's in the police. A **rotten**② **bounder**③."

"I should hardly have expected him to be that. His uncle is my friend Lord Barraclough. I had a letter from Lady Barraclough only the other day asking me to look out for him."

"I heard he was related to somebody or other. I suppose that's how he got the job. He's been to Eton and Oxford and he doesn't forget to let you know it."

"You surprise me," said Mr. Warburton. "All his family have been at Eton

食，而且开动脑筋，发挥聪明才智，充分利用好食材。

“您想要看一看食谱吗？”他说着，一边把菜谱递给库珀。

食谱是用法文写的，上面写着的菜都有响亮的名字。两个男仆在旁边伺候着他们。房间另一端的两个角上，还有两个仆人扇着大扇子，这样一来，房间里闷热的空气便流动起来了。美食佳肴奢华丰盛，还有优质香槟。

① sumptuous ['sʌmptjuəs] *a.* 奢侈的

“您每天都给自己配这么丰盛的餐食吗？”库珀问了一声。

沃伯顿先生若无其事地瞥了一眼食谱。

“我看不出这顿饭跟平常的有什么不同，”他说，“我本人吃得很少，但每晚一定要吩咐厨子给我提供像样的晚餐。这样一来，厨子一直练着手艺，对仆人们也是很好的锻炼。”

交谈进行得颇为费劲。沃伯顿先生周到礼貌，或许是因为他这样做让他的同伴感到有点尴尬，而他却从这种尴尬中觉察到了一丝略显恶意的戏谑。库珀待在森布鲁还不到几个月，所以，沃伯顿先生问到了关于他在瓜拉索洛的朋友的情况时，该话题很快便进行不下去了。

“顺便问一声，”他不一会儿便问，“您遇到过一位名叫亨纳雷年轻人吗？他是最近到海外驻地来的，我认为。”

② rotten ['rɔtən] *a.* 极坏的

③ bounder ['baundə] *n.* 行为不端的人

“噢，遇到过，他在警察队伍中，是个行为不端的恶劣之徒。”

“我根本没有想到他会是那种人。他伯父巴拉克拉夫爵士是我的朋友。就在几天前，我还收到了巴拉克拉夫爵士的来信，请我去寻找他呢。”

“我听说过，他和什么人物有关系。我估摸着，这就是他谋到这份差事的原因。他在伊顿公学[1]和牛津念过书，而且不会忘记向人炫耀这一点的。”

“您让我感到很惊讶啊，”沃伯顿先生说，“几百年

1　伊顿公学（Eton）坐落在离伦敦二十英里远的温莎小镇，是英国最著名的贵族中学。伊顿以“精英摇篮”、“绅士文化”而闻名世界，学生大都成绩十分优异，被公认是英国最好的中学，是英国王室、政界、经济界精英的培训之地。

and Oxford for a couple of hundred years. I should have expected him to take it as a matter of course."

"I thought him a damned **prig**①."

"To what school did you go?"

"I was born in Barbadoes. I was educated there."

"Oh, I see."

Mr. Warburton managed to put so much offensiveness into his brief reply that Cooper flushed. For a moment he was silent.

"I've had two or three letters from Kuala Solor," continued Mr. Warburton, "and my impression was that young Hennerley was a great success. They say he's a first-rate sportsman."

"Oh, yes, he's very popular. He's just the sort of fellow they would like in K. S. I haven't got much use for the first-rate sportsman myself. What does it amount to in the long run that a man can play golf and tennis better than other people? And who cares if he can make a break of seventy-five at billiards? They attach a damned sight too much importance to that sort of thing in England."

"Do you think so? I was under the impression that the first-rate sportsman had come out of the war certainly no worse than anyone else."

"Oh, if you're going to talk of the war then I do know what I'm talking about. I was in the same regiment as Hennerley and I can tell you that the men couldn't stick him at any price."

"How do you know?"

"Because I was one of the men."

"Oh, you hadn't got a commission."

"A fat chance I had of getting a commission. I was what was called a Colonial. I hadn't been to a public school and I had no influence. I was in the ranks the whole damned time."

Cooper frowned. He seemed to have difficulty in preventing himself from breaking out into violent invective. Mr. Warburton watched him, his little blue eyes narrowed, watched him and formed his opinion. Changing the conversation,

① prig [prig] *n.* 自命不凡者

来，他家族的人都是从伊顿和牛津出来的。我觉得，他会把这事看成是很平常的。”

“我觉得他就是个可恶的自命不凡之徒。”

“您上的是哪所学校啊？”

“我出生在巴巴多斯[1]，我是在那儿接受教育的。”

“噢，我明白啦。”

沃伯顿先生处心积虑地用简略的回答透出冒犯之意，所以让库珀的脸绯得通红。他沉默了一会儿。

“我收到了从瓜拉索洛寄来的两三封信，”沃伯顿先生接着说，“我有个印象，感觉小亨纳雷是个很成功的人。大家都说他是个一流的运动家。”

“噢，是这么回事，他很受欢迎。他属于那种在瓜拉索洛很吃香的人。我本人却不喜欢什么一流的运动家。从长远来说，一个人打高尔夫球或者网球比别人水平更高，那又有什么用呢？谁又在乎他玩台球时能够连续打出七十五分呢？他们在英国把这种事情看得太那么回事了。”

“您是这么认为的吗？我的感觉是，一流的运动家打起仗来肯定不会逊色于其他人啊。”

“噢，您若是谈起打仗来，那我是更加有得说了。我和亨纳雷待在同一个团里，所以，可以告诉您，团里的人都无法容忍他。”

“您怎么知道呢？”

“因为我是其中的一员呀。”

“噢，您没有取得军衔。”

“我取得军衔的机会微乎其微啊。我是位所谓的殖民地居民，没有上过公立学校，没有任何影响力。那该死的日子可难受啦。”

库珀眉头紧锁，似乎很难控制住自己不说出难听的话来。沃伯顿先生注视着他，蓝色的小眼睛眯缝了起来，注视着他，心里有了判断了。他转换了话题，开始对库

1　巴巴多斯（Barbadoes）是一个拉丁美洲国家，原为英国殖民地，1966 年宣布独立，成为英联邦成员。位于东加勒比海小安得列斯群岛最东端，为珊瑚石灰岩海岛。

he began to speak to Cooper about the work that would be required of him, and as the clock struck ten he rose.

"Well, I won't keep you any more. I daresay you're tired by your journey."

They shook hands.

"Oh, I say, look here," said Cooper, "I wonder if you can find me a boy. The boy I had before never turned up when I was starting from K. S. He took my kit on board and all that, and then disappeared. I didn't know he wasn't there till we were out on the river."

"I'll ask my head-boy. I have no doubt he can find you someone."

"All right. Just tell him to send the boy along and if I like the look of him I'll take him."

There was a moon, so that no lantern was needed Cooper walked across from the Fort to his bungalow.

"I wonder why on earth they've sent me a fellow like that?" reflected Mr. Warburton. "If that's the kind of man they're going to get out now I don't think much of it."

He strolled down his garden. The Fort was built on the top of a little hill and the garden ran down to the river's edge; on the bank was an **arbour**①, and hither it was his habit to come after dinner to smoke a **cheroot**②. And often from the river that flowed below him a voice was heard, the voice of some Malay too **timorous**③ to venture into the light of day, and a complaint or an accusation was softly wafted to his ears, a piece of information was whispered to him or a useful hint, which otherwise would never have come into his official ken. He threw himself heavily into a long rattan chair. Cooper! An envious, ill-bred fellow, bumptious, self-assertive and vain. But Mr. Warburton's irritation could not withstand the silent beauty of the night. The air was scented with the sweet-smelling flowers of a tree that grew at the entrance to the arbour, and the fire-flies, sparkling dimly, flew with their slow

珀谈到了需要展开的工作。时钟敲响十点时，他站起了身。

“行啊，我不就留您啦，您旅途过后一定很疲倦了。”

他们握了握手。

“噢，对啦，您看看，”库珀说，“不知道您能否替我物色到一位男仆。我过去的那位男仆打我从瓜拉索洛启程出发时便没有再露面了。他把我的行李搬到了船上，然后就不见了踪影。直到我们的船驶出了河道之后，我才知道他不在船上。”

“我去问一问我那位领头的仆人，毫无疑问，他一定可以物色到一位。”

“好啊，吩咐他把人领着过来就行，只要其相貌我看得上，我就雇佣他。”

晚上有月亮，所以，库珀无需提灯照耀便可以从“要塞”走到他居住的孟加拉平房。

“我真是弄不明白，他们为何派遣这样一个家伙过来啊？”沃伯顿先生思忖着，“他们若是派遣这种货色过来，我是不会看重的。”

他在花园里信步走着。“要塞”建在一座小山的顶端，花园延伸到了河畔。岸边有座凉亭，他饭后到此抽上一支方头雪茄烟，这已经成了他的习惯了。他下方流淌着的河面上常常可以听见有说话的声音传来，说话的是马来人。他们过于畏缩胆怯，不敢冒险大白天出来。他的耳畔还会听见轻柔的抱怨声或者责怪声。某一则信息会窃窃私语地传到他这儿，或者是某种有帮助的暗示。若非如此，这样的一些声音绝不可能进入他代表的官方领域。他把身子重重地坐到一把长藤椅上。库珀！一个心怀嫉妒而且缺乏教养的家伙。傲慢无礼，刚愎自用，爱慕虚荣。但是，沃伯顿先生满腔的怨气抵挡不了眼前沉静美妙的夜景。凉亭入口处生长着一棵树，树上鲜花盛开，空气中弥漫着鲜花散发出的清香。萤火虫幽光闪烁，缓慢地在空中飞舞，发出银光。月光在宽阔的河面上替湿婆神的新娘[1]那轻盈的双脚铺好了一条路。河对岸是

① arbour ['ɑːbə] *n.* 凉亭

② cheroot [ʃə'ruːt] *n.* 方头雪茄烟

③ timorous ['timərəs] *a.* 胆小的

1 湿婆神（Siva）是印度教神话中的最高神之一，其新娘是乌摩，也称为雪山女神，是光明和美丽的象征。

and silvery flight. The moon made a pathway on the broad river for the light feet of Sila's bride, and on the further bank a row of palm trees was delicately **silhouetted**① against the sky. Peace stole into the soul of Mr. Warburton.

He was a queer creature and he had had a singular career. At the age of twenty-one he had inherited a considerable fortune, a hundred thousand pounds, and when he left Oxford he threw himself into the gay life which in those days (now Mr. Warburton was a man of four and fifty) offered itself to the young man of good family. He had his flat in Mount Street, his private hansom, and his hunting-box in Warwickshire. He went to all the places where the fashionable **congregate**②. He was handsome, amusing, and generous. He was a figure in the society of London in the early nineties, and society then had not lost its exclusiveness nor its brilliance. The Boer War which shook it was unthought of; the Great War which destroyed it was **prophesied**③ only by the pessimists. It was no unpleasant thing to be a rich young man in those days, and Mr. Warburton's chimney-piece during the season was packed with cards for one great function after another. Mr. Warburton displayed them with **complacency**④. For Mr. Warburton was a **snob**⑤. He was not a timid snob, a

一排棕榈树，在天空的衬托下，显现出精妙的轮廓。不知不觉中，沃伯顿先生的内心深处滋生起了一种平静的感觉。

① silhouetted [ˌsiluːˈetid] *a.* 显出轮廓的

沃伯顿先生是个颇为古怪的人，经历了一段奇特的人生历程。二十一岁时，他继承了一笔可观的遗产——十万英镑。牛津大学毕业后，他沉溺于放荡不羁的生活。那时候（沃伯顿如今已经五十有四了），富家公子们都会享受那种生活。他在芒特街[1]有自己的寓所，有自己的私家马车，在沃里克郡[2]有属于自己的狩猎小屋。他涉足于各种上流社会汇集的场所。他仪表堂堂，言谈风趣，为人豪爽，算得上是90年代伦敦社交界的一个人物。当时的社交界还不失为独立王国，依旧熠熠生辉。动摇社交界的布尔战争[3]令人始料未及，而摧毁社交界的第一次世界大战只是悲观主义者的预言而已。那时候，做一名富家公子可是件舒心惬意的事情。社交季[4]期间，沃伯顿先生家里的壁炉架上便会堆满这样那样的请柬，都是邀请他出席各种盛大宴会的。沃伯顿先生沾沾自喜地把请柬展示出来，因为沃伯顿先生是个势利眼，但不

② congregate [ˈkɔŋgriˌgeit] *v.* 聚集

③ prophesy [ˈprɔfisai] *v.* 预言

④ complacency [kəmˈpleisənsi] *n.* 洋洋自得

⑤ snob [snɔb] *n.* 势利眼

1 芒特街（Mount Street）是伦敦西区梅费尔高级住宅区的一条街道。

2 沃里克郡（Warwickshire）英格兰的一个郡，其东北与莱斯特郡相邻，东与北安普敦郡相邻，东南与牛津郡相邻，西南与格洛斯特郡相邻。

3 布尔战争（Boer War, 1899—1902，也称为第二次布尔战争）是指英国人和布尔人之间为了争夺南非殖民地而展开的战争。荷兰殖民者于17世纪抵达南非，他们和葡萄牙、法国殖民者的后裔被称为布尔人。19世纪晚期，德兰士瓦共和国和奥兰士自由国相继发现世界上最大的钻石矿和金矿。英国殖民者觊觎那些宝藏，于1899年8月与布尔人爆发战争。战争初期，英军在人数上处于劣势，在轻捷灵便的布尔人面前多次遭到失败，随着援军的抵达，英军逐渐掌握主动权。第一次发生在1880年至1881年间。

4 此处指伦敦社交季（London season）。它源于18世纪的英国上流社会每年都要举行的社交活动。活动多种多样，如宫廷舞会、晚宴、慈善活动、赛马会、板球赛、网球赛都会集中在社交季内举办。根据《德布雷特英国贵族年鉴》（Debrett's Peerage）的解释，社交季每年的4—8月，长达四个月之久。期间是不列颠小岛最美丽的季节，由于地处高纬度，每天日照时间相当长，早上四点钟就天亮了，晚上十点钟户外景物还看得很清楚，加上气温不高，降雨不多，户外活动舒心惬意。舞会通常在晚上十点钟开始，次日凌晨三点结束。白天，要么上邦德大街、摄政大街购物，要么骑马、打马球。关系特别亲密的还会相互串门做客。

little ashamed of being impressed by his betters, nor a snob who sought the intimacy of persons who had acquired celebrity in politics or notoriety in the arts, nor the snob who was dazzled by riches; he was the naked, unadulterated common snob who dearly loved a lord. He was touchy and quick-tempered, but he would much rather have been snubbed by a person of quality than flattered by a commoner. His name figured insignificantly in Burke's Peerage, and it was marvellous to watch the ingenuity he used to mention his distant relationship to the noble family he belonged to; but never a word did he say of the honest Liverpool manufacturer from whom, through his mother, a Miss Gubbins, he had come by his fortune. It was the terror of his fashionable life that at Cowes, maybe, or at Ascot, when he was with a duchess or even with a prince of the blood, one of these relatives would claim acquaintance with him.

His failing was too obvious not soon to become notorious, but its extravagance saved it from being merely despicable. The great whom he adored laughed at him, but in their hearts felt his adoration not unnatural. Poor Warburton was a dreadful snob, of course, but after all he was a good fellow. He was always ready to back a bill for an **impecunious**[1] nobleman, and if you were in a tight corner you could safely count on him for a hundred pounds. He gave good dinners. He played whist badly, hut never minded how much he lost if the company was select. He happened to be a gambler, an unlucky one, hut he was a good loser, and it was impossible not to admire the coolness with

属于那种胆怯怕事的势利眼，不会因为比自己地位更高的人而受到影响，有些许自惭不如之感。他也不是那种处心积虑巴结政界名流或者艺术精英的势利眼，也不是那种见钱眼开的势利眼。他是那种赤裸裸不含杂质的平常势利眼，由衷地热爱贵族。他生性敏感，脾气暴躁，但是，他宁可被贵族冷落，也不愿意受到平民的恭维。他的名字在《伯克英国贵族年鉴》[1]中处在很不起眼的位置。令人感到惊叹不已的是，他言谈当中会巧妙地提及某个名门望族，并说自己同该家族有远亲关系，但是，却缄口不言自己母亲那边的那位诚实守信的利物浦制造业主，而正是有了自己的母亲——出嫁前名叫格宾斯小姐——这一层关系，他才继承到了那笔遗产。他可能会在考斯[2]或者阿斯科特[3]陪伴着某位公爵夫人或者某位王室贵胄，这种时候，若是那些亲戚中有某一位认出他来，那对他的上流社会生活而言可是一件恐怖的事情啊。

他的缺点过于明显，不久便众人皆知了。但是，出手阔绰大方，他的缺点倒是没有让人完全鄙视。他所崇敬的那些大人物嘲笑他，但是，他们的内心深处对他的崇敬之情还是感同身受的。可怜兮兮的沃伯顿当然是个十足的势利眼，但是，他毕竟还算得上是个好人。他会随时愿意替某位身无分文的贵族支付账单，而您若是身处绝境，您一定可以从他那儿借到一百英镑。他会提供丰盛的餐食。他的惠斯特牌戏[4]技术很拙劣，但是，一

① impecunious [ˌimpiˈkjuːnjəs] *a.* 贫穷的

1 《伯克英国贵族年鉴》（*Burke's Peerage*）类似于《德布雷特英国贵族年鉴》(初版于 1803 年)，最初由爱尔兰谱系学家约翰·伯克（John Burke, 1787—1848）于 1826 年编成。

2 考斯（Cowes）是英格兰南部港口城市，以帆船比赛著称。

3 阿斯科特（Ascot）是伯克郡的一座城镇，以赛马会著称。

4 惠斯特牌戏（whist）是包括惠斯特桥牌、竞叫桥牌和定约桥牌在内的纸牌游戏的统称。这三种桥牌都是从最初的惠斯特牌相继发展而成的。惠斯特纸牌游戏的主要特点是，通常四人分成两组，互相对抗；将一副五十二张的纸牌发出，每人十三张牌，每人每次出一张牌，以赢墩为目的。开局前可把一种花色定为王牌。任何一张王牌都可赢过其他花色的任何一张牌，以最后发出的一张牌的花色为王牌花色。惠斯特牌戏于 17 世纪起源于英国。起初是民间的一种娱乐形式，到了 18 世纪初，有闲阶层开始在伦敦的咖啡馆里把它作为消愁解闷的手段之一。

which he lost five hundred pounds at a sitting. His passion for cards, almost as strong as his passion for titles, was the cause of his undoing. The life he led was expensive and his gambling losses were formidable. He began to plunge more heavily, first on horses, and then on the Stock Exchange. He had a certain simplicity of character, and the unscrupulous found him an ingenuous prey. I do not know if he ever realised that his smart friends laughed at him behind his back, but I think he had an obscure instinct that he could not afford to appear other than careless of his money. He got into the hands of money-lenders. At the age of thirty-four he was ruined.

He was too much **imbued**① with the spirit of his class to hesitate in the choice of his next step. When a man in his set had run through his money, he went out to the colonies. No one heard Mr. Warburton repine. He made no complaint because a noble friend had advised a disastrous speculation, he pressed nobody to whom he had lent money to repay it, he paid his debts (if he had only known it, the despised blood of the Liverpool manufacturer came out in him there), sought help from no one, and, never having done a stroke of work in his life, looked for a means of livelihood. He remained cheerful, unconcerned and full of humour. He had no wish to make anyone with whom he happened to be uncomfortable by the recital of his misfortune. Mr. Warburton was a snob, but he was also a gentleman.

The only favour he asked of any of the great friends in whose daily company he had lived for years was a recommendation. The able man who was at that time Sultan of Sembulu took him into his service. The night before he sailed he dined for the last time at his club.

"I hear you're going away, Warburton," the old Duke of Hereford said to him.

"Yes, I'm going to Borneo."

"Good God, what are you going there for?"

同玩牌的人若是上等人士，他可就不会在乎输掉多少了。他是位赌徒，而且是位运气不佳的赌徒，但却是个挺有风度的输家，一次输掉五百英镑，但却还能够保持镇定自若的姿态，这不能不让人心生敬意。他对牌戏的热衷几乎同对贵族头衔一样强烈，而这正是他落魄的原因。他的生活很奢侈，开支巨大，赌博场上的输额更是大得惊人。他开始越赌越大了，起初把钱押在赛马上，继而把钱投入在证券上。他的性格中自然有质朴的一面，而那些肆无忌惮之徒看准了他是个城府不深的猎物。我不知道他是否意识到了，他的那些精明的朋友们都在背地里嘲笑他。但是，我觉得他有一种模糊的直觉，这种直觉告诉他必须要表现出不在乎那些钱。他落到了放债人的手上了。三十岁时，他彻底落败了。

① imbue [im'bjuː] *v.* 使充满

他耳濡目染，深受自己所属阶层的精神世界的影响，所以，面临自己下一步的抉择时，显得犹豫踌躇。他那种类型的人一旦花光了钱之后，往往会离开家乡前往殖民地。没有任何人听到过沃伯顿先生有过一声抱怨。他之所以不抱怨，那是因为他曾经在一位贵族朋友的建议下做过一次灾难性的投机。他没有逼迫任何一位向他借钱的人还钱。他还清了债务（他其实并不知道，正是那位被瞧不起的利物浦制造业主在他身上流淌的血统起了作用），没有寻求任何人的帮助，虽说生平从未干过活儿，但他还是寻求谋生之路。他保持乐观豁达，无忧无虑，幽默风趣。他不愿意喋喋不休地复述自己倒霉的经历，从而让同他在一块儿人感到不爽。沃伯顿先生是个势利眼，但同时也是位绅士。

他向同自己朝夕相处的上流社会朋友只开口求情过一次，那就是写封推荐信。当时，那个正好能够帮上忙的朋友是森布鲁的苏丹，他替沃伯顿谋到了职位。他起航出发的头一天晚上，他在自己所属的俱乐部里用了最后一顿晚餐。

“我听说你要走了，沃伯顿。”赫里福德老公爵对他说。

“是啊，我打算去婆罗洲。”

“天哪，你去那儿干什么啊？”

"Oh, I'm broke."

"Are you? I'm sorry. Well, let us know when you come back. I hope you have a good time."

"Oh yes. Lots of shooting, you know."

The Duke nodded and passed on. A few hours later Mr. Warburton watched the coast of England recede into the mist, and he left behind everything which to him made life worth living.

Twenty years had passed since then. He kept up a busy correspondence with various great ladies and his letters were amusing and chatty. He never lost his love for **titled**① persons and paid careful attention to the announcements in *The Times* (which reached him six weeks after publication) of their comings and goings. He perused the column which records births, deaths, and marriages, and he was always ready with his letter of congratulation or **condolence**②. The illustrated papers told him how people looked and on his periodical visits to England, able to take up the threads as though they had never been broken, he knew all about any new person who might have appeared on the social surface. His interest in the world of fashion was as vivid as when himself had been a figure in it. It still seemed to him the only thing that mattered.

But insensibly another interest had entered into his life. The position he found himself in flattered his vanity; he was no longer the **sycophant**③ craving the smiles of the great, he was the master whose word was law. He was gratified by the guard of Dyak soldiers who presented arms as he passed. He liked to sit in judgement on his fellow men. It pleased him to compose quarrels between rival chiefs. When the head-hunters were troublesome in the old days he set out to **chastise**④ them with a thrill of pride in his own behaviour. He was too vain not to be of dauntless courage, and a pretty story was told of his coolness in adventuring single-handed into a stockaded village and demanding the surrender

“噢，我破产了。”

“是嘛？很遗憾啊。对啦，你回来后给我们说一声。希望你过的快乐啊。”

“噢，那是当然的，狩猎活动多的是，您知道的。”

公爵点了点头，然后走过去了。几个小时之后，沃伯顿先生看着英格兰的海岸渐渐消失在迷雾中。他抛开了让他值得为之生活的一切。

从那之后，时间过去了二十年。他一直同多位贵妇人保持频繁的通信联系。他在信中的行文妙趣横生，娓娓道来。他从未失却对名门贵族的崇敬之情，密切关注《泰晤士报》[1]（不过，报纸要在出版之后六个星期才能到他的手上）上关于他们行踪轨迹的报道。他会仔细阅读记录着出生、死亡和婚姻状况的专栏。他会随时准备写信表示祝贺或者吊唁之情。通过图文并茂的报纸版面，他得知了那些人的音容相貌，所以，当他定期返回英国时，可以重续他们的联系，好像从未中断过一样。他熟悉任何一张可能在社交界斩露头角的新面孔。他对上流社会的兴趣如同当初自己置身其中时一样鲜活。对他来说，那依然是唯一要紧的事情。

但是，不知不觉之中，他在生活中培养起了另外一种兴趣。他现在所处的位置满足了他的虚荣心。他不再是那个为了博上等人一笑而溜须谄媚的人了。他是主人了，可谓一言九鼎。他对于自己经过时那些迪雅克卫兵举枪致意的情景感到很满意。他喜欢坐下来，对他的那些手下做出公断。他能够调停那些首领之间的争端，为此感到舒心惬意。昔日里，当那些割下敌人首级当作战利品的人滋扰生事时，他会身体力行，荣耀感顿生，对其实施讨伐。他虚荣心过强，不会显得气馁。他曾经镇定自若，冒着风险，单枪匹马冲进一处四周有围栏的村

① titled ['taitld] *n.* 有头衔的；有爵位的

② condolence [kən'dəuləns] *n.* 哀悼

③ sycophant ['sikəfənt] *n.* 奉承者

④ chastise [tʃæs'taiz] *v.* 责罚

1 《泰晤士报》（*The Times*）是英国的一份综合性全国发行的日报，对全世界政治、经济、文化影响巨大。该报创办于1785年元旦，创办人是约翰·沃尔特，初为《每日环球纪录报》（*The Daily Universal Register*），1788年1月1日，改为现名。

of a bloodthirsty pirate. He became a skilful administrator. He was strict, just, and honest.

And little by little he conceived a deep love for the Malays. He interested himself in their habits and customs. He was never tired of listening to their talk. He admired their virtues, and with a smile and a shrug of the shoulders **condoned**① their vices.

"In my day," he would say, "I have been on intimate terms with some of the greatest gentlemen in England, but I have never known finer gentlemen than some well-born Malays whom I am proud to call my friends."

He liked their courtesy and their distinguished manners, their gentleness and their sudden passions. He knew by instinct exactly how to treat them. He had a genuine tenderness for them. But he never forgot that he was an English gentleman, and he had no patience with the white men who yielded to native customs. He made no surrenders. And he did not imitate so many of the white men in taking a native woman to wife, for an **intrigue**② of this nature, however **sanctified**③ by custom, seemed to him not only shocking but undignified. A man who had been called George by Albert Edward, Prince of Wales, could hardly be expected to have any connection with a native. And when he returned to Borneo from his visits to England it was now with something like relief. His friends, like himself, were no longer young, and there was a new generation which looked upon him as a tiresome old man. It seemed to him that the England of to-day had lost a good deal of what he had loved in the England of his youth. But Borneo remained the same. It was home to him now. He meant to remain in service as long as was possible, and the hope in his heart was that he would die before at last he was forced to retire. He had stated in his will that wherever he died he wished his body to be brought back to Sembulu, and buried among the people he loved within the sound of the softly flowing river.

But these emotions he kept hidden from the eyes of men; and no one, seeing this **spruce**④, stout, well-set-up man, with his clean-shaven strong face and his

落，命令一位嗜血成性的海盗缴械投降。他的这一事迹被传为佳话。他成了一位老练娴熟的执政官。他严格、公正和诚实。

久而久之，他对马来人怀有一份深深的爱意，对他们的风俗习惯乐此不疲。他对他们的言语谈话百听不厌。他敬佩他们的美德，但面对他们的恶行时，会报以微笑，并且耸一耸肩膀，以示容忍。

“过去，”他会说，“我同一些英国上流社会的绅士交往密切，但是，一些出身高贵的马来人，我以称他们为我的朋友为荣，我从未遇过比他们更加卓越的绅士。”

他喜爱他们谦逊礼让的风度，尊贵高雅的举止。他们温文尔雅，他们热情奔放。他凭着直觉便能够清楚地知道，该如何对待他们。他对他们怀有一种真正的和蔼之情。但是，他从未忘记，自己是位英国绅士，无法容忍屈从土著人习惯的白种人。他从不屈服投降。他没有效仿许多白人的做法，娶个土著妇女为妻，因为在他看来，虽遵行习俗，性情使然，但此事显得既令人震惊，又有失尊严。一个曾经被艾伯特·爱德华[1]威尔士亲王直呼乔治的人绝不可能同一位土著妇女联姻。他从英国返回到婆罗洲时，有一种如释重负之感。和他本人一样，他的朋友们已经不再年轻了，年轻一代的人把他看成是碍手碍脚的老人了。他觉得，相对于他年轻时代挚爱的英国，当今的英国已经失去了许多风采。但是，婆罗洲风采依旧。这儿现在是他的家了。他打算尽可能长久地留下来履职。他内心怀有的希望是，自己最后离世之前，不要被迫退休。他已经立下了遗嘱，无论在何处离世，希望遗体能够运回森布鲁，葬在他深爱着的人们中间，能够倾听到河水缓缓流淌的声音。

但是，他把这些情感藏匿于心，从不在人前流露。他整洁大方，身强体壮，装扮讲究，方正的脸庞修刮得

① condone [kən'dəun] *v.* 宽恕

② intrigue ['intri:g] *n.* 诡计

③ sanctify ['sæŋktifai] *v.* 使合法化

④ spruce [spru:s] *a.* 整洁的

1　此处指英国国王（1901—1910）爱德华七世（Edward VII, 1841—1910），即维多利亚女王之子，讲究穿着，性喜交际，到欧洲各国旅游，促进相互了解，改善英法关系。

whitening hair, would have dreamed that he cherished so profound a sentiment.

He knew how the work of the station should be done, and during the next few days he kept a suspicious eye on his assistant. He saw very soon that he was painstaking and competent. The only fault he had to find with him was that he was **brusque**① with the natives.

"The Malays are shy and very sensitive," he said to him. "I think you will find that you will get much better results if you take care always to be polite, patient and kindly."

Cooper gave a short, **grating**② laugh.

"I was born in Barbados and I was in Africa in the war. I don't think there's much about niggers that I don't know."

"I know nothing," said Mr. Warburton acidly. "But we were not talking of them. We were taking of Malays."

"Aren't they niggers?"

"You are very ignorant," replied Mr. Warburton.

He said no more.

On the first Sunday after Cooper's arrival he asked him to dinner. He did everything ceremoniously, and though they had met on the previous day in the office and later, on the Fort veranda where they drank a gin and bitters together at six o'clock, he sent a polite note across to the bungalow by a boy. Cooper, however unwillingly, came in evening dress and Mr. Warburton, though gratified that his wish was respected, noticed with **disdain**③ that the young man's clothes were badly cut and his shirt ill-fitting. But Mr. Warburton was in a good temper that evening.

"By the way," he said to him, as he shook hands, "I've talked to my head-boy about finding you someone and he recommends his nephew. I've seen him and he seems a bright and willing lad. Would you like to see him?"

"I don't mind."

"He's waiting now."

Mr. Warburton called his boy and told him to send for his nephew. In

干净，头发渐次灰白。面对这样的一个人，谁都不可能想象得到，他会怀着一份如此深沉的情愫。

他深谙这处海外驻地的运行方式。随后的几天当中，他对他的助手持一种怀疑态度。他很快便看出来了，助手吃苦耐劳，能力很强。他从他身上发现的唯一缺点便是，对待土著居民态度粗暴。

① brusque [brusk] *a.* 粗暴的

“马来人很羞怯，很敏感，”沃伯顿对库珀说，“我觉得，您若是注意一直保持礼貌、忍耐和友好的态度，您便会发现，您可以取得更加理想的结果。”

库珀哈哈大笑起来，笑得短促而又刺耳。

② grating ['greitiŋ] *a.* 刺耳的

“我出生在巴巴多斯，战争期间[1]待在非洲。我觉得，关于那些黑鬼的情况，我是知晓的。”

“我倒是不知晓，”沃伯顿先生说，语气中透着讥讽，“但是，我们不是在说黑人，我们是在说马来人。”

“他们不是黑鬼吗？”

“您真是一无所知啊，”沃伯顿先生回应说。

他没有再多说什么。

库珀到达后的第一个星期天，沃伯顿先生请他吃晚饭。他在礼节上做得十分周全，尽管他们头天在办公室见过面，随后六点钟时，还在“要塞”的露台上一块儿喝过杜松子酒和苦啤酒，但他还是打发一位男仆给孟加拉平房那边送去了一封措辞彬彬有礼的请柬。库珀不管有多么不愿意，但还是身穿着晚礼服到场了。尽管沃伯顿先生因自己的意愿受到了尊重而感到很高兴，但却注意到，年轻人的衣服裁剪的很不得体，衬衫也很不合身，不禁有些鄙夷。不过，沃伯顿先生当晚的性情很好。

③ disdain [dis'dein] *n.* 鄙夷

“对啦，”他们握手时，他对库珀说，“关于您要物色一位男仆的事情，我已经对我领头的仆人说过了，他推荐了他的侄子。我见过他，看起来是个聪明勤快的小伙子。您愿意见见他吗？”

“可以。”

“他正等着呢。”

1　此处指布尔战争（1899—1902）。

a moment a tall, slender youth of twenty appeared. He had large dark eyes and a good profile. He was very neat in his sarong, a little white coat, and a fez, without a **tassel**①, of **plum**②-coloured velvet. He answered to the name of Abas. Mr. Warburton looked on him with approval, and his manner insensibly softened as he spoke to him in fluent and idiomatic Malay. He was inclined to be sarcastic with white people, but with the Malays he had a happy mixture of **condescension**③ and kindliness. He stood in the place of the Sultan. He knew perfectly how to preserve his own dignity and at the same lime put a native at his ease.

"Will he do?" said Mr. Warburton, turning to Cooper.

"Yes, I dare say he's no more of a **scoundrel**④ than any of the rest of them."

Mr. Warburton informed the boy that he was engaged, and dismissed him.

"You're very lucky to get a boy like that," he told Cooper. "He belongs to a very good family. They came over from Malacca nearly a hundred years ago."

"I don't much mind if the boy who cleans my shoes and brings me a drink when I want it has blue blood in his veins or not. All I ask is that he should do what I tell him and look sharp about it."

Mr. Warburton pursed his lips, but made no reply.

They went in to dinner. It was excellent, and the wine was good. Its influence presently had its effect on them, and they talked not only without **acrimony**⑤, but even with friendliness. Mr. Warburton liked to do himself well, and on Sunday night he made it a habit to do himself even a little better than usual. He began to think he was unfair to Cooper. Of course he was not a gentleman, but that was not his fault, and when you got to know him it might be that he would turn out a very good fellow. His faults, perhaps, were faults of manner. And he was certainly good at his work, quick, conscientious, and

① tassel ['tæsəl] *n.* 缨
② plum[plʌm] *n.* 紫红色
③ condescension [ˌkɔndi'senʃən] *n.* 谦卑
④ scoundrel ['skaundrəl] *n.* 恶棍
⑤ acrimony ['ækriməni] *n.* 尖刻

沃伯顿先生喊来了他的仆人，吩咐他把他侄子叫来。片刻之后，一位又高又瘦的二十岁的年轻人出现了。他长着一双大大的黑眼睛，长相英俊。他衣着整洁，围着围裙，穿着白色小外套，头戴一顶紫红色天鹅绒料子非斯帽[1]，但帽子上面没有缨带。他回话说自己名叫阿巴斯。沃伯顿先生看着他，目光中透着赞许。当他用流畅地道的马来语同年轻人交谈时，他的态度不知不觉中变得柔和了。他往往会以讥讽的态度对待白人，但是，面对马来人时，他会显露出优越和友善完美结合的态度。他所处的地位相当于苏丹。他很清楚如何才能维持自己的尊严，同时又让土著居民觉得自在。

“他可以吧？”沃伯顿先生问了一声，一边转向库珀。

“可以，我肯定，他和其他那些人一样，不过是混蛋一个罢了。”

沃伯顿先生告诉小伙子说，他被录用了，于是打发他离开。

“您物色到了这样一位男仆，真算是运气啊，”他告诉库珀说，“他家庭背景很好。他们家族是在大约一百年前从马六甲[2]过来的。”

“仆人不过是替我擦皮鞋和端饮料的，他有没有贵族血统我并不在乎。我所要求的是，我想要他干什么他就干什么，而且行动利索。”

沃伯顿先生噘起嘴唇，但没有回话。

他们进入餐厅吃饭了，饭菜味美，葡萄酒纯正。不一会儿，他们受其影响，交谈不仅没有了尖刻的言辞，甚至充满了友好气氛。沃伯顿先生喜欢好好款待自己，星期天晚上更加比平常要款待得更加好一些。他开始觉得，自己对库珀有失公平。当然，他不是位绅士，但不是他的过错，但是，您一旦了解他了，便会发现，他其实是个很优秀的人。他的缺点或许体现在举止态度上。

1 非斯帽（fez）是地中海东岸各国男子所戴的一种圆筒形无边毡帽，红色，并饰有长黑缨。

2 马六甲（Malacca）是马来西亚马来地区西南部的港口。

thorough. When they reached the dessert Mr. Warburton was feeling kindly disposed towards all mankind.

"This is your first Sunday, and I'm going to give you a very special glass of port. I've only got about two dozen of it left and I keep it for special occasions."

He gave his boy instructions and presently the bottle was brought. Mr. Warburton watched the boy open it.

"I got this port from my old friend Charles Hollington. He'd had it for forty years, and I've had it for a good many. He was well-known to have the best **cellar**① in England."

"Is he a wine merchant?"

"Not exactly," smiled Mr. Warburton. "I was speaking of Lord Hollington of Castle Reagh. He's one of the richest peers in England. A very old friend of mine. I was at Eton with his brother."

This was an opportunity that Mr. Warburton could never resist, and he told a little anecdote of which the only point seemed to be that he knew an Earl. The port was certainly very good; he drank a glass and then a second. He lost all caution. He had not talked to a white man for months. He began to tell stories. He showed himself in the company of the great. Hearing him, you would have thought that at one time ministries were formed and policies decided on his suggestion whispered into the ear of a duchess or thrown over the dinner-table to be gratefully acted on by the confidential adviser of the Sovereign. The old days at Ascot, Goodwood, and Cowes lived again for him. Another glass of port. There were the great house-parties in Yorkshire and in Scotland to which he went every year.

"I had a man called Foreman then, the best valet I ever had, and why do you think he gave me notice? You know in the Housekeeper's Room the

① cellar ['selə] *n.* 酒窖

毫无疑问，他在工作方面很优秀，动作利索，态度认真，考虑周到。当他们开始吃甜点时，沃伯顿先生感觉到自己对整个人类都充满了善意。

“这是您到这儿后的第一个星期天，我要请您喝一杯特别的波尔图葡萄酒[1]。我只剩下两打了。我是留着特殊场合喝的。”

他吩咐男仆去拿酒来，男仆很快拿来了一瓶酒。沃伯顿先生看着仆人把酒瓶打开。

“我是从我的老朋友查尔斯·霍林顿那儿弄到这种波尔图葡萄酒的。他珍藏了四十年，我也已经珍藏了好多年了。他因在英国拥有最好的酒窖而闻名遐迩。”

“他是位酒商吗？”

“不完全是，”沃伯顿先生微笑着说，“我说的是雷格城堡的霍林顿爵士。他是英国最富有的贵族之一，是一位同我交往时间长久的老朋友。我在伊顿公学时和他兄弟是同学。”

碰到了这样的机会，沃伯顿先生无论如何是不会轻易放过的。他讲述了一些趣闻轶事，目的只有一个，那就是他认识一位伯爵。波尔图葡萄酒无疑是纯正优质的，他喝了一杯，然后又喝了第二杯。他谨言慎行的态度不见了踪影。他已经有好几个月没有同白人说过话了，于是开始讲起了故事，凸显自己当初如何与上流社会的大人物相伴相随。倾听他讲述着往事，您会觉得，曾几何时，内阁的组建，政策的确立，都是有赖于他的建议，因为那些建议他曾在某位公爵夫人的耳边窃窃私语提出，或者在餐桌上抛出，由君王枢密院的顾问们满怀着感激之情加以执行。阿斯科特、古德伍德[2]和考斯的昔日时光再次浮现在他的眼前。又喝了一杯波尔图葡萄酒。接着讲述他每年前往约克郡和苏格兰参加盛大的家庭聚会的情况。

“我曾经雇佣了一位男仆，我管他叫‘领班’，那可是我雇佣过的最优秀的仆人。您知道他为何向我提出

1　波尔图葡萄酒（port）常为深红色，产于葡萄牙北部杜罗河流域波尔图市，那儿有着悠久的酿酒文化。

2　古德伍德（Goodwood）是英国苏塞克斯郡境内的城镇，以赛马会著称。

ladies' maids and the gentlemen's gentlemen sit according to the precedence of their masters. He told me he was sick of going to party after party at which I was the only commoner. It meant that he always had to sit at the bottom of the table, and all the best bits were taken before a dish reached him. I told the story to the old Duke of Hereford, and he roared. 'By God, Sir,' he said, 'if I were King of England, I'd make you a viscount just to give your man a chance.' 'Take him yourself, Duke,' I said. 'He's the best valet I've ever had.' 'Well, Warburton,' he said, 'if he's good enough for you he's good enough for me. Send him along.'"

Then there was Monte Carlo, where Mr. Warburton and the Grand Duke Fyodor, playing in partnership, had broken the bank one evening; and there was Marienbad. At Marienbad Mr. Warburton had played baccarat with Edward VII.

"He was only Prince of Wales then, of course. I remember him saying to me, 'George, if you draw on a five you'll lose your shirt.' He was right; I don't think he ever said a truer word in his life. He was a wonderful man. I always said he was the greatest diplomatist in Europe. But I was a young fool in those days, I hadn't the sense to take his advice. If I had, if I'd never drawn on a five, I dare say I shouldn't be here today."

Cooper was watching him. His brown eyes, deep in their sockets, were hard and **supercilious**①, and on his lips was a mocking smile. He had heard a good deal about Mr. Warburton in Kuala Solor, not a bad sort, and he ran his district like clockwork, they said, but by heaven, what a snob! They laughed at him good-naturedly, for it was impossible to dislike a man who was so generous

辞职吗？您要知道，‘管家餐厅’里，贵妇人的侍女和贵族大人的侍从的座位是根据他们主人的身份来安排的。他对我说，他对没完没了地去参加聚会感到烦腻了，聚会当中，我是唯一的平民。这就是意味着，他总是坐在餐桌的末位，等到盘子传到他身边时，好东西都被人家给挑拣走了。我把这件事情告诉给了赫里福德老公爵，他听后大声嚷嚷起来。‘我向上帝保证，先生，’公爵说，‘我若是当上了英国的国王，即便是给你的仆人一次机会，我也要让你封个子爵。’‘您接过去使唤他好啦，公爵，’我说，‘他是我雇佣过的最优秀的仆人。’‘那好吧，沃伯顿，’他说，‘你若是觉得他足够优秀，那我也会觉得他足够优秀的。那就把他送过来吧。’”

随后讲到了蒙特卡洛[1]，沃伯顿先生和费奥多尔大公[2]两人搭档，一个晚上让赌博场的庄家破了产。接着又讲到了马林巴德[3]。在马林巴德，沃伯顿先生同爱德华七世一块儿玩巴卡拉[4]。

“当然啦，他当时只是威尔士亲王。我记得他对我说过，‘乔治，你若是再投五块钱，恐怕衬衫都要输掉啦。’他说得对，我觉得，他一辈子说的话，没有一次比这次应验的。他是个了不起的人物。我一直都说，他是欧洲最伟大的外交家。但是，我那时候少不更事，不懂得接受他的劝告。我若是接受了，若是当时没有投下五块钱，我可以肯定，如今不可能在这儿了。”

库珀注视着他。他棕褐色的双眼深深地陷入在眼窝里，目光冷峻而傲慢。他的嘴边挂着一丝讥讽的微笑。他在瓜拉索洛时便已经听说过了关于沃伯顿先生的许多情况。不是很糟糕的一个人。大家都说，沃伯顿先生把自己管辖的区域治理得井然有序。不过，天哪，就是个十

① supercilious [ˌsjuːpəˈsiliəs] *a.* 傲慢的

---

1 蒙特卡洛（Monte Carlo，也可译为蒙的卡罗）是摩洛哥城市，世界著名赌城。

2 大公（grand duke）指仅次于国王的爵位，大公国的统治者。

3 马林巴德（Marienbad）是捷克共和国玛利亚温泉市的旧称。

4 巴卡拉（baccarat）是指流行于欧洲赌场的一种牌戏，通常有三个人玩。

and so kindly, and Cooper had already heard the story of the Prince of Wales and the game of baccarat. But Cooper listened without indulgence. From the beginning he had resented the Resident's manner. He was very sensitive, and he **writhed**① under Mr. Warburton's polite sarcasms. Mr. Warburton had a **knack**② of receiving a remark of which he disapproved with a **devastating**③ silence. Cooper had lived little in England and he had a peculiar dislike of the English. He resented especially the public-school boy since he always feared that he was going to **patronise**④ him. He was so much afraid of others putting on airs with him that, in order as it were to get in first, he put on such airs as to make everyone think him **insufferably**⑤ conceited.

"Well, at all events the war has done one good thing for us," he said at last. "It's smashed up the power of the aristocracy. The Boer War started it, and 1914 **put the lid on**⑥."

"The great families of England are doomed," said Mr. Warburton with the complacent melancholy of an ***émigré***⑦ who remembered the court of Louis XV. "They cannot afford any longer to live in their splendid palaces and their princely hospitality will soon be nothing but a memory."

"And a damned good job too in my opinion."

"My poor Cooper, what can you know of the glory that was Greece and the grandeur that was Rome?"

Mr. Warburton made an ample gesture. His eye for an instant grew dreamy with a vision of the past.

"Well, believe me, we're fed up with all that rot. What we want is a business government by business men. I was born in a Crown Colony, and I've lived practically all my life in the colonies. I don't give a row of pins for a lord. What's wrong with England is snobbishness. And if there's anything that gets

① writhe [raið] *v.* 感到痛苦
② knack [næk] *n.* 本事
③ devastating ['devəsteitiŋ] *a.* 使人泄气的
④ patronise ['peitrənaiz] *v.* 保护
⑤ insufferably [in'sʌfərəbli] *ad.* 不能忍受地
⑥ put the lid on 完成，结束
⑦ émigré ['emigrei] *n.* 流亡者

足的势利眼！他们并非恶意嘲笑他，因为面对一个慷慨大度并且热情友好的人士，他们不可能不喜欢。库珀已经听说过了关于威尔士亲王与用巴卡拉牌戏赌博的故事。但是，库珀听故事时并没有宽容忍让。从一开始，他便痛恨这位驻地专员的做派。他非常敏感，置身于沃伯顿先生礼貌而又讥讽的氛围中十分痛苦。沃伯顿先生具备一种本领，因为面对一种自己不赞成的看法时，他会以一种咄咄逼人的沉默来加以应对。库珀几乎没有在英国生活过，所以特别反感英国人。他特别痛恨公立学校的学生，因为他总是担心，对方会对他颐指气使。他非常害怕别人在他面前拉架子，于是，他往往会先发制人，摆出一副架势，让大家都觉得，他是个傲慢的人，难以容忍。

“是啊，不管怎么说，战争总归还是替我们做了一件好事，”他终于说话了，“战争摧毁了贵族势力。布尔战争算是肇始，1914 年[1]则大功告成。”

“英国的名门望族遭受了灭顶之灾，”沃伯顿说，语气中充满了傲慢与忧伤，犹如一位法国大革命时代流亡国外但依然怀念路易十五的宫廷贵族。“他们再也承担不起居住在自己豪华的宫殿里的开支用度了，他们那亲王气派的热情待客气势也将很快消失，只停留在人们的记忆中了。”

“我倒是觉得，这事真他妈干得漂亮。”

“可怜的库珀啊，‘光荣属于希腊，伟大属于罗马[2]。’您哪里会知道这一点啊？”

沃伯顿先生做了个引人注目的动作。瞬间，他的眼神变得迷离起来，仿佛眼前呈现出昔日的光景。

“啊，说实在的，那些腐朽不堪的东西我们已经听够了。我们需要的是经商的人管理着经商的政府。我出生在一个由英国政府直辖的殖民地，实际上，我的整个人生都是在不同的殖民地度过的。我才不在乎什么贵族呢。英国的问题是，势利世故。若说有什么东西会让我

1　指 1914 年第一次世界大战爆发。
2　典出爱伦·坡的诗《致海伦》。

my goat it's a snob."

A snob! Mr. Warburton's face grew purple and his eyes blazed with anger. That was a word that had pursued him all his life. The great ladies whose society he had enjoyed in his youth were not inclined to look upon his appreciation of themselves as unworthy, but even great ladies are sometimes out of temper and more than once Mr. Warburton had had the dreadful word flung in his teeth. He knew, he could not help knowing, that there were odious people who called him a snob. How unfair it was! Why, there was no vice he found so **detestable**① as snobbishness. After all, he liked to mix with people of his own class, he was only at home in their company, and how in heaven's name could anyone say that was snobbish? Birds of a feather.

"I quite agree with you," he answered. "A snob is a man who admires or despises another because he is of a higher social rank than his own. It is the most vulgar failing of our English middle-class."

He saw a flicker of amusement in Cooper's eyes. Cooper put up his hand to hide the broad smile that rose to his lips, and so made it more noticeable. Mr. Warburton's hands trembled a little.

Probably Cooper never knew how greatly he had offended his chief. A sensitive man himself he was strangely insensitive to the feelings of others.

Their work forced them to see one another for a few minutes now and then during the day, and they met at six to have a drink on Mr. Warburton's veranda. This was an old-established custom of the country which Mr. Warburton would not for the world have broken. But they ate their meals separately. Cooper in his bungalow and Mr. Warburton at the Fort. After the office work was over they walked till dusk fell, but they walked apart. There were but few paths in this country, where the jungle pressed close upon the plantations of the village, and when Mr. Warburton caught sight of his assistant passing along with his loose stride, he would make a circuit in order to avoid him. Cooper, with his bad manners, his conceit in his own judgement, and his intolerance, had already got

生气，那就是势利眼。”

势利眼！沃伯顿先生脸都是紫的，眼睛里冒出怒火。“势利眼”这个词一辈子同他如影随形。年轻时代，他置身于贵妇人的社交圈，乐此不疲。她们不会把他对她们的欣赏看成毫无价值，但是，贵妇们有时候甚至也会生气失态，而沃伯顿先生不止一次被她们用这个难听的词当面羞辱过。他知道，他不可能不知道，有些可恶的人管他叫“势利眼”。多么不公平啊！啊，他认为，最恶劣的秉性莫过于势利。毕竟，说到底他还是喜欢与自己同一阶层的人们相处。只有同他们在一块儿时，他心里才觉得踏实自在。上帝呀，怎么有人偏偏会说，这是势利呢？志趣相投才相聚啊。

“我很赞同您的观点，”他回答说，“说一个人是势利眼，那是说别人拥有的社会地位比他的更高，而他则巴结或者鄙视人家。这是我们英国中产阶级最为俗不可耐的缺点。”

沃伯顿先生看见库珀的眼中闪烁着一丝戏谑的神情。库珀抬起一只手挡住自己嘴边露出的灿烂的微笑，这样反而显得更加明显了。沃伯顿先生的双手微微抖动着。

库珀可能怎么也不知道自己已经大大地得罪了他的长官。他本人倒是个敏感的人，但是，奇怪的是，对于别人的感受怎么就那么不敏感呢。

由于工作的原因，他们必须在白天里时不时地会面几分钟。他们六点钟见面，在沃伯顿先生的露台上喝上一杯。这是在英国形成的老习惯，沃伯顿先生无论如何也不会破除。但是，他们用餐是分别进行的。库珀在他的孟加拉平房，沃伯顿先生在他的“要塞”。公务结束之后，他们便开始散步，一直到暮色降临，不过他们是分开散步的。当地有几条小路，丛林紧挨着村上的种植园。沃伯顿先生瞥见自己的助手漫不经心地走着时，便会兜一个圈，以便回避他。库珀举止不雅，心高气傲，心胸狭隘，凡此种种，已经令他很伤脑筋了。

① detestable [di'testəbl] *a.* 可憎的

on his nerves; but it was not till Cooper had been on the station for a couple of months that an incident happened which turned the Resident's dislike into bitter hatred.

Mr. Warburton was obliged to go up-country on a tour of inspection, and he left the station in Cooper's charge with mere confidence, since had definitely come to the conclusion that he was a capable fellow. The only thing he did not like was that he had no indulgence. He was honest, just, and painstaking, but he had no sympathy for the natives. It bitterly amused Mr. Warburton to observe that this man who looked upon himself as every man's equal should look upon so many men as his own inferiors. He was hard, he had no patience with the native mind, and he was a bully. Mr. Warburton very quickly realized that the Malays disliked and feared him. He was not altogether displeased. He would not have liked it very much if his assistant had enjoyed a popularity which might rival his own. Mr. Warburton made his elaborate preparations, set out on his expedition, and in three weeks returned. Meanwhile the mail had arrive. The first thing that struck his eyes when he entered his sitting-room was a great pile of open newspapers. Cooper had met him, and they went into the room together. Mr. Warburton turned to one of the servants who had been left behind, and sternly asked him what was the meaning of those open papers. Cooper hastened to explain.

"I wanted to read all about the Wolverhampton murder, and so I borrowed your *Times*. I brought them back again. I knew you wouldn't mind."

Mr. Warburton turned on him, while with anger.

"But I do mind. I mind very much."

"I'm sorry," said Cooper, with composure. "The fact is, I simply couldn't wait till you came back."

"I wonder you didn't open my letters as well."

Cooper, unmoved, smiled at his chief's exasperation.

"Oh, that's not quite the same thing. After all, I couldn't imagine you'd mind my looking at your newspapers. There's nothing private in them."

但是，直到库珀到达这处海外驻地几个月之后，发生了一件事情，令这位驻扎专员的厌恶感转化为了刻骨的仇恨。

沃伯顿先生必须前往内地进行一次例行巡视，他完全放心地把驻地交给库珀管理，因为他心里完全有数，认为库珀很能干。他唯一不喜欢的有点是，库珀没有宽容忍让之心。他诚实，公正，吃苦耐劳，但对土著居民没有同情心。有一点令沃伯顿先生看到既痛苦有好笑，此人一方面认为人皆平等，另一方面竟然会认为许多人不如他。他很严厉，不能耐着性子倾听土著居民的想法，是个颐指气使的人。沃伯顿先生很快便意识到，马来人厌恶他，惧怕他。他对此并非完全不开心。他的助手若是比他自己更加受欢迎，那他倒是会开心不起来了。沃伯顿先生精心地做好了各项准备，开始了自己的巡视之旅，三个星期之后返回。期间，邮件也到达了。他走进起居室时，首先看到的是那一大堆摊开的报纸。库珀迎接了他，他们一同进入房间。沃伯顿先生转身对着自己身后的一位仆人，态度严厉地问他，报纸摊开着是什么意思。库珀急忙做出了解释。

“我想要浏览一下关于沃尔弗汉普顿谋杀案的全部报道，所以借阅您的《泰晤士报》。我看后送回来了。我知道您不会介意的。”

沃伯顿先生面对着他，气得脸色煞白。

“但是，我很介意，非常介意。”

“对不起啊，”库珀说，态度显得很平静，“实际情况是，我不能等到您回来后再看。”

“我寻思着，您怎么没有连我的信都拆开来看看呢。”

库珀无动于衷，面对自己的长官火冒三丈的气势，报以微笑。

“噢，这不是一回事儿。毕竟，我没有想到，您会介意我浏览您的报纸，因为报纸上面不存在什么隐私啊。”

"I very much object to anyone reading my paper before me." He went up to the pile. There were nearly thirty numbers there. I think it extremely **impertinent**① of you. They're all mixed up."

"We can easily put them in order," said Cooper, joining him at the table.

"Don't touch them," cried Mr. Warburton.

"I say, it's childish to make a scene about a little thing like that."

"How dare you speak to me like that?"

"Oh, go to hell," said Cooper, and he flung out of the room.

Mr. Warburton, trembling with passion, was left contemplating his papers. His greatest pleasure in life had been destroyed by those **callous**②, brutal hands. Most people living in out-of-the-way places when the mail comes tear open impatiently their papers and taking the last ones first glance at the latest news from home. Not so Mr. Warburton. His newsagent had instructions to write on the outside of the wrapper the date of each paper he despatched, and when the great bundle arrived Mr. Warburton looked at these dates and with his blue pencil numbered them. His headboy's orders were to place one on the table every morning in the veranda with the early cup of tea and it was Mr. Warburton's especial delight to break the wrapper as he sipped his tea, and read the morning paper. It gave him the illusion of living at home. Every Monday morning he read the Monday *Times* of six weeks back, and so went through the week. On Sunday he read the *Observer*. Like his habit of dressing for dinner it was a tie to civilisation. And it was his pride that no matter how exciting the news was he had never yielded to the temptation of opening a paper before its allotted time. During the war the suspense sometimes had been intolerable, and when he read one day that a push was begun he had undergone agonies of suspense which he might have saved himself by the simple expedient of opening a later paper which lay waiting for him on a shelf. It had been the severest trial to which he had ever exposed himself, but

① impertinent [im'pəːtinənt] *a.* 无礼的

② callous ['kæləs] *a.* 起老茧的

“我强烈反对任何人先于我看我的报纸。”他走到那堆报纸旁边，这堆报纸差不多有三十份。“我觉得，你这样做是极为不礼貌的，报纸都乱成一团了。”

“我们可以轻而易举就把报纸整理好啊。”库珀说，走到了桌子边他的身旁。

“别碰报纸。”沃伯顿先生大声说。

“我说啊，为这么一点小事大动肝火，未免显得有点幼稚吧。”

“你竟敢这么对我说话？”

“噢，见鬼去吧。”库珀说着，冲出了房间。

沃伯顿先生激动得浑身颤抖，独自一人面对报纸出神。他人生当中最大的乐趣被那双粗糙兽性的手给糟蹋了。对于大多数生活在偏僻地方的人们而言，每当有邮件到达了，他们都会迫不及待地打开，拿出最新的那一份，浏览一下来自自己家乡的新闻。但沃伯顿先生不会这样做。他嘱咐过了他的报纸经办人，要在包装纸上注明每一份报纸派送的日期。当一大捆报纸送达时，沃伯顿先生会看看那些日期，并且用蓝色铅笔标明序号。他吩咐自己领头的仆人，每天早上，要把一份报纸连同一杯早茶放置在露台的桌子上。一边品着早茶，一边打开报纸，看着早报，这是沃伯顿先生特殊的乐趣。这样做让他产生一种置身家乡的幻觉。每个星期一早上，他阅读着六个星期以前的《泰晤士报》，一个星期就是以这样的方式度过的。到了星期天，他便阅读《观察家报》[1]。如同他衣着妥帖用晚餐的习惯一样，这一点也是同文明世界保持联系的纽带。无论新闻有多么令人激动，他决不会受到诱惑，在规定的时间之前打开报纸，这是他感到自豪的一点。战争期间，悬念有时候令人无法忍受。有一天，他在报纸上看到，军队的攻势开始了。他当时就经历着那种悬念带来的痛苦煎熬。其实，他只要费举手之劳，打开架子上后面的报纸看一看，便可以让自己

1 《观察家报》（*The Observer*）是英国一家创刊最早的星期日报纸，创办于 1791 年，常披露一些独家新闻，广受中上层知识分子欢迎。

he victoriously surmounted it. And that clumsy fool had broken open those neat tight packages because he wanted to know whether some **horrid**① woman had murdered her odious husband.

Mr. Warburton sent for his boy and told him to bring wrappers. He folded up the papers as neatly as he could, placed a wrapper round each and numbered it. But it was a melancholy task.

"I shall never forgive him," he said. "Never."

Of course his boy had been with him on his expedition; he never travelled without him, for his boy knew exactly how he liked things, and Mr. Warburton was not the kind of jungle traveller who was prepared to dispense with his comforts; but in the interval since their arrival he had been gossiping in the servants' quarters. He had learnt that Cooper had had trouble with his boys. All but the youth Abas had left him. Abas had desired to go too, but his uncle had placed him there on the instructions of the Resident, and he was afraid to leave without his uncle's permission.

"I told him he had done well, Tuan," said the boy. "But he is unhappy. He says it is not a good house, and he wishes to know if he may go as the others have gone."

"No, he must stay. The Tuan must have servants. Have those who went been replaced?"

"No, Tuan, no one will go."

Mr. Warburton frowned. Cooper was an insolent fool, but he had an official position and must be suitably provided with servants. It was not seemly that his house should be improperly conducted.

"Where are the boys who ran away?"

"They are in the kampong, Tuan."

"Go and see them tonight, and tell them that I expect them to be back in Tuan Cooper's house at dawn tomorrow."

"They say they will not go, Tuan."

① horrid ['hɔrid] *a.* 可恶的

从中摆脱出来。这是他所经历的最为严厉的考验，但是，他最终还是取得了胜利。而那个拙劣的蠢货竟然拆开了密封得严严实实的包装，就因为想要知道某个丑恶的女人是否谋杀了她下三滥的丈夫。

沃伯顿先生叫来了他的仆人，吩咐他去取些包装纸来。他把报纸尽量卷紧，给每一张都裹上包装纸，标好序号。但是，这是一桩令人感到忧伤的任务。

“我决不会原谅他，”他说，“决不会。”

当然，他巡视途中，他的男仆一直都跟随着他。他从没有撇下男仆独自旅行的情况，因为仆人对他的喜好知道得一清二楚。况且，沃伯顿先生也不属于那种在丛林中旅行而轻易放弃享受的人。但是，他们到家后的一段时间里，他往往会到仆人的住处去闲聊。他了解到，库珀同他的仆人们相处得不融洽。除了那位叫阿巴斯的，其他仆人全都离开了他。阿巴斯也想要离开来着，但他叔叔有了驻扎专员的吩咐才给他谋到了这个职位，没有得到他叔叔的许可，他不敢擅自离开。

“我告诉他说，他做得很好，*Tuan*[1]，”仆人说，“但是，他很不开心。他说，这不是一个好人家，他想要知道，自己可不可以离开，因为其他人都离开了。”

“不行，他必须留下来。那位 *Tuan* 必须要有仆人。那些离开了的已经有人补充上了吗？”

“没有呢，*Tuan*，没有谁愿意去。”

沃伯顿先生紧锁眉头。库珀是个傲慢无礼的蠢货，但他拥有一份公职，必须要有仆人伺候好。他的住处不能得体地收拾好，那也不像话啊。

“那些跑掉的仆人到哪儿去啦？”

“他们都待在村上呢，*Tuan*。”

“今晚看他们去，告诉他们，我希望他们明天黎明时回到库珀 *Tuan* 的住处去。”

“他们说，他们不去呢，*Tuan*。”

1 此处为马来语，意为“先生，老爷”。

"On my order?"

The boy had been with Mr. Warburton for fifteen years, and he knew every **intonation**① of his master's voice. He was not afraid of him, they had gone through too much together, once in the jungle the Resident had saved his life, and once, upset in some rapids, but for him the Resident would have been drowned; but he knew when the Resident must be obeyed without question.

"I will go to the **kampong**②," he said.

Mr. Warburton expected that his **subordinate**③ would take the first opportunity to apologise for his rudeness, but Cooper had the ill-bred man's inability to express regret; and when they met next morning in the office he ignored the incident. Since Mr. Warburton had been away for three weeks it was necessary for them to have a somewhat prolonged interview. At the end of it, Mr. Warburton dismissed him.

"I don't think there's anything else, thank you." Cooper turned to go, but Mr. Warburton stopped him. "I understand you've been having some trouble with your boys."

Cooper gave a harsh laugh.

"They tried to blackmail me. They had the damned cheek to run away, all except that incompetent fellow Abas—he knew when he was well off—but I just sat light. They've all come to heel again."

"What do you mean by that?"

"This morning they were all back on their jobs, the Chinese cook and all. There they were, as cool as cucumbers; you would have thought they owned the place. I suppose they'd come to the conclusion that I wasn't such fool as I looked."

"By no means. They came back on my express order."

Cooper flushed slightly.

"I should be obliged if you wouldn't interfere with my private concerns."

"They're not your private concerns. When your servants run away it makes you ridiculous. You are perfectly free to make a fool of yourself, but I cannot

① intonation [ˌintəu'neiʃən] *n.* 语调

② kampong [kæm'pɔŋ] *n.* 小村庄

③ subordinate [sə'bɔːdinət] *n.* 下属

“若是有了我的命令呢？”

这个男仆跟随沃伯顿先生已经十五年了。他明白自己主人说话时每一种语调的用意。他不是惧怕他，他们一同经历了风风雨雨。有一次，在丛林中，驻地专员救了他的命。还有一次，在激流中翻了船，幸亏有了他，否则驻地专员一定会淹死。但是，仆人知道，对于驻地专员的吩咐，什么时候应该毫无疑问遵从。

“我这就到村上去。”他说。

沃伯顿先生预料他的助手会第一时间替自己的粗鲁行为道歉。但是，库珀是个没有修养的人，不至于表达悔恨之意。他们翌日上午在办公室见面时，他根本就没有提起那件事情。由于沃伯顿先生离开了三个星期，按理他们这次见面有必要延长时间。会面结束时，沃伯顿先生表示他可以离开了。

“我看没有什么别的事情了，谢谢啊。”库珀转身离开，但是，沃伯顿先生拦住了他。“我了解到，你和你的仆人相处得不融洽。”

库珀发出了刺耳的笑声。

“他们想要对我敲诈勒索，全都厚颜无耻地跑了，全都跑了，只剩下那个无能的阿巴斯——他知道什么时候好过日子——但是，我不动声色地坐着，他们全都又回来了。”

“你这话是什么意思啊？”

“他们今天早上全部返回到自己的工作岗位上了，那位华人厨子和所有人。他们镇定自若，好像什么事情都没有发生一样。你还会以为那是他们的家呢。我估摸着，他们认定了，我毕竟不像看起来那么愚蠢吧。”

“根本不是那么回事啊。他们之所以回来，那是我责令他们那么干的。”

库珀脸上涨得有点红了。

“你若是不来干涉我的私事，我会感激不尽的。”

“他们不是你的私事。你的仆人跑掉了，让你显得荒谬可笑。你尽可以把自己当作笑料，但我不允许让你

allow you to be made a fool of. It is unseemly that your house should not be properly staffed. As soon as I heard that your boys had left you, I had them told to be back in their places at dawn. That'll do."

Mr. Warburton nodded to signify that the interview was at an end. Cooper took no notice.

"Shall I tell you what I did? I called them and gave the whole bally lot the sack. I gave them ten minutes to get out of the compound."

Mr. Warburton shrugged his shoulders.

"What makes you think you can get others?"

"I've told my own clerk to see about it."

Mr. Warburton reflected for a moment.

"I think you behaved very foolishly. You will do well to remember in future that good masters make good servants."

"Is there anything else you want to teach me?"

"I should like to teach you manners, but it would be an arduous task, and I have not the time to waste. I will see that you get boys."

"Please don't put yourself to any trouble on my account. I'm quite capable of getting them for myself."

Mr. Warburton smiled acidly. He had an inkling that Cooper disliked him as much as he disliked Cooper, and he knew that nothing is more galling than to be forced to accept the favours of a man you detest.

"Allow me to tell you that you have no more chance of getting Malay or Chinese servants here now than you have of getting an English **butler**① or a French **chef**②. No one will come to you except on an order from me. Would you like me to give it?"

"No."

"As you please. Good morning."

Mr. Warburton watched the development of the situation with acrid humour. Cooper's clerk was unable to persuade Malay, Dyak, or Chinese to enter the house of such a master. Abas, the boy who remained faithful to him, knew how

被当成笑料。你的食宿起居不能妥当料理好，这不像话。我一听说你的仆人全都离开你了，我便打发人去告诉他们，黎明时分一定要返回。事情就是这样的。”

沃伯顿先生点了点头，示意会面结束了。库珀未加理会。

“我需要告诉你我做了些什么吗？我把他们叫到一块儿，然后全部把他们给解雇了。我限定他们十分钟之内滚出那个住处。”

沃伯顿先生耸了耸肩膀。

“你凭什么觉得自己还能够物色到别的人呢？”

“我吩咐了我自己的秘书去负责物色。”

沃伯顿先生思忖了片刻。

“我感觉，你的行为很愚蠢。你将来定会好好地记住，好主人才能成就好仆人。”

“你还有什么别的事情要教导我的吗？”

“我倒是想要教导你如何具备好的行为举止，不过，那是个艰巨的任务。我没有时间可以浪费。我来负责帮你物色仆人的事情吧。”

“请你不要替我的事情操心了。我能够自己物色到仆人的。”

沃伯顿先生露出了酸楚的微笑。他隐约地觉察到，库珀不喜欢他，如同他不喜欢库珀一样。他知道，没有什么事情比勉为其难地接受一位你所厌恶的人帮忙更加别扭的。

“请允许我告诉你，你在此地找到马来或华人仆人的机会并不比找到英国管家或者法国厨师更大啊。除非我发了话，任何人都不会到你那儿去了。你要我发个话吗？”

“不要。”

“随你便吧，再见。”

沃伯顿先生关注着事态的进展，有点幸灾乐祸。库珀的秘书说服不了马来人、迪雅克人或者中国人给这样一个主儿当仆人。那位留在他身边的阿巴斯只会烹饪本地风格的食物。库珀本是一位口粗的食客，连他见到那一成不变

① butler ['bʌtlə] *n.* 男仆
② chef [ʃef] *n.* 厨师

to cook only native food, and Cooper, a coarse feeder, found his **gorge**① rise against the everlasting rice. There was no water-carrier, and in that great heat he needed several baths a day. He cursed Abas, but Abas opposed him with sullen resistance and would not do more than he chose. It was galling to know that the lad stayed with him only because the Resident insisted. This went on for a fortnight and then, one morning, he found in his house the very servants whom he had previously dismissed. He fell into a violent rage, but he had learnt a little sense, and this time, without a word, he let them stay. He swallowed his humiliation, but the impatient contempt he had felt for Mr. Warburton's idiosyncrasies changed into a sullen hatred: the Resident with this malicious stroke had made him the laughing-stock of all the natives.

The two men now held no communication with one another. They broke the time-honoured custom of sharing, notwithstanding personal dislike, a drink at six o'clock with any white man who happened to be at the station. Each lived in his own house as though the other did not exist. Now that Cooper had fallen into the work, it was necessary for them to have little to do with one another in the office. Mr. Warburton used his orderly to send any message he had to give his assistant, and his instructions he sent by formal letter. They saw one another constantly, that was inevitable, but did not exchange half a dozen words in a week. The fact that they could not avoid catching sight of one another got on their nerves. They brooded over their antagonism, and Mr. Warburton, taking his daily walk, could think of nothing but how much he detested his assistant.

And the dreadful thing was that in all probability they would remain thus, facing each other in deadly enmity, till Mr. Warburton went on leave. It might be three years. He had no reason to send in a complaint to headquarters: Cooper did his work very well, and at that time men were hard to get. True, vague complaints reached him and hints that the natives found Cooper harsh. There was certainly a feeling of dissatisfaction among them. But when Mr. Warburton looked into specific cases, all he could say was that Cooper had shown severity where mildness would not have been **misplaced**②, and had

① gorge [gɔːdʒ] *n.* 食道

② misplace [ˌmisˈpleis] *v.* 使（言行等）不合时宜

的米饭都觉得反胃。挑水的人也没有，但天气闷热得很，他一天需要冲几次澡。他咒骂阿巴斯，但阿巴斯沉默不语，以示反抗，而且绝不干自己不愿意干的活儿。小伙子之所以愿意留下来，只是因为驻扎专员坚持要他这么做。当他知道这个情况时，心里感到不是滋味。这种情况持续了两个星期。后来，一天早上，他发现自己先前解雇了的那些仆人出现在了他家里。他感到义愤填膺，但学得理智了一些。这一次，他没有吭声，让他们留下来了。面对羞辱，他忍气吞声，但是，对于沃伯顿先生特有的个人习性，他怀有难以克制的轻蔑感，而这种轻蔑感已经转化为默默的仇恨了。由于驻扎专员这个充满了恶意的招数，库珀成了所有土著居民的笑料。

现如今，两人之间互不交流了。过去，尽管两人之间互存厌恶感，但是，每天六点钟时还是会同正好在驻地的白人喝上一杯。他们打破了这个长期坚持的习惯了。各自生活在自己的住处，好像对方压根儿就不存在似的。库珀全身心投入工作，他们在办公室便极少打交道了。沃伯顿先生会让自己的勤务员把信息转送给助手，他要吩咐什么事情都是以正式的信函传递的。他们常常不可避免地会照面，但一个星期当中也说不上几句话。实际情况是，他们之间无法避免见面，这让他们心里感到很别扭。他们处在这样的对立状态，内心感到很沮丧。沃伯顿先生每天散步时，不会想别的事情，满脑子就想着自己有多么仇视那位助手。

可怕的情况是，很有可能，他们会一直维持这种相互敌视的状态，直到沃伯顿先生离开岗位。如此看来，可能要持续三年，因为他没有任何理由向总部抱怨。库珀工作很出色，那个时候，又很难招募到人手。确实，他也听到过一些含糊其辞的抱怨，还有些暗示，说土著居民发现库珀为人粗暴。毫无疑问，他们中间有一种不满情绪。但是，当沃伯顿先生调查一些具体事情时，他能够说得出的也无非就是，库珀本来可以态度和蔼一些的时候却表现得很严厉。库珀过于冷酷，而若是换了他

been unfeeling when himself would have been sympathetic. He had done nothing for which he could be **taken to task**[①]. But Mr. Warburton watched him. Hatred will often make a man clear-sighted, and he had a suspicion that Cooper was using the natives without consideration, yet keeping within the law, because he felt that thus he could exasperate his chief. One day perhaps he would go too far. None knew better than Mr. Warburton how irritable the **incessant**[②] heat could make a man and how difficult it was to keep one's self-control after a sleepless night. He smiled softly to himself. Sooner or later Cooper would deliver himself into his hand.

When at last the opportunity came, Mr. Warburton laughed aloud. Cooper had charge of the prisoners; they made roads, built sheds, rowed when it was necessary to send the prahu up or down stream, kept the town clean, and otherwise usefully employed themselves. If well-behaved they even on occasion served as house-boys. Cooper kept them hard at it. He liked to see them work. He took pleasure in devising tasks for them; and seeing quickly enough that they were being made to do useless things the prisoners worked badly. He punished them by lengthening their hours. This was contrary to the regulations, and as soon as it was brought to the attention of Mr. Warburton, without referring the matter back to his subordinate, he gave instructions that the old hours should be kept; Cooper, going out for his walk, was astounded to see the prisoners strolling back to the gaol; he had given instructions that they were not to knock off till dusk. When he asked the warder in charge why they had left off work he was told that it was the Resident's bidding.

White with rage he strode to the Fort. Mr. Warburton, in his spotless white ducks and his neat topee, with a walking-stick in his hand, followed by his dogs, was on the point of starting out on his afternoon stroll. He had watched Cooper go, and knew that he had taken the road by the river. Cooper jumped up the steps and went straight up to the Resident.

"I want to know what the hell you mean by countermanding my order that the prisoners were to work till six," he burst out, beside himself with fury.

① take to task 责备

② incessant [in'sesənt] *a.* 持续不断的

自己则会表现出同情心。库珀没有做什么应该受到指责的事情。但是，沃伯顿先生在盯着他。仇恨往往会让一个人目光变得犀利。他怀疑，库珀利用土著居民做事，却从不替人家着想，不过，仍然是在法律允许的范围内行事，因为库珀觉得，通过这样做，他可以激怒他的长官。说不定有朝一日，他会做得太过分。没有任何人比沃伯顿先生更加清楚，没完没了的炎热天气会让一个人变得多么烦躁不安，而经历过一个不眠之夜后，要控制住自己的情绪有多么困难。他暗自微笑了起来。库珀迟早会栽到他手里的。

最后，机会来了，沃伯顿哈哈大笑了起来。库珀负责管理囚犯。囚犯们修路，建造棚屋，有马来帆船上下时需要拉纤。他们还负责小镇的清洁，以及干用得上他们干的其他活儿。他们若是表现得好，有时候甚至会叫去当家里的仆人。库珀迫使他们卖力干活儿。他喜欢看他们干活儿时的情形，享受给他们安排活儿带来的乐趣。囚犯们很快便发现，他们干的全是一些毫无意义的活儿，于是干活时开始磨蹭起来。他便延长他们的劳动工时，以此来惩罚他们。这种做法是违规的。沃伯顿先生刚一注意到这种情况时，并没有同他的助手协商，便吩咐说，要执行过去的干活时间。库珀外出散步时，看到囚犯们返回监舍，感到很震惊，因为他先前吩咐过了，不到暮色降临，不准收工。他询问监舍的看守为何囚犯们收工了，对方告诉他说，是驻扎专员下达的命令。

他气得脸色煞白，大步走向"要塞"。沃伯顿先生身穿洁白的帆布裤，头戴整洁的遮阳帽，手上拿着一个手杖，身后跟随着他的几条狗，正准备出发开始自己下午的散步。他早就注意到库珀出门了，而且知道他走的是河畔那条路。库珀跳跃着跑上了门前的台阶，直接到了驻扎专员的跟前。

"我有令在先，囚犯们不到六点钟不准收工。你竟然撤销我的命令，我想知道，你这到底是什么意思啊？"他一上来便嚷嚷着，愤怒导致他情绪失控。

Mr. Warburton opened his cold blue eyes very wide and assumed an expression of great surprise.

"Are you out of your mind? Are you so ignorant that you do not know that that is not the way to speak to your official superior?"

"Oh, go to hell. The prisoners are my pidgin, and you've got no right to interfere. You mind your business and I'll mind mine. I want to know what the devil you mean by making a damned fool of me. Everyone in the place will know that you've countermanded my order."

Mr. Warburton kept very cool.

"You had no power to give the order you did. I countermanded it because it was harsh and tyrannical. Believe me, I have not made half such a damned fool of you as you have made of yourself."

"You disliked me from the first moment I came here. You've done everything you could to make the place impossible for me because I wouldn't lick your boots for you. You got your knife into me because I wouldn't flatter you."

Cooper, **spluttering**① with rage, was nearing dangerous ground, and Mr. Warburton's eyes grew on a sudden colder and more piercing.

"You are wrong. I thought you were a **cad**②, but I was perfectly satisfied with the way you did your work."

"You snob. You damned snob. You thought me a cad because I hadn't been to Eton. Oh, they told me in K.S. what to expect. Why, don't you know that you're the laughing-stock of the whole country? I could hardly help bursting into a roar of laughter when you told your celebrated story about the Prince of Wales. My God, how they shouted at the club when they told it. By God, I'd rather be the cad I am than the snob you are."

He got Mr. Warburton on the raw.

"If you don't get out of my house this minute I shall knock you down," he cried.

The other came a little closer to him and put his face in his.

"Touch me, touch me," he said. "By God, I'd like to see you hit me. Do you

沃伯顿先生蓝色的眼睛睁得大大的，透出冷漠的神情，显得大为惊讶。

“你脑袋出问题了吗？你难道不知道这不是对自己长官说话的方式吗？”

“噢，见鬼去吧。囚犯们是归我管的，你无权干涉。你管你自己该管的事情，我管我的。我想要知道，你让我丢脸献丑，这到底是什么意思？这儿所有的人都会知道，你撤销了我下达的命令。”

沃伯顿先生镇定自若。

“你没有权力下达那样的命令。我之所以撤销它，那是因为那个命令苛刻而又残暴。你相信我好啦，我并没有让你丢脸献丑，你让你自己丢脸献丑还差不多。”

“从我刚一到达这儿开始，你就厌恶我。你做出的每一件事情都让我无法在此地安身，就因为我不对你溜须拍马。你对我怀恨在心，就因为我不对你恭维奉承。”

库珀义愤填膺，唠唠叨叨地说着，已经接近危险的边缘了。沃伯顿先生的目光变得更加冷漠，更加犀利。

“你错了。我心里面觉得你是个无赖，但是，对你的工作还是十分满意的。”

“你这个势利眼，该死的势利眼。你认为我是个无赖，就因为我没有进过伊顿念书。噢，在瓜拉索洛时，他们就告诉过我，我到这儿来会遇到什么样的情形。啊，你难道不知道自己是整个这个地区的笑料吗？当你讲述你那个关于威尔士亲王的著名故事时，我都忍不住要哈哈大笑起来。天哪，他们大声嚷嚷着在俱乐部里讲述那个故事呢。天哪，我宁愿做个无赖，也不愿意做你这样的势利眼啊。”

他触到了沃伯顿先生的痛处。

“你若不立刻从我这儿滚出去，我就会揍得你趴下。”他大声说。

对方反而挨他更近了，脸朝着他的脸。

“碰我试试，碰我试试，”他说，“天哪，我倒是想要看看你是如何揍我的。你还想要我再说吗？势利眼，

① splutter ['splʌtə] *v.* 急切地说

② cad [kæd] *n.* 下等人

want me to say it again? Snob. Snob."

Cooper was three inches taller than Mr. Warburton, a strong, muscular young man. Mr. Warburton was fat and fifty-four. His clenched fist shot out. Cooper caught him by the arm and pushed him back.

"Don't be a damned fool. Remember I'm not a gentleman. I know how to use my hands."

He gave a sort of hoot, and grinning all over his pale, sharp face jumped down the veranda steps. Mr. Warburton, his heart in his anger pounding against his ribs, sank exhausted into a chair. His body tingled as though he had prickly heat. For one horrible moment he thought he was going to cry. But suddenly he was conscious that his head-boy was on the veranda and instinctively regained control of himself. The boy came forward and filled him a glass of whisky and soda.

Without a word Mr. Warburton took it and **drank it to the dregs**①.

"What do you want to say to me?" asked Mr. Warburton, trying to force a smile on to his strained lips.

"Tuan, the assistant Tuan is a bad man. Abas wishes again to leave him."

"Let him wait a little. I shall write to Kuala Solor and ask that Tuan Cooper should go elsewhere."

"Tuan Cooper is not good with the Malays."

"Leave me."

The boy silently withdrew. Mr. Warburton was left alone with his thoughts. He saw the club at Kuala Solor, the men sitting round the table in the window in their flannels, when the night had driven them in from golf and tennis, drinking whiskies and gin pahits, and laughing when they told the celebrated story of the Prince of Wales and himself at Marienbad. He was hot with shame and misery. A snob! They all thought him a snob. And he had always thought them very good fellows, he had always been gentleman enough to let it make no difference to him that they were of very second-rate position. He hated them now. But his hatred for them was nothing compared with his hatred for Cooper. And if it had

势利眼。”

库珀比沃伯顿先生高出三英寸，青春年华，体格健壮，肌肉发达。沃伯顿先生体型肥胖，已经五十四岁了。他紧握的拳头挥了出去，但库珀抓住了他的一条胳膊，把他向后一推。

“别他妈冒傻气了，别忘了我可不是什么绅士啊。我知道该如何使用自己的双手来着。”

他发出一声呼哧声，苍白而五官分明的脸上堆满狞笑，跳下了露台的台阶。沃伯顿先生怒不可遏，心砰砰直跳，身子瘫坐在一把椅子上。他浑身感到刺痛，好像生了痱子一样。恐惧瞬间袭来，他觉得自己都快要哭出来了。但是，突然，他意识到领头的仆人就在露台上，于是便本能地恢复了平静。男仆走向前，给他斟了一杯威士忌兑苏打水。

沃伯顿先生没有吭声，接过杯子，一饮而尽。

“你想要对我说什么来着？”沃伯顿先生问了一声，想要从绷紧的嘴唇上挤出一丝微笑来。

“*Tuan*，助手 *Tuan* 是个坏人。阿巴斯又想要离开他了。”

“让他再等一等。我会给瓜拉索洛那边写信的，请求把库珀 Tuan 调到别的什么地方去。”

“库珀 *Tuan* 对马来人不友好。”

“你走吧。”

男仆默默地走开了。沃伯顿先生独自一人待着，陷入了沉思。他仿佛看到了瓜拉索洛的俱乐部，夜幕降临后，身穿法兰绒衣服的男人们不得不从高尔夫球场和网球场撤退，围坐在窗户边的桌子旁，喝着威士忌和杜松子酒，一边讲述着威尔士亲王和他自己在马林巴德的那个著名故事，一边哈哈大笑。他羞得脸上发烫，痛苦不已。势利眼！他们全都认为他是势利眼。但他一直都认为他们是非常好的人。尽管他们在地位上属于二流，但他一直都怀着君子的风度，把他们当成同自己平起平坐的人。他现在痛恨他们了。但是，他对他们的仇恨无法

① drink to the dregs 喝干

come to blows Cooper could have **thrashed**① him. Tears of **mortification**② ran down his red, fat face. He sat there for a couple of hours smoking cigarette after cigarette, and he wished he were dead.

At last the boy came back and asked him if he would dress for dinner. Of course! He always dressed for dinner. He rose wearily from his chair and put on his stiff shirt and the high collar. He sat down at the prettily decorated table, and was waited on as usual by the two boys while two others waved their great fans. Over there in the bungalow, two hundred yards away, Cooper was eating a filthy meal **clad**③ only in a sarong and a baju. His feet were bare and while he ate he probably read a detective story. After dinner Mr. Warburton sat down to write a letter. The Sultan was away, but he wrote, privately and confidentially, to his representative. Cooper did his work very well, he said, but the fact was that he couldn't get on with him. They were getting dreadfully on each other's nerves and he would look upon it as a very great favour if Cooper could be transferred to another post.

He despatched the letter next morning by special messenger. The answer came a fortnight later with the month's mail. It was a private note, and ran as follows:

My dear Warburton,

I do not want to answer your letter officially, and so I am writing you a few lines myself. Of course if you insist I will put the matter up to the Sultan, but I think you would be much wiser to drop it. I know Cooper is a rough diamond, but he is capable, and he had a pretty thin time in the war, and I think he should be given every chance. I think you are a little too much inclined to attach importance to a man's social position. You must remember that times have changed. Of course it's a very good thing for a man to be a gentleman, but it's better that he should be competent and hard-working. I think if you'll exercise a little tolerance you'll get on very well with Cooper.

Yours very sincerely,

Richard Temple.

① thrash [θræʃ] *v.* 彻底打败
② mortification [ˌmɔːtifiˈkeiʃən] *n.* 羞愧感
③ clad [klæd] *v.*clothe 的一种过去分词

同对库珀的仇恨相比拟。他们若是真的打起架来，库珀可能会揍扁他。屈辱的泪水从他通红肥胖的脸颊上流下来。他在那儿做了两三个小时，一支接着一支抽烟。心里面觉得还不如死了的好。

最后，男仆进来了，问他是否着装准备用晚餐。当然啦！他一直都是着好装用晚餐的。他从坐着的椅子上站起身，疲惫不堪，穿上浆洗得梆硬的衬衫和高领子。他在装点精致的餐桌边坐下来，还和平常一样，两位仆人伺候用餐，另外两位扇着大扇子。距离两百码的另外一处孟加拉平房内，库珀只围着一条短裙和穿着一件长袖衫，正在吃着脏兮兮的晚餐。双脚是光着的，他可能在边吃边看一部侦探小说。晚餐过后，沃伯顿先生坐下来写信。苏丹离开了，于是，他私下里秘密地给苏丹的代表写信。他说，库珀工作很出色，但是，实际情况是，他与自己相处不了。他们相互之间看着对方都很别扭，若是能够把库珀调换到另外一个驻地去，他将感激不尽。

翌日上午，他派遣特使把信送走了。两个星期之后，回信随着当月的邮件送到了。这是一封私人信件，内容如下：

亲爱的沃伯顿：

我不想用公函的形式给你回复，于是亲笔给你写上几句话。当然，你若是坚持走官方程序，我自会把这件事情向苏丹回报。不过，我觉得，更加明智的做法是放下此事。我了解库珀，他是一枚粗糙的钻石，但很有能力。他在战场上经历过磨难，我觉得，你应该给他每一个机会。我觉得，你过于看重一个人的社会地位了。你必须要记住，时代发生了变化。当然，一个人若是绅士，那是件好事情，但是，有能力和能吃苦更加重要。我觉得，你若是多磨砺一下自己的忍耐性，可能会同库珀相处得很融洽的。

你诚挚的

理查德·坦普尔

The letter dropped from Mr. Warburton's hand. It was easy to read between the lines. Dick Temple, whom he had known for twenty years, Dick Temple, who came from quite a good county family, thought him a snob, and for that reason had no patience with his request. Mr. Warburton felt on a sadden discouraged with life. The world of which he was a part had passed away and the future belonged to a meaner generation. Cooper represented it and Cooper he hated with all his heart. He stretched out his hand to fill his glass, and at the gesture his head-boy stepped forward.

"I didn't know you were there."

The boy picked up the official letter. Ah, that was why he was waiting.

"Does Tuan Cooper go, Tuan?"

"No."

"There will be a misfortune."

For a moment the words conveyed nothing to his **lassitude**①. But only for a moment. He sat up in his chair and looked at the boy. He was all attention.

"What do you mean by that?"

"Tuan Cooper is not behaving rightly with Abas."

Mr. Warburton shrugged his shoulders. How should a man like Cooper know how to treat servants? Mr. Warburton knew the type: he would be grossly familiar with them at one moment and rude and inconsiderate the next.

"Let Abas go back to his family."

"Tuan Cooper holds back his wages so that he may not run away. He has paid him nothing for three months. I tell him to be patient. But he is angry, he will not listen to reason. If the Tuan continues to use him ill there will be a misfortune."

"You were right to tell me."

The fool! Did he know so little of the Malays as to think he could safely injure them? It would serve him damned well right if he got a **kris**② in his back. A kris. Mr. Warburton's heart seemed on a sudden to miss a beat. He had only to

信从沃伯顿先生的手上掉落了。字里行间的意思一目了然。迪克·汤普尔，一个他认识长达二十年之久的人，迪克·汤普尔，一个来自于体面乡村家族的人，竟然会认为他是个势利眼。因为这个理由，他竟然没有耐性来对待他的请求。沃伯顿先生突然觉得垂头丧气了，对人生失去了勇气。他曾经拥有过的世界已经逝去了，未来则属于更加猥琐平庸的一代了。库珀代表了未来的一代。他发自内心地仇视库珀。他伸出一只手，把酒杯斟满。领头的仆人看见这个动作后走上前来。

"我不知道你在这儿呢。"

男仆捡起公函。啊，他这正是为了这个等候着的。

"库珀 *Tuan* 会走吧，*Tuan*？"

"不会。"

"那可是会出大事情啊。"

一时间，他由于困乏无力，没有听出话里的意思。他在椅子上坐直了身子，看着男仆。他聚精会神起来。

① lassitude ['læsitjuːd] *n.* 疲乏

"你这话什么意思啊？"

"库珀 *Tuan* 对阿巴斯的态度不对劲儿。"

沃伯顿先生耸了耸肩膀。库珀这种人怎么会知道该如何对待仆人呢？沃伯顿先生了解这种人：对待仆人，一会儿亲切随和得让人受不了，一会儿便会翻脸不认人。

"那就叫阿巴斯回到家人身边去吧。"

"库珀 *Tuan* 扣住了他的薪水，所以他跑不了。他已经有三个月没有支付给他一个子儿了。我对他说要耐心点。但他很生气，不听劝告。*Tuan* 若是继续虐待他，那是会出大事情的。"

"你告诉我这个情况，做得对。"

蠢货！他难道对马来人这么无知，以至于觉得可以随意伤害人家吗？他若是哪一天背上被人刺上一曲刃短剑，那才真是活该呢。曲刃短剑啊。沃伯顿先生的心脏似乎突然停止了跳动。他只能任由事态发展了。遇上某

② kris [kriːs] *n.* 波状刃短剑

let things take their course and one fine day he would be rid of Cooper. He smiled faintly as the phrase, a masterly inactivity, crossed his mind. And now his heart beat a little quicker, for he saw the man he haled lying on his face in a pathway of the jungle with a knife in his back. A fit end for the cad and the bully. Mr. Warburton sighed. It was his duty to warn him, and of course he must do it. He wrote a brief and formal note to Cooper asking him to come to the Fort at once.

In ten minutes Cooper stood before him. They had not spoken to one another since the day when Mr. Warburton had nearly struck him. He did not now ask him to sit down.

"Did you wish to see me?" asked Cooper.

He was untidy and none too clean. His face and hands were covered with little red blotches where mosquitoes had bitten him and he had scratched himself till the blood came. His long, thin face bore a sullen look.

"I understand that you are again having trouble with your servants. Abas, my head-boy's nephew, complains that you have held back his wages for three months. I consider it a most arbitrary proceeding. The lad wishes to leave you, and I certainly do not blame him. I must insist on your paying what is due to him."

"I don't choose that he should leave me. I am holding back his wages as a pledge of his good behaviour."

"You do not know the Malay character. The Malays are very sensitive to injury and ridicule. They are passionate and revengeful. It is my duty to warn you that if you drive this boy beyond a certain point you run a great risk."

Cooper gave a contemptuous chuckle.

"What do you think he'll do?"

"I think he'll kill you."

"Why should you mind?"

"Oh, I wouldn't," replied Mr. Warburton, with a faint laugh. "I should bear it with the utmost **fortitude**①. But I feel the official obligation to give you a proper warning."

"Do you think I'm afraid of a damned nigger?"

个好日子，他总会摆脱掉库珀的。“静观其变”，当这个短语掠过他的心头时，他会心地微笑了。他的心跳得更快些了，因为他看到他所仇恨的那个人俯卧在丛林的小路上，背上插着一把刀。这是那个流氓恶棍应有的下场。沃伯顿先生叹息了一声。他有责任提醒他，当然，他必须得这样做。他给库珀写了一封简短而正式的信函，请他立刻到“要塞”来。

十分钟过后，库珀便站立在他面前了。自从沃伯顿先生几乎要打他的那天开始，他们相互之间就没有说过话。他现在也没有请他坐下。

“你想要见我？”库珀问了一声。

他显得很邋遢，很不整洁。脸上和手上满是蚊虫叮咬后留下的小红包。他用手挠出血来了。他又长又瘦的面容上挂着闷闷不乐的神态。

“我听说，你又和仆人们闹别扭了。我那位领头仆人的侄子阿巴斯抱怨说，你克扣了他三个月的薪水。我认为这是一种太过任性的做法。小伙子想要离开你，我肯定不会责备他，但我必须坚持要求你把应该付给他薪水支付给他。”

“他要离开我，我不愿意。我克扣他的薪水那是作为他好好表现的保证。”

“你不了解马来人的性格啊。马来人对伤害和嘲笑十分敏感。他们容易激动，而且耿耿于怀。我有责任提醒你，你若是把小伙子逼急了，那可是在冒巨大的风险呢。”

库珀轻蔑地咯咯笑了起来。

“你觉得他会干什么呢？”

“我觉得他会宰了你。”

“你为何要操这份心呢？”

“噢，我才不操这份心呢，”沃伯顿先生回答说，淡淡地笑了一下，“我会以最坚强的意志忍受的。但是，我觉得，公事公办，我有责任适当提醒你一声。”

“你觉得我会惧怕一个该死的黑鬼吗？”

① fortitude ['fɔːtitjuːd] *n.* 刚毅

"It's a matter of entire indifference to me."

"Well, let me tell you this, I know how to take care of myself; that boy Abas is a dirty, thieving rascal, and if he tries any monkey tricks on me, by God, I'll wring his bloody neck."

"That was all I wished to say to you," said Mr. Warburton. "Good evening."

Mr. Warburton gave him a little nod of dismissal. Cooper flushed, did not for a moment know what to say or do, turned on his heel, and stumbled out of the room. Mr. Warburton watched him go with an icy smile on his lips. He had done his duty. But what would he have thought had he known that when Cooper got back to his bungalow, so silent and cheerless, he threw himself down on his bed and in his bitter loneliness on a sudden lost all control of himself? Painful sobs tore his chest and heavy tears rolled down his thin cheeks.

After this Mr. Warburton seldom saw Cooper, and never spoke to him. He read his *Times* every morning, did his work at the office, took his exercise, dressed for dinner, dined, and sat by the river smoking his cheroot. If by chance he ran across Cooper he cut him dead. Each, though never for a moment unconscious of the propinquity, acted as though the other did not exist. Time did nothing to **assuage**① their **animosity**②. They watched one another's actions and each knew what the other did. Though Mr. Warburton had been a keen shot in his youth, with age he had acquired a distaste for killing the wild things of the jungle, but on Sundays and holidays Cooper went out with his gun: if he got something it was a triumph over Mr. Warburton; if not, Mr. Warburton shrugged his shoulders and chuckled. These counter-jumpers trying to be sportsmen! Christmas was a bad time for both of them: they ate their dinners alone, each in his own quarters, and they got deliberately drunk. They were the only white men within two hundred miles and they lived within shouting distance of each other. At the beginning of the year Cooper went down with fever, and when Mr. Warburton caught sight of him again he was surprised to see how thin he had grown. He looked ill and worn. The solitude, so much more unnatural because

“你惧不惧怕与我毫无关系。”

“那好，那就让我告诉你吧。我知道该如何照顾好自己。那个名叫阿巴斯的男仆是个行为不端、手脚不干净的流氓。他若是想要对我玩弄什么把戏，上帝作证，我会拧断他的脖子的。”

“我要对你说的话已经说过了，”沃伯顿先生说，“再见吧。”

沃伯顿先生对他微微点了点头，打发他离开。库珀的脸涨得通红，一时间不知道该说什么，该做什么。他转过身，踉踉跄跄地走出了房间。沃伯顿先生看着他离开，嘴边挂着冷漠的微笑。他履行了自己的义务。但是，库珀返回到他自己的孟加拉平房之后，沉默不语，闷闷不乐，一跃身子躺在自己的床上，痛苦孤独之中，突然控制不了自己的情绪。痛苦的抽泣撕心裂肺，泪珠子从他瘦削的脸颊上流淌下来。沃伯顿先生若是知道这个情况，他会怎么想啊？

从那以后，沃伯顿先生极少看到库珀，也从未同他说过话。他每天早晨都浏览着自己的《泰晤士报》，在办公室里干自己的工作，锻炼身体，穿着妥帖后用晚餐，坐在河畔抽方头雪茄烟。他若是偶尔遇到了库珀，便不予理睬。尽管他们每时每刻都意识到彼此其实近在咫尺，但各自都表现得似乎对方根本就不存在。时间无法消弭他们之间的怨恨。他们都注视着对方的行为，而且都知道，对方在干什么。虽说沃伯顿先生年轻时喜爱狩猎，而随着年龄的增长，他开始反感杀戮丛林中的野生动物的行为了。但是，每逢星期天和节假日，库珀便会带着猎枪外出：若是有所收获，那便是一次盖过沃伯顿先生的胜利。若是没有收获，沃伯顿先生便会耸耸肩膀，咯咯发笑。那些站柜台的人还想方设法想当运动家呢！圣诞节对他们两个人而言都是难过的时刻：他们孤零零地吃晚餐，各自在自己的住处，而且有意喝醉。方圆二百英里之内，唯有他们两个是白人，而他们之间的距离叫喊起来对方都可以听见。新年伊始，库珀发起了

① assuage [ə'sweidʒ] *v.* 减轻

② animosity [ˌæni'mɔsəti] *n.* 敌意

it was due to no necessity, was getting on his nerves. It was getting on Mr. Warburton's too, and often he could not sleep at night. He lay awake brooding. Cooper was drinking heavily and surely the breaking point was near; but in his dealings with the natives he took care to do nothing that might expose him to his chief's **rebuke**[①]. They fought a grim and silent battle with one another. It was a test of endurance. The months passed, and neither gave sign of weakening. They were like men dwelling in regions of eternal night, and their souls were oppressed with the knowledge that never would the day dawn for them. It looked as though their lives would continue for ever in this dull and hideous monotony of hatred.

And when at last the inevitable happened it came upon Mr. Warburton with all the shock of the unexpected. Cooper accused the boy Abas of stealing some of his clothes, and when the boy denied the theft took him by the **scruff**[②] of the neck and kicked him down the steps of the bungalow. The boy demanded his wages and Cooper flung at his head every word of abuse he knew. If he saw him in the compound in an hour he would hand him over to the police. Next morning the boy **waylaid**[③] him outside the Fort when he was walking over to his office, and again demanded his wages. Cooper struck him in the face with his clenched fist. The boy fell to the ground and got up with blood streaming from his nose.

Cooper walked on and set about his work. But he could not attend to it. The blow had calmed his irritation, and he knew that he had gone too far. He was worried. He fell ill, miserable, and discouraged. In the adjoining office sat Mr. Warburton, and his impulse was to go and tell him what he had done; he made a movement in his chair, but he knew with what icy scorn he would listen to the story. He could see his patronising smile. For a moment he had an uneasy fear of what Abas might do. Warburton had warned him all right. He sighed. What a fool he had been! But he shrugged his shoulders impatiently. He did not care; a fat lot he had to live for. It was all Warburton's fault; if he hadn't put his back up nothing like this would have happened. Warburton had

高烧。当沃伯顿先生再次见到他时，惊讶不已，他竟然消瘦成那副样子。他看上去一副病态，憔悴不堪。由于这种孤独寂寞的生活状态并非是必要的，所以更加显得不自然，让他在精神上备受折磨。孤独感也同样折磨着沃伯顿先生，他常常夜不能寐，躺在床上醒着，思前想后。库珀酗酒无度，快要到不可收拾的地步了。不过，他在同土著居民打交道时，却是谨小慎微，尽量不做出格的事情，免得长官斥责。他们彼此之间进行着一场严峻而又无声的搏斗。这是对耐力的考验。时间过去了几个月，彼此都没有显现缓和的迹象。他们好比是两个永远居住在漫漫长夜中的人，灵魂受到压抑，因为他们知道，永远都迎不来黎明。看起来，他们的人生将要在这种单调乏味而又恐怖可怕的仇恨中永远持续下去。

① rebuke [ri'bju:k] *n.* 训斥

当不可避免的事情终于发生时，面对突如其来的事情，沃伯顿先生还是感到十分震惊。库珀指责男仆阿巴斯偷盗了自己的一些衣服。而男仆拒不承认，库珀便揪着人家的后脖子，用脚把他踹下孟加拉平房处的台阶。男仆向库珀索要薪水，库珀便劈头盖脸地骂他，什么难听的话都骂出来了。若是再过一个小时看见他还在院落内，就会把他送交警察局。翌日早上，库珀去上班时，那男仆把他堵在“要塞”的外面，再次向他索要薪水。库珀用拳头击打他的脸部。男仆倒在了地上，站立起来时，鼻腔流淌着鲜血。

② scruff [skrʌf] *n.* 后脖子

③ waylay [ˌwei'lei] *v.* 阻拦

库珀继续向前走，开始工作。但是，他的心思集中不到工作上。那一拳让他解了自己的怨气。他知道，自己做得过分了。他担心受怕了。他感到闷闷不乐，痛苦难受，垂头丧气。隔壁的办公室就坐着沃伯顿先生。他的心里突然有了一种冲动，想要去把刚才自己做过的事情告诉他。他在椅子上挪动一下身子，但他知道，沃伯顿先生会以冷漠而又鄙视的态度听他讲述事情的经过。他可以想到他脸上的那种傲慢的笑容。一时间，他忐忑不安起来，担心阿巴斯会做出什么事情来。沃伯顿先生提醒得对。他叹息了一声。他真是个十足的蠢货啊！但

made life a hell for him from the start. The snob. But they were all like that: it was because he was a Colonial. It was a damned shame that he had never got his commission in the war; he was as good as anyone else. They were a lot of dirty snobs. He was damned if he was going to **knuckle**[①] under now. Of course Warburton would hear of what had happened; the old devil knew everything. He wasn't afraid. He wasn't afraid of any Malay in Borneo, and Warburton could go to blazes.

He was right in thinking that Mr. Warburton would know what had happened. His head-boy told him when he went in to tiffin.

"Where is your nephew now?"

"I do not know, Tuan. He has gone."

Mr. Warburton remained silent. After luncheon as a rule he slept a little, but today he found himself very wide awake. His eyes involuntarily sought the bungalow where Cooper was now resting.

The idiot! Hesitation for a little was in Mr. Warburton's mind. Did the man know in what peril he was? He supposed he ought to send for him. But each time he had tried to reason with Cooper, Cooper had insulted him. Anger, furious anger welled up suddenly in Mr. Warburton's heart, so that the veins on his temples stood out and he clenched his fists. The cad had had his warning. Now let him take what was coming to him. It was no business of his, and if anything happened it was not his fault. But perhaps they would wish in Kuala Solor that they had taken his advice and transferred Cooper to mother station.

He was strangely restless that night. After dinner he walked up and down the veranda. When the boy went away to his own quarters, Mr. Warburton asked him whether anything had been seen of Abas.

"No, Tuan, I think maybe he has gone to the village of his mother's brother."

Mr. Warburton gave him a sharp glance, but the boy was looking down, and their eyes did not meet. Mr. Warburton went down to the river and sat in his

① knuckle ['nʌkl] *v.* 屈服

是，他不耐烦地耸了耸肩膀。他不在乎，他的人生中还有许多事情要做。一切都是沃伯顿的错。他若是不惹毛他，这样的事情绝不可能发生。沃伯顿从一开始就把他的人生变成了地狱。势利眼。但是，世人都是一丘之貉：因为他是殖民地的居民。他战争中没能弄到个军衔，这简直是奇耻大辱。他跟任何人相比都差不多。他们中有大量可恶的势利眼。他现在若是认软服输了，那才真他妈丢脸呢。当然，沃伯顿会听到发生了的事情，老魔鬼什么事情都知道。他并不感到害怕。他不害怕婆罗洲的任何马来人，让沃伯顿见鬼去吧。

库珀的感觉是对的，沃伯顿先生一定知道发生了情况。他在吃午饭时，他那位领头的仆人把事情告诉了他。

"你侄子这会儿在哪儿呢？"

"我不知道啊，*Tuan*。他已经走了。"

沃伯顿先生缄口不言。吃过午饭后，他一般会睡一会儿，但今天，他感觉自己毫无睡意。他不由自主地把目光转向库珀正在休息的那幢孟加拉平房。

那个白痴！沃伯顿先生的心里迟疑了片刻。难道此人没有意识到他正处在危险之中吗？我觉得，自己应该派个人去把他叫过来。但是，但凡他试图同库珀讲道理时，库珀都会羞辱他。愤怒，难以抑制的愤怒，突然在沃伯顿先生的心里升腾，他额头上青筋毕露，拳头紧握。那个无赖已经得到警示了。那现在就让他罪有应得吧。这不关他的什么事。如若发生了什么什么事情，那也不是他的过错。但是，兴许瓜拉索洛那边的人还会后悔自己没有听从他的建议把库珀调到别的驻地去呢。

真是奇怪，沃伯顿先生当晚格外心神不宁。晚餐过后，他在露台上来回踱步。仆人离开要返回到自己住处时，沃伯顿先生问他是否见过阿巴斯。

"没有啊，*Tuan*。我估计他可能到他舅舅的村上去了。"

沃伯顿先生瞥了他一眼，目光严厉，但是，仆人朝下看着，他们的目光没有相遇。沃伯顿先生走到下方的

arbour. But peace was denied him. The river flowed ominously silent. It was like a great serpent gliding with sluggish movement towards the sea. And the trees of the jungle over the water were heavy with a breathless menace. No bird sang. No breeze ruffled the leaves of the cassias. All around him it seemed as though something waited.

He walked across the garden to the road. He had Cooper's bungalow in full view from there. There was a light in his sitting-room, and across the road floated the sound of rag-time. Cooper was playing his gramophone. Mr. Warburton shuddered; he had never got over his instinctive dislike of that instrument. But for that he would have gone over and spoken to Cooper. He turned and went back to his own house. He read late into the night, and at last he slept. But he did not sleep very long, he had terrible dreams, and he seemed to be awakened by a cry. Of course that was a dream too, for no cry—from the bungalow for instance—could be heard in his room. He lay awake till dawn. Then he heard hurried steps and the sound of voices, his head-boy burst suddenly into the room without his **fez**①, and Mr. Warburton's heart stood still.

"Tuan, Tuan."

Mr. Warburton jumped out of bed.

"I'll come at once."

He put on his slippers, and in his sarong and pyjama jacket walked across his compound and into Cooper's. Cooper was lying in bed, with his mouth open, and a kris sticking in his heart. He had been killed in his sleep. Mr. Warburton started, but not because he had not expected to see just such a sight, he started because he fell in himself a sudden glow of exultation. A great burden had been lifted from his shoulders.

Cooper was quite cold. Mr. Warburton took the kris out of the wound, it had been thrust in with such force that he had to use an effort to get it out, and looked at it. He recognised it. It was a kris that a dealer had offered him some weeks before, and which he knew Cooper had bought.

河畔，坐在他常到的那座凉亭里。但是，他内心无法平静。河水静静地流淌着，给人一种不详的感觉。它犹如一条巨蛇懒洋洋地扭动着身子滑向大海。河畔生长着丛林树木，沉重的树干仿佛因恐惧而屏声静气。听不见鸟儿鸣唱。没有一丝风掠过肉桂树的树叶。他周围的一切都似乎在等待着什么。

他横过花园走向大路，那儿可以将库珀的孟加拉平房尽收眼底。起居室里亮着灯。路的另一边传来雷格泰姆音乐。库珀在播放着留声机。沃伯顿先生不寒而栗。他从来都克服不了对那种机器本能的厌恶感。要不是因为这一点，他本来是可以过去同库珀说一说的。他转身返回到了自己的住处。他当晚看书看到很晚，最后睡着了。但是，他没有睡多长时间，噩梦连连，好像是被一声叫喊惊醒了。当然，那也是一个噩梦，其实，他在自己的房间里是听不见叫喊声的——比如从孟加拉平房那边传来的叫喊声。他一直醒着，直到天亮。后来，他听见了急促的脚步声，还有说话的声音。他那位领头的仆人突然闯进了他的房间，连非斯帽都没有戴。沃伯顿先生心都提到嗓子眼了。

① fez［fez］*n.* 圆筒形无边毡帽

"*Tuan, Tuan*。"

沃伯顿先生跳下床。

"我立刻就去。"

他趿着拖鞋，围着围裙，穿着睡衣，走过了自己的院落，来到库珀的住处。库珀躺在床上，嘴巴张开着，一把曲刃短剑刺进了他的心脏。他是睡着时遇刺的。沃伯顿先生怔了一下，不是因为他没有预料到会看到如此情形。他怔了一下是因为自己的心里突然升腾起了一阵狂喜。他肩膀上的那副重担终于卸下了。

库珀身子冰凉了。沃伯顿先生把那把曲刃短剑从伤口处拔了出来，短剑刺进去用的力气很大，他费了很大的劲儿才拔出来。然后看着短剑，他认出来了，几个星期前，有位做买卖的要把短剑卖给他，结果后来被库珀买下来了。

"Where is Abas?" he asked sternly.

"Abas is at the village of his mother's brother."

The sergeant of the native police was standing at the foot of the bed.

"Take two men and go to the village and arrest him."

Mr. Warburton did what was immediately necessary. With set face he gave orders. His words were short and **peremptory**①. Then he went back to the Fort. He shaved and had his bath, dressed, and went into the dining-room. By the side of his plate *The Times* in its wrapper lay waiting for him. He helped himself to some fruit. The head-boy poured out his tea while the second handed him a dish of eggs. Mr. Warburton ate with a good appetite. The head-boy waited.

"What is it?" asked Mr. Warburton.

"Tuan, Abas, my nephew, was in the house of his mother's brother all night. It can be proved. His uncle will swear that he did not leave the kampong."

Mr. Warburton turned upon him with a frown.

"Tuan Cooper was killed by Abas. You know it as well as I know it. Justice must be done."

"Tuan, you would not hang him?"

Mr. Warburton hesitated an instant, and though his voice remained set and stern a change came into his eyes. It was a flicker which the Malay was quick to notice and across his own eyes flashed an answering look of understanding.

"The **provocation**② was very great. Abas will be sentenced to a term of imprisonment." There was a pause while Mr. Warburton helped himself to **marmalade**③. "When he has served a part of his sentence in prison I will take him into this house as a boy. You can train him in his duties. I have no doubt that in the house of Tuan Cooper he got into bad habits."

"Shall Abas give himself up, Tuan?"

"It would be wise of him."

The boy withdrew. Mr. Warburton took his *Times* and neatly slit the wrapper. He loved to unfold the heavy, rustling pages. The morning, so fresh and cool, was delicious and for a moment his eyes wandered out over the garden

“阿巴斯在哪儿呢？”他问了一声，语气很严厉。

“阿巴斯在他舅舅村上呢。”

当地警署的警长站立在床边。

“带两个人到村子里去逮捕他。”

沃伯顿先生立刻采取了必要的行动。他铁青着脸下达了命令，言辞简单，不容争辩。他随后返回到“要塞”，刮脸，洗澡，穿衣，然后用早餐。《泰晤士报》卷在包装纸里放在餐盘旁边，等待他拆开。他吃了点水果。领头的仆人给他倒茶，第二位仆人端给他一盘子鸡蛋。沃伯顿先生美滋滋地吃了起来。领头的仆人在一边等待着。

“有什么事吗？”沃伯顿先生问了一声。

“*Tuan*，我侄子阿巴斯整宿都在他舅舅家里。这一点有人可以证明。他舅舅发誓说，阿巴斯整宿都没有离开村庄。”

沃伯顿先生转身对着他，皱眉蹙眼。

“阿巴斯刺杀了库珀 *Tuan*。你和我一样清楚这件事情。此事必须公正处理。”

“*Tuan*，您不会绞死他吧？”

沃伯顿先生迟疑了片刻，尽管他说话的声音沉稳而严厉，但眼神还是发生了变化。目光闪现，马来人很快便觉察到了，并报之以心领神会的眼神。

“这个马蜂窝捅得够大的。阿巴斯会被处以监禁的。”沃伯顿先生抹果酱时停顿了片刻。“等到他服一段时间刑后，我会让他到这儿来当仆人。你可以训练他如何做事。我毫无怀疑，他在库珀 *Tuan* 那儿一定养成了坏习惯。”

“阿巴斯应该自首吗，*Tuan*?”

“这是他明智的做法。”

仆人退下了。沃伯顿先生拿起《泰晤士报》，精心地撕开包装纸。他喜爱展开分量厚实、沙沙作响的报纸版面。早晨空气新鲜，清凉宜人，令人神清气爽。一时间，他游离的目光转到了那边的花园，目光中透着友善。他

① peremptory [pə'remptəri] *a.* 命令式的

② provocation [ˌprɔvə'keiʃən] *n.* 挑衅

③ marmalade ['mɑːməleid] *n.* 果酱

with a friendly glance. A great weight had been lifted from his mind. He turned to the columns in which were announced the births, deaths, and marriages. That was what he always looked at first. A name he knew caught his attention. Lady Ormskirk had had a son at last. By George, how pleased the old **dowager**① must be! He would write her a note of congratulation by the next mail.

Abas would make a very good house-boy.

That fool Cooper!

的心头卸下了沉重的负担。他把报纸翻到告示出生、死亡和婚姻的专栏。那一直都是他首先要浏览的内容。一个他熟悉的名字引起了他的注意。奥姆斯柯克夫人终于生了个儿子了。天哪，老妇人该有多么开心啊！他要在接来下的邮件中给她写一封贺信。

阿巴斯会成为一位很称职的仆人的。

库珀那个蠢货！

① dowager ['dauədʒə] *n.* 老年贵妇人